1/93

DEVELOPING WOMEN
THROUGH TRAINING
A PRACTICAL HANDBO

S.Victor Stepp
Feb 1993

Further titles in the McGraw-Hill Training Series

Details of these and other titles in the series are available from:

The Product Manager, Professional Books,
McGraw-Hill Book Company Europe,
Shoppenhangers Road, Maidenhead,
Berkshire, SL6 2QL.
Telephone: 0628 23432 Fax: 0628 770224

Developing women through training

A practical handbook

Liz Willis and Jenny Daisley

McGRAW-HILL BOOK COMPANY

London · New York · St Louis · San Francisco · Auckland
Bogotá · Caracas · Hamburg · Lisbon · Madrid · Mexico · Milan
Montreal · New Delhi · Panama · Paris · San Juan · São Paulo
Singapore · Sydney · Tokyo · Toronto

Published by
McGRAW-HILL Book Company Europe
Shoppenhangers Road, Maidenhead, Berkshire SL6 2QL, England.
Telephone 0628 23432
Fax 0628 770224

British Library Cataloguing in Publication Data
Willis, Liz
  Developing women through training.
  I. Title II. Daisley, Jenny
  658.31245

  ISBN 0-07-707566-8

Library of Congress Cataloging-in-Publication Data
Willis, Liz.
    Developing women through training : a practical handbook / Liz
  Willis and Jenny Daisley.
      p. cm. — (McGraw-Hill training series)
    Includes bibliographical references and index.
    ISBN 0-07-707566-8 :
    1. Women white collar workers—Training of—Handbooks, manuals,
  etc. 2. Occupational training for women—Handbooks, manuals, etc.
  3. Career development—Handbooks, manuals, etc. I. Daisley, Jenny.
  II. Title.   III. Series.
  HF5549.5.T7W493   1992
  658.3'124'082—dc20   91-26775
                                                                 CIP

1234 CL 932

Typeset by Book Ens Limited, Baldock, Herts
Printed in England by Clays Ltd, St Ives plc

Contents

Series preface

Training and development are now firmly centre stage in most organizations, if not all. Nothing unusual in that—for some organizations. They have always seen training and development as part of the heart of their businesses—but more and more must see it the same way.

The demographic trends through the 1990s will inject into the marketplace severe competition for good people who will need good training. Young people without conventional qualifications, skilled workers in redundant crafts, people out of work, women wishing to return to work—all will require excellent training to fit them to meet the job demands of the 1990s and beyond.

But excellent training does not spring from what we have done well in the past. T&D specialists are in a new ball game. 'Maintenance' training—training to keep up skill levels to do what we have always done—will be less in demand. Rather, organization, work and market change training are now much more important and will remain so for some time. Changing organizations and people is no easy task, requiring special skills and expertise which, sadly, many T&D specialists do not possess.

To work as a 'change' specialist requires us to get to centre stage—to the heart of the company's business. This means we have to ask about future goals and strategies and even be involved in their development, at least as far as T&D policies are concerned.

This demands excellent communication skills, political expertise, negotiating ability, diagnostic skills—indeed, all the skills a good internal consultant requires.

The implications for T&D specialists are considerable. It is not enough merely to be skilled in the basics of training, we must also begin to act like business people and to think in business terms and talk the language of business. We must be able to resource training not just from within but by using the vast array of external resources. We must be able to manage our activities as well as any other manager. We must share in the creation and communication of the company's vision. We must never let the goals of the company out of our sight.

In short, we may have to grow and change with the business. It will be hard. We shall not only have to demonstrate relevance but also value for money and achievement of results. We shall be our own boss, as accountable for results as any other line manager, and we shall have to deal with fewer internal resources.

The challenge is on, as many T&D specialists have demonstrated to me over the past few years. We need to be capable of meeting that challenge. This is why McGraw-Hill Book Company (UK) Limited have planned and launched this major new training series—to help us meet that challenge.

The series covers all aspects of T&D and provides the knowledge base from which we can develop plans to meet the challenge. They are practical books for the professional person. They are a starting point for planning our journey into the twenty-first century.

Use them well. Don't just read them. Highlight key ideas, thoughts, action pointers or whatever, and have a go at doing something with them. Through experimentation we evolve; through stagnation we die.

I know that all the authors in the McGraw-Hill Training Series would want me to wish you every success. Have a great journey into the twenty-first century.

ROGER BENNETT
Series Editor

About the series editor

Roger Bennett has over twenty years' experience in training, management education, research and consulting. He has long been involved with trainer training and trainer effectiveness. He has carried out research into trainer effectiveness and conducted workshops, seminars and conferences on the subject around the world. He has written extensively on the subject including the book *Improving Trainer Effectiveness*, Gower. His work has taken him all over the world and has involved directors of companies as well as managers and trainers.

Dr Bennett has worked in engineering, several business schools (including the International Management Centre, where he launched the UK's first masters degree in T&D) and has been a board director of two companies. He is the editor of the *Journal of European Industrial Training* and was series editor of the ITD's *Get In There* workbook and video package for the managers of training departments. He now runs his own business called The Management Development Consultancy.

Acknowledgements

We would like to thank the many people who have contributed to our own development and to the development of the content of this book:

- the thousands of women who've attended our courses, workshops and conferences and from whom we've learned so much
- the men and women who have worked with us in pioneering women's development training inside organizations
- the many others who have given us help along the way, in particular Marjo Boeschoten, Julia Cleverdon, Yvonne Collymore, Zoë Fairbairns, Pippa Isbell, Janice Leary, Kirsty Peake, Pat Richards, Margaret Thomson Davis and Anne Watts
- Jean Buswell of the Gloucestershire and West of England Training Initiative for her contributions of examples for women returners
- Carroll Beard for all her support and word processing, transforming the manuscript from handwritten squiggles, through its many drafts to its finished state
- Dianne Brackley for her comments and help in gathering information for the appendices
- and finally, all those who have contributed material and case studies which make the ideas in the book come alive: Annabel Perahia, Sun Microsystems, Isobel Macdonald, BBC Scotland, Rita Bryant, Kent County Council, Valerie Fawcett, Oxford Women in Publishing, Helen Loughlin, Grand Metropolitan Foods Europe, Liz Bargh, The Domino Consultancy Ltd, Shelley Simmons, Sun Alliance, Diana Balsdon, National Westminster Bank plc, Anne Munroe, Bull HN Information Systems, Christine Kerr, Thames Television plc, and Zoë Gruhn, Midland Bank plc.

About the authors

Liz Willis

Liz Willis is one of the UK's leading women's development consultants and is well known as a consultant, writer and broadcaster on women's development issues. She runs her own consultancy following six years at the Industrial Society where she set up and ran the Pepperell Unit—the first department of its kind specializing in developing opportunities for women at work.

Liz has ten years' experience in the women's development field enabling women to develop the skills and determination to make things happen for themselves.

She is well known for her enthusiastic, positive and practical approach, and works with organizations in both the private and public sectors, as well as with women's groups. She works at all levels in organizations, developing overall women's development strategies as well as designing and delivering a variety of training and development, from in-depth residential courses with small groups, to one-day workshops with hundreds.

All of Liz's work is enhanced by her diverse background which includes being a line manager in industry and a professional marketing manager. This gives her an unusual blend of the practical manager and the experienced creative developer.

Jenny Daisley

Jenny Daisley has worked for over 20 years at the leading edge of training and development consultancy, enabling individuals and organizations to become more effective through her work as a holistic development consultant, and has a track record as a pioneer and innovator.

She has run her own consultancy for the last ten years and set up Biographic Management Ltd, of which she is managing director, in 1984. In the 1970s she pioneered women's development—biography work for women, 'Managing Transitions' for women managers and developing equal opportunities policies and practice with employers.

She has developed courses for women at all levels in organizations, and for people with disabilities. She has trained women of all ages and races as trainers to run women's development programmes, and recently trained women from 13 different countries as biographical counsellors, in a 3-year programme.

In her counselling practice she works in depth with women, enabling them to understand the past, heal the present and take new action steps for the future.

Liz and Jenny have collaborated on many women's development programmes, particularly training trainers events. Most notably, they developed the Springboard Women's Development Programme for non-management women for the BBC, which was awarded the 1989 Lady Platt Award for Equal Opportunity training. This is the second book which they have written jointly.

Introduction

This book is written for anyone who wants to run women's development training. It is a practical handbook filled with down-to-earth ideas, do's and don'ts, hints and tips. Everything in this book is the result of our 30 years' combined experience of experimenting, refining, falling flat on our faces and consolidating successes! So we're writing from experience, not from theory; from what works in practice, not from wishful thinking. This means that much of the book is common sense.

If you're already an experienced trainer, you may think that you've heard and seen all of it before; do not be misled. Much of women's development training is good training practice anyway, but the success of women's development training lies in the nuances, the throw-away lines, the subtle emphases and, more than in any other form of training, in the assumptions, prejudices and behaviour of the trainer. So keep an eye open for the things that make women's development training different, and build on your experience of the things that are the same. We've tried to point these out along the way.

If you're not a trainer, but are coming to this book because you have the job of initiating women's development training, then you may want to read this in conjunction with wider women's development issues. This is not a book on equal opportunities strategies or human resources policy. This book takes the training part of your overall strategy and pulls it down to earth.

You may work inside an organization, you may be involved in a women's group, you may be a freelance trainer or you may be an individual woman wanting to start some training locally. This book has all these possibilities in mind, and we have kept the approach as broad as possible. However, the book is written primarily for the in-house trainer and/or personnel specialist, who is faced with running women's development training for the first time.

We are acutely aware of the wide range of special needs which are currently being addressed by many tailored versions of women's development training: women returners, women with disabilities, women in rural areas, women in housing associations, unemployed women, black women, etc. Each of these could fill a book of their own, so we have made a conscious decision to keep the content and material of this book as broad and general as possible. We have referred to the special needs of women returners from time to time, as such a large proportion of women attending women's development training at the moment are returners, but if you're embarking on training with any other groups with special needs, we'd ask you to interpret and transfer the ideas in this book to your specific situation.

We've taken all the elements needed for women's development training and structured the book chronologically, so the sequence of events roughly follows on. However, life is never that neat and tidy, so we'd urge you to read the book through before embarking on a women's development training initiative, as there may be issues raised in the later chapters which will have an influence on your earlier thoughts.

The word 'organization' is used throughout to refer to any organization in which you or your participants may be involved. It could just as easily be a local charity group or community association as a company or trade union, so you'll have to interpret it for yourself as relevant.

At the end of most chapters is a case study. These are real examples of how women's development training is being used in a variety of ways, written by a representative of the organization or group concerned. As such, they give ideas and inspiration on a range of issues and sometimes give alternative ideas to those in the chapters. We have written an introductory paragraph to each one, otherwise they aren't amended or edited at all. As each one covers so many aspects of women's development training, they stand complete on their own, and may have a strong or only a tenuous link with the preceding chapter.

Writing a book on development training specifically for women has its own advantages and disadvantages, just as any book looking at a particular group. The advantages are that it can focus on the issues of specific importance to women, and enable you to design and run a course of greater relevance and sensitivity. The disadvantages are that we have been forced reluctantly into making gross generalizations about men and women, and that focusing on their special needs produces a distorted and negative impression of women. Many of the practices outlined in this book would be just as relevant for a group of men who had identified that they wanted to work on such issues as low self-esteem, low aspirations, lack of self-confidence and lack of assertiveness. However, there is an added dimension of something very special about a women-only development course and that is what we shall be highlighting throughout this book.

As you flick through or work through this book, women's development training may appear to be fraught with difficulties and you may wonder why anyone ever bothers! From our experience as women's development trainers, women's development training is one of the most exciting and rewarding forms of training. The women who come on the courses are courageous people who are seeking to become more themselves. They simply need some support, inspiration, ideas and a kick in the right direction to get them started. If you can supply this you will be quickly rewarded with remarkably fast changes in behaviour and the satisfaction of seeing people grow.

Over to you!

1 Setting the scene

As you have opened this book, we are assuming that you have at least some interest in women's development training, but—why bother with it and what are your objectives in running women's development training? After all, isn't it rather passé and undoubtedly patronising? Isn't there an inbuilt assumption that women simply can't cope and need extra help?

This opening chapter looks at the overall situation for women in the UK, briefly identifies the legal position on women-only training and defines women's development training. It will describe the main reasons why organizations run women's development training and help you to set or clarify your own objectives.

The present state of play

Women's development training is a controversial subject. Few people are neutral about it and it almost always provokes an automatic positive or negative response from both men and women. From women this can range from downright hostility: 'Are you implying there's something wrong with us? Go away, we're not women's libbers!' through neutrality: 'I've never found problems on the graduate training scheme', to warm enthusiasm: 'At last—about time they gave us a chance. Let's make the most of this'.

From men the reaction ranges from the traditional resistance to change: 'We don't want anything like that here/it doesn't apply in our organization/women should stay at home' (yes—still!), to the perplexed: 'I don't really know what all the fuss is about—what is women's development training anyway?' to the patronizing and paternalistic: 'I think we should be thinking about giving them a little course of their own'. And from both sexes there is also the large body of people who go very silent at the mention of women's development and disappear into the wallpaper: 'I don't want to get involved'.

These, of course, are stereotypes and there are many other and more complex reactions in this range of examples, but when you embark on any form of women's development training you will be dealing with all these prejudices and assumptions, and often with deep-seated feelings. People get angry or frightened about women's development training in a way that doesn't occur with most other forms of training.

These feelings arise because developing women represents a huge change from the norm that has existed since the Industrial Revolution. Through conditioning and upbringing, people have been used to men dominating the upper layers of the workforce and women being at the bottom. Any substantial change from this deep-rooted traditional stance is bound to give rise to considerable fear of the unknown from men and women alike; from men, because they have little experience of women as bosses or senior colleagues, and from women because they are being challenged to stand up and be counted in the world of work. There are few examples of women at the top of organizations—so few that some people can name them!

In the UK, we have had a woman prime minister—proof enough that there is no longer a problem, surely? We have women at increasingly senior levels in business, local authorities, the trade unions—in all walks of life. We hear regularly of large organizations introducing career-break schemes, workplace nurseries and flexible ways of working. 'Surely women's development training is no longer needed—it's a hangover from the bra-burning women's libbers of the 1970s, and not relevant for today's egalitarian enlightened world. It is simply not an issue any more', we are told, and anyway (the conclusive argument!) a smart woman will always make it to the top without any special treatment.

What is women's development training?

Many personnel managers, and some women themselves, connect the idea of women's development training with the equal opportunities legislation of the mid-1970s. It started off as one of a whole range of initiatives taken at that time to help right injustices. Other issues were equal pay, equal rights, and initiatives around sexism, sexual harassment, and civil liberties.

This raises the question of exactly what women's development training *is* and also contributes to the issues of 'remedial' versus 'developmental' training, and 'positive action' versus 'positive discrimination'. It is important to be clear about these terms and the ideas that lie behind them, as they provide foundation stones for this book and for your own women's development training programmes.

Here are our definitions:

Remedial training happens when someone has a problem with a particular skill and is sent on a course to get her 'up to scratch'.
Developmental training happens when someone who is already doing fine attends a course to 'grow' further and develop her full potential, preferably by her own choice and not by being 'sent'.

Before running any women's development training you need to be clear about what is acceptable and what infringes the law.

Positive discrimination means appointing a woman for the job or giving her access to training just because she's a woman and not necessarily because she's the right person for the job or the training. This results in tokenism and doesn't help the individual woman, other women in the organization or the organization itself. *It's also illegal in the UK.* As the Hansard Society Commission reports in *Women at the Top*:[1]

The Sex Discrimination Act does not permit discrimination in favour of women in making appointments to public offices and posts, nor in recruitment. However, goals and targets are not unlawful, provided they do not result in 'reverse discrimination' of this kind.

Positive action means taking any action at all, short of appointment, to enable the woman to *be* the right person for the job. This is what we mean by real equal opportunities—flexitime, career-break schemes, workplace nurseries, access to training, access to experience, access to risk taking, mentoring, and setting targets for numbers of women in jobs/grades are all examples of positive action, as is women's development training. Again, the Hansard Society Commission helpfully outlines the legal position:[1]

We draw attention to little-used provisions of the Sex Discrimination Act allowing positive action to be taken without breaching the principle of non-discrimination. Section 47 permits training bodies to afford women only access to facilities for training which would help fit them for work in which they are significantly under-represented or to encourage women only to take advantage of opportunities for doing that work. Section 48 contains a similar provision in relation to employers. Section 49 provides that trade unions, employer's associations, and any other organisation whose members carry on a particular profession or trade for the purposes of which the organisation exists, may take important positive steps in certain circumstances.

Definition Women's development training aims to help all women gain an opportunity to win or succeed at what they want in life. It is not about taking a group of women who have a 'problem' and patronizingly giving them a women's development course to make them feel better.

What do we mean by 'women's development training' and what differentiates it from any other form of training?

In practice the loose term 'women's development training' can cover a wide range of subjects and material, such as career planning, assertiveness skills, biography work, goal setting, presentation skills and interview techniques. Indeed, many women's development courses include a little bit of all these subjects. Obviously, these topics are not specifically women's issues, or particular to women—all are just as relevant to men.

So tackling certain subject material in itself does not constitute a women's development course—there's a lot more to it than that. The definition of 'women's development training' for the purposes of this book is:

Women's development training is a form of training where the needs are defined, objectives set and the course designed and run with the developmental needs of women especially in mind.

Of course, any form of good training will be developmental for both women and men, and women can perfectly well attend mixed courses and benefit enormously. Women's development training, however, gives priority to women's issues and perspectives.

A common question which arises with this type of training is: 'What about men's development training then?' To which our reply is that there is already an abundance of men's development training happening, because most training in the world of work is designed by men, to address issues defined by men, with courses organized by men, using material developed by men, and attended mostly by men. Run your eye down almost any employer's training schedule and you'll see that most of the content is aimed at predominantly male concerns, whether it's management training or technical training, and a majority of the total course delegates will probably be men.

In most organizations, training is conducted at times to fit male work patterns, in venues that suit men, with subject matter, processes and teaching styles appropriate to men. Of course, women attend these courses too, but by definition they will be in the minority and will be in a foreign land. Women at senior levels often report being the only woman on the course.

Courses attended predominantly by women tend to tackle technical skills and reinforce the roles that women already occupy e.g. secretarial skills, word processing, working better with your boss, and telephonist and receptionist skills, with venue and budget to match. Just as women's work is undervalued and underpaid, so any training specifically seen as 'for women' tends to be undervalued and underfunded.

Our definition of women's development training does not tell you the subject matter or material to be covered (this will vary from group to group) but it does tell you where the emphasis lies—with and for women.

If you are used to designing and running courses mostly for men, you may find this rather like walking through a looking glass—you're still doing the same things, such as assessing needs, designing a programme, organizing a course, delivering and then evaluating it, but it looks and feels different!

Women's development training, as with all training, takes place on many, often subtle, levels. However, from our experience, we believe that in women's development training the emphasis is more on the hidden, subtle, unspoken processes than in any other form of training. It explains, too, why women's development training programmes appear so ordinary when written down, often looking very similar to each other, but also explains why some courses work, while others transform!

The ingredients of women's development training

There are many intangible aspects of women's development training. Trying to pin down these invisible, intangible elements is rather like trying to separate out the different ingredients of a mysterious cocktail, once it has been shaken! You can see the colour and texture of the mixture, and your eye is caught by the umbrella on top, but what exactly is it? And what is the special ingredient that makes it so different? The active ingredients in any form of women's development training are:

- the material
- networking
- role models
- you as trainer
- comparing notes, swapping experiences, support from each other

These ingredients mix and blend with each other through the whole process of women's development training so they will be referred to in later chapters. Each of us may gain the hint of different flavours which will make us say 'This cocktail is the right one for me', but all the ingredients have to be there for the recipe to work.

So being involved in women's development training in your organization is challenging, thought-provoking and rewarding. It's also one of the most important developmental activities you can do, and has more long-term *organizational* development implications than most. If you are a woman and haven't personally experienced that being a woman has held you back or deprived you of opportunities, then we ask you to keep an open mind because:

- Many women have experienced hurdles.
- Women with your experience, qualities and qualifications may experience hurdles at a different time or in different circumstances.
- You may be a true pioneer and true pioneers often have the skills, abilities, confidence or drive to be first into your area and simply never see the hurdles that seem so insurmountable to others. Some pioneers go on for ever and some burn out or level off.

The evidence

The need for women's development training is borne out by extensive statistical and attitudinal evidence.

The statistics

In most organizations women are well represented at the bottom but the higher up one looks the fewer women there are. Figures 1.1 and 1.2 show statistics from two very different organizations. The organizations differ but the pattern is the same: very few women above middle management level. This is typical of the majority of organizations in the UK.

The Manpower Services Commission (MSC)[2] outlines three main reasons why there are so few women in management:

- the organizational climate
- women's attitudes and behaviour
- career paths and personnel procedures

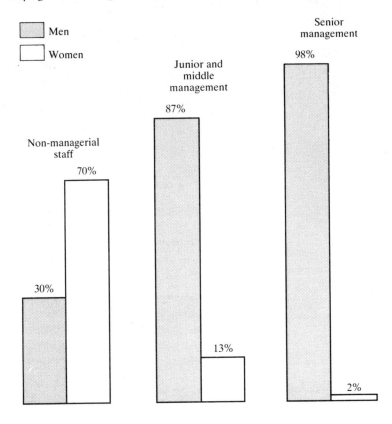

Men

Women

Non-managerial staff

30%

70%

Junior and middle management

87%

13%

Senior management

98%

2%

Figure 1.1 *Organization A: statistics*

Percentage of women	
Grade 8 (most senior)	0
Grade 7	0
Grade 6	0
Grade 5	5.5
Grade 4	17.4
Grade 3	45
Grade 2	74
Grade 1	76

Figure 1.2 *Organization B: statistics*

Career paths and personnel procedures These were established when most women did not work for long periods of time and men tended to spend anything up to 40 years with an organization. Women have to be more dedicated than men to reach the top. Career guidance for men stresses the need to think long-term while women are encouraged to concentrate on their current jobs.

The organizational climate

There is a general lack of awareness about women's capabilities. Senior executives, usually male, make incorrect assumptions about women's real interests and abilities and tend to channel them into highly specialized work rather than mainstream management.

Women's attitudes and behaviour

The MSC reports that women are less positive and less confident about themselves than men. They present themselves less positively and assume that they will be rewarded with promotion for work well done. They tend not to push themselves forward for promotion. Rather, they wait for someone to encourage them to apply for it.

Access to training

The other piece of evidence lies in the reporting of access to training for women. The MSC[2] recorded:

Training is the main process by which the composition of the existing workforce can be changed. It therefore has a central role in promoting similar career progression among men and women.

In terms of training and development women often appear to be at a disadvantage. They tend to receive less training than men of comparable ability and in general their training tends to be narrower and more job specific. This may be due, in part, to initial job choice.

Women tend to enter occupations where there is limited access to training. However, even where men and women receive comparable basic job training, women typically receive less career development. This can inhibit subsequent career progress for women since they do not obtain the necessary breadth of experience and training in their early careers.

Training is expensive and to optimise the returns it should be based on a careful analysis of job and individual needs. The training needs of men and women of comparable ability may be similar, but programmes should take account of individual differences as well. This ensures that women's training needs, which may sometimes have a different emphasis from those of men, are accommodated.

Some women by virtue of their qualifications, experience or life/work patterns may have specific training requirements that are not successfully met by existing programmes. Organisations may find it beneficial to adapt their training to meet these needs for women of identified ability.

Morag Alexander writes in *Training 2000 News*[3] about the research of the Equal Opportunities Commission (EOC) into training for women:

Training potentially offers women an opportunity to redress some of the inequalities they suffer in employment, says the Equal Opportunities Commission, introducing its review of recent research and policy initiatives in training in Britain. Training can enable women to enter occupations that have traditionally been the preserve of men, or to move up the hierarchy to levels from which they have previously been excluded. And today, more than ever before, training can be the key that helps women returners update and refresh their skills so they can re-enter the labour market at a level similar to the one they left before taking time out to raise a family. Faced with the decline in the number of young people coming on to the labour market, are employers making use of training for women to ensure that they have the skilled workforce they need?

The EOC's review shows that employers often treat women as second class employees when it comes to access to training.

Some employers appear to have different and lower expectations of young women, and these are reflected in their poorer access to training overall, says the EOC. Furthermore, the training provided for young women in full-time employment tends to be of shorter duration than that for young men. One in three young men in full-time employment and receiving training expected it to last three years or more, compared with one in ten equivalent young women.

Do adult women fare any better in access to training? There is a growing need for continuing training for all adults—to keep pace with technological change, to update skills after time out of the labour market, to develop careers. However, the EOC's review shows that the occupational segregation of women and men, and the different levels of continuing training associated with different occupations, result in women getting less than their fair share of training. Women part-time workers (42 per cent of all women workers) are much less likely to get training than women full-timers or men. In addition, training is grade-related, so women's concentration in lower grades means they have less access to training, and the training they do get is likely to be of short duration. Women are also disproportionately concentrated in small establishments, which are less likely than large employers to provide training for their employees.

A close look at training opportunities of all types, and in all age groups, shows that women in Britain get a raw deal. But the EOC review shows that women *want* training to update their skills, to help build confidence to re-enter the labour market, to enable them to change their occupations; and they also want new technology training.

What can employers do?
- Recognize training for women as an essential investment.
- Raise their expectations of their women employees.
- Develop the neglected resource represented by their women employees.
- Broaden the range of training opportunities offered to women.
- Provide training opportunities for part-time workers.

Small employers in particular should make sure the Training Enterprise Councils and Local Enterprise Companies know the training needs of their women employees, and that they meet those needs as part of mainstream training provision.

So in any organization the evidence shows that you can't pin the blame purely on the women themselves, or the organization; it's a multi-faceted problem which demands a multi-faceted solution of which women's development training is just a part.

Why organizations implement training

In our work in women's development over the last 20 years, we've come to the conclusion that there are almost as many reasons for initiating women's development training as there are organizations. Each set of circumstances, and therefore each set of reasons, is unique.

If you are the sort of person who only opens a book for the 'how to do it' bits, bear with us, because your motivation for initiating women's development training will have a powerful influence on the effectiveness of your training.

Here are some of the main reasons, although most organizations usually have a combination of more than one:

- the chairman said so
- business needs
- as a public relations exercise
- social justice

The chairman said so This occasionally happens in organizations when the person at the top (or, in large organizations, a group of people at the top) simply makes the decision that women's development training is to happen. The decision is imposed from on high, sometimes without consultation.

Advantages
- It happens, and often quickly.
- There is support from the top for anyone who wants to take it further.
- The decision leap-frogs the 'frozen layer' of middle management (who often obstruct women's development training initiatives) to give encouragement to the women (who are often at the bottom).
- It gives it a high profile.
- It brings the issues into the open.
- Budgets are set up to make it happen.
- The chairman keeps asking for progress reports on action.
- It gets press coverage.
- It looks good in recruitment literature.

Disadvantages
- The people implementing it aren't necessarily committed to it.
- No one really knows why it is happening.
- It's seen as the latest gimmick.
- It has no roots.
- It provokes a cynical reaction.
- It gives it a high profile.
- It may become too closely associated with that one person, and may die when he/she moves on.
- It may be implemented by others just to get a pat on the back.

Usually, the powerful people at the top are middle-aged white *men*, who are themselves subject to personal influence. *For example*

Up until last year I really thought that equal opportunities and special initiatives for women were fringe issues for organisations. Something blown up by the media and militant feminist types. However, I had to have a re-think when my daughter, with her Honours degree and several years of management experience, encountered a lot of difficulty in returning to work after a two-year break to have her son. I was so angry at the hurdles that were placed in her way, and at the way in which her male colleagues were treated so differently. It was then that I began to see that this is a vital issue for organisations and that the lead has to come from the top.
(Board director)

Business needs Most organizations running women's development training do so to address straightforward business needs and can see the sound common sense in it. Kent County Council says this clearly in its case study. These reasons vary enormously according to which business sector you are in, your market position, size, geographical situation, and so on. Here are some of the most usual reasons.

Skills shortages and demography

The workforce for the year 2000 has already been born and cannot be increased or decreased except by emigration or immigration. There will be 1.25 million fewer school leavers in 1993 than there were in 1983. The number of young people aged 16 to 25 will fall by 1.4 million between 1987 and 2000. Employers are acutely aware of this shrinking pool of labour and talent and are waking up to the fact that they cannot rely on new people coming in; they are forced to develop the people they already have within.

This means that for this period employers are searching around for underdeveloped groups of people. Traditionally, these tend to be people from ethnic minority groups, people with disabilities, older people, women generally and women returning to work.

As Business in the Community points out in its literature,[4] the predictions are:

- By 1995, 90 per cent of new jobs will be filled by women, mostly women with family responsibilities.
- By 1995, 50 per cent of the entire workforce will be women.
- Thirty-three per cent of new businesses are owned by women, as business start-ups by women have doubled between 1979 and 1989.
- At the same time, work is demanding a more highly educated and skilled workforce.
- By the year 2000, 40 per cent of UK jobs will require degree-level qualifications or higher.
- By 2000, 80 per cent of UK jobs will be designated as requiring 'thinking skills'.
- About 1 million of the 1.7 million new jobs forecast for the mid-1990s will be in professional and related areas.

All these trends mean that employers are being forced to look more flexibly and creatively at underdeveloped sources of ability—ethnic minorities, people with disabilities, older people and women. The largest source of untapped potential is women. Particularly women with family responsibilities.

Already organizations are beginning to 'woo' these women with career-break schemes, childcare arrangements, more flexible work patterns and enhanced maternity schemes, as these quotes from senior policy makers demonstrate:

The labour market is tightening. Individuals are more likely to be selective and have special requirements in their choice of employers. Employers will be forced to offer more flexible approaches to patterns of work.

Dr Ann Robinson, Head of the Policy Unit,
Institute of Directors

It is time companies sat up and took notice of what is going on around them. They will lose their high flying women managers to more responsive organisations, if they fail to heed the warnings.

> Peter Benton, Director General,
> British Institute of Management

Employers in the United Kingdom are fully aware of the need to encourage women to return to work, in view of the skill and experience which they contribute to the workforce in so many of our member companies.

> John Banham, Director General
> of the Confederation of British Industry

Offering women's development training as an inducement to retain, recruit or retrain is often part of an overall strategy.

Changing organizations

As technological breakthroughs speed up our pace of life, and as changes in society also accelerate, the world of work is discovering that the old ways of working are increasingly redundant. Management styles based on hierarchical organizational structures are too rigid for the speed of tomorrow. Large centralized organizations are too cumbersome to respond to the light-footedness needed for tomorrow. Rigid work patterns and traditional career structures are becoming simply irrelevant in a world of telecommuting, franchising, self-employment, second and third careers, and contracting out. Everything is changing. Charles Handy's *The Age of Unreason*[5] puts us in no doubt of this, and the prediction made by John Harvey-Jones[6] when he became chairman of ICI—'At the moment ICI UK has 66 000 employees. By the year 2015 I anticipate us employing some 3000 full-time staff plus a hell of a lot of part-timers'—does not mean that ICI is on its knees! Quite the reverse; it is simply a symptom of the radical shake-up that is upon us of the ways in which we structure and perform our work.

Some farsighted employers have put two and two together and realized the profound implications that this has for management styles. They will need people who do things differently: people who use cooperation, not confrontation; who are good at listening, not just giving orders; who are sensitive communicators; who lead alongside, not from in front; and who treat people as whole beings, with personal lives which are important, as well as their lives at work. A very, very few organizations are slowly realizing that there is a group of people who naturally prefer to work that way already and have the requisite skills and talent, and that group is *women*. Women work in a way which is different to men. They use different processes and skills and often work out of a different value system. They are just as effective, but go about it differently. Of course, there's nothing to stop employers training men in these different processes and skills, and many do, but soon there simply won't be enough of them to go round.

This is a radical and farsighted reason for supporting the development of women in the organization. We don't know of anyone doing it for this reason alone, but we anticipate that it will gain greater ground in the future.

Recruitment   Clearly, with a diminishing pool of school leavers and graduates to recruit from, competition between organizations to find and attract the best people is hotting up. A real and demonstrable commitment to women's development training, together with a package of other 'women-friendly' initiatives, can give an organization the edge over its competitor in a specific area or industry. Organizations which offer women's development training as an inducement at the point of recruitment tend to talk about it loudly and demonstrate with evidence the career prospects and support available.

Women want more   It would be misleading to suggest that it is always the organization that initiates women's development training, as it is often the women themselves who organize group pressure and lobby for training opportunities. This is less so now, as organizations slowly wake up to the good business sense of offering women's development training, but in the 1970s and 1980s it was not unusual for us to be approached primarily by an individual woman or a small group of women who were determined to make things happen.

Women are increasingly aware of their own potential and are no longer content with second best. Young women, in particular, now assume that they will be able to have a satisfying and fulfilling career, as well as a family life. Any employer who isn't prepared to offer these women opportunities to develop and fulfil themselves at work must beware. Women have a greater awareness and confidence than ever before, and organizations run the risk of losing them to a competitor who is prepared to take their development seriously.

Wasted resources   After the pressing case created by the demographic profile dip, wasted resources is the most compelling reason for offering any women's development initiatives, including women's development training. It is cheaper to retain and develop a woman that you already employ, than to have her leave and then have the expensive business of recruiting, training and settling in someone new.

For example   A large corporate organization initiated a massive women's development training programme throughout the organization, simply to check the flow of highly qualified secretarial staff leaving. Offering them women's development training was risky—for a small minority the training strengthened their resolve to leave—but it gave the vast majority the determination and confidence to stretch themselves in their existing jobs and to apply for other jobs, within the organization, often involving moving house or further technical training.

Career-break schemes are introduced to retain the valuable women who wish to leave for a few years to bring up children. It is more cost effective to have a career-break scheme, supported by training opportunities, than it is to let them go, recruit and train a replacement.

All the women working in an organization have undeveloped skills, abilities and ideas that could be of use to the organization. Of course, this probably applies to most of the men, too, but statistics show that there is no shortage of men at the top of organizations, no shortage of men on training courses, no shortage of men earmarked as high-flyers and no shortage of men being groomed for the board, even in organizations and industries where the majority of employees are women.

Wasted resources as a reason for initiating women's development training simply means acknowledging that an organization which turns its back on a largely untapped and enormous pool of talent already within its doors is simply not running cost effectively.

As a public relations exercise
This is the most negative and, often, cynical reason for embarking on women's development training. It hides a lack of real commitment to developing the women in the organization—the work is being done simply to look good. No one cares whether the women really develop their skills, confidence and experience, or whether they progress further in the organization. Here are the advantages and disadvantages of this exercise.

Advantages
- It promotes you as an enlightened employer.
- It enables you to keep up with competitors.
- It gets good media coverage.
- It looks good in recruitment.
- It makes you appear a genuinely progressive employer.

Disadvantages
- You'll get found out!
- Media coverage may push you into doing more than you want.
- It may work and bring about changes you don't want!
- Once it gets going it will be difficult to stop.

This may be the wrong reason for doing women's development training, but if that is why your organization is doing it, there's no need to stop! Fortunately, there are very few organizations that are quite so cynical, but they are on the increase. The women inside such organizations may be temporarily taken in, but they quickly see through the insincerity and can become cynical themselves about the organization. To such women we would say: 'Never mind *why* the organization is offering you this training. Even if you suspect that they don't mean a word of it, grab the training and use it for yourselves'. It could also be expressed: 'Don't look a gift horse in the mouth'!

A trainer being asked to deliver women's development training in this environment is in a difficult position. If you are genuine in your commitment to women's development training while you suspect the organization as a whole is cynical, then hijack the opportunity, establish the precedent, and fight the overall battle another day. We'll look further at comprehensive strategies in Chapter 3. However, if *you* are cynical, only jumping on a bandwagon to raise *your* profile while caring nothing for the progression of women in the organization, you cannot deliver good quality women's development training.

Social justice   This reason for implementing women's development training comes from the conscience of the organization and of society itself. It is the same impulse that acknowledges the inbuilt unfairness in a system where women doing the same work receive less pay than their male colleagues. This means acknowledging the innate prejudices and hurdles that are placed in the way of women in our society, and in the world of work, and consciously taking steps to compensate. It appeals to the altruistic streak in organizations and in individual decision makers.

Occasionally, women's development training does take place purely for this reason, but it is more likely to be in conjunction with a pressing business need. Since this is an emotionally charged debate, here are some of the facts which provoke a sense of social justice:

Women constitute half the world's population, perform nearly two-thirds of its work hours, receive one-tenth of the world's income, and own less than one-hundredth of the world's property.[7]

Women constitute 51.3 per cent of the UK population,[8] 43 per cent of the working population,[8] 26 per cent of management[8] and 0.4 per cent of chief executives.[9]

Table 1.1   *Women MPs in the House of Commons in 1990*[10]

Party	Women MPs	Men MPs
Conservative	17	356
Labour	23	220
Liberal Democrats	1	18
Scottish Nationalist	1	3
Independent	1	2
Ulster Unionists	0	8
Total	43	607

Women constituted over a third of trade union members in the 10 biggest unions in 1988, but less than a tenth of full-time officials are women.[11]

In 1988, in Great Britain, female manual workers earned on average 70.8 per cent of the hourly earnings of male manual workers; female non-manual workers earned an average of 62.2 per cent of the hourly wage of their male equivalents. All data refer to persons working full-time only.[8]

Women have just as much commitment, loyalty, intelligence, ability for hard work, creativity and persistence as their male colleagues. What they do not have are opportunities and support in a world of work which is structured and run by men, to suit men. Offering women's development training acknowledges this imbalance and attempts to redress it.

Your motivation

Most organizations are provoked into action by a subtle combination of more than one of these main reasons, with the most compelling influence coming from business needs.

Here are the Midland Bank Group's published reasons for providing a specific women's development programme as part of its LEAP initiative:

Why is Midland providing this programme for all female staff?
- It is one way of attracting women who might be thinking of returning to work, whether for a job or a career.
- It will show Midland to be supportive to working women by helping to ease their return to work.
- Having attracted women to work for Midland, it will encourage them to remain loyal.
- It will attract more women undergraduates who, research shows, are concerned about equal opportunities at work and about the support available for managing the home/work conflict.
- It shows Midland commitment to good training practices, especially through a self-development process.
- It shows to people within and outside the bank that Midland is committed to developing the skills and talents of *all* employees.
- It enables Midland to provide itself with a larger pool from which to select its managers and other senior staff.
- It achieves visible results within an equal opportunities field.
- It increases loyalty among existing female staff who may themselves be considering a career break.
- It increases the motivation of those staff concerned.
- There will be improved competency at work and better customer service given through implementation of the training.

Whatever your motivation for offering women's development training, it will permeate the training itself and the strategy you employ. Pause for a moment and clarify your own and your organization's reasons for bothering to initiate this training. Are you clear what you want to achieve in your organization? There may be a mixture of reasons. Consider your motivation now so that you'll know what you are aiming for and will be able to measure your success later. Consider, also, how you will know when you have succeeded. Will there be any measurable, tangible signs? Chapter 10 deals with evaluation.

Tick the reasons for providing training that apply to you.

To retain staff	☐
To recruit staff	☐
To get more women higher up the organization	☐
To get women into specific areas in the organization	☐
To free the bottleneck of women in certain areas and at certain levels	☐
To look good internally/externally	☐
To change the management style in the organization	☐
To keep up with your competitors	☐

To keep the women quiet ☐
To help women become better qualified ☐
To help women retrain ☐
To help women return after a career break ☐
To change the culture ☐
To create more balanced management teams ☐
To make better use of the creative resources already in the
    organization ☐
Other reasons ☐

Summary

In this chapter we've looked at the context of women's development training, clarified what it is and examined the different reasons why organizations bother with it.

The main messages from this chapter are:

- There is undisputed evidence to support the need for women's development training.
- Women's development training is a vital part of your overall human resource development and equal opportunities programmes.
- Every organization has its own reasons for implementing women's development training. It is important to be clear about *your* reasons.

References

1. Report of the Hansard Society Commission, *Women at the Top*, 1990.
2. Manpower Services Commission, *No Barriers Here*, 1980.
3. Morag Alexander, 'Second Class Training for Women?', *Training 2000 News*, December 1990.
4. Business in the Community, 'TECS and Women', 1990.
5. Charles Handy, *The Age of Unreason* (Arrow, 1989).
6. Quote from Francis Kinsman, *Millenium* (W.H. Allen, 1990).
7. UN Report, 1980.
8. Equal Opportunities Commission, *Women and Men in Britain 1990* (HMSO, 1990).
9. 'Women move into the executive chair', *The Times*, 30 April 1987.
10. *300 Group News*, 1990/91, Issue 18.
11. 'Unions fail to give women a full role', *The Guardian*, 4 March 1988.

2 The ground rules

Whatever form your women's development training takes, at whatever level and at whatever depth, there are several golden ground rules which apply to both the content and delivery. Take account of these ground rules all the way through. Some of them will influence specifics, such as the way you develop your strategy, run the course or evaluate it. Others run like themes through every aspect of women's development training, and influence your own performance.

Taken one by one, they provide you with the criteria to assess your strategy, course design and your own performance. Taken collectively they provide a whole approach to and philosophy of training. We've evolved these ground rules over the past 20 years as the vital ingredients which really make women's development training work. Each one is there for a very specific reason, and makes demands on the trainer. As the ground rules provide the threads that weave throughout women's development training, most of them are developed further in other parts of this book. This chapter gives you an overall picture by introducing each ground rule and looking at the practical implications for you of each one. They are:

 1 Women only
 2 Self-nomination
 3 Holistic approach
 4 Confidentiality
 5 Demonstrate equality
 6 Practise what you preach
 7 Role models
 8 No magic answers
 9 Stretching and small steps
10 Keep positive
11 Accept where people are
12 Build people up
13 Believe in them
14 It's their course
15 Practical and participative
16 Networking

Women only

Women's development training only works in a single-sex environment. It provides a safe place in which women can raise issues, knowing they will not be ridiculed or harassed (verbally or physically), an environment where common themes and issues will be taken seriously, and where they will be able to compare notes and gain encouragement and support.

Most women work in a mixed environment. Our aim is not to be separatist: rather, as one takes a holiday in a healing and restoring place, or goes to exciting and encouraging new climes, women-only training can bring the special qualities needed to face the reality of daily life.

You may say that this safe and supportive environment could just as easily be supplied by a mixed group, and some development courses do run along these lines. However, from our own experience of running women-only and mixed groups, and our male colleagues' experiences of running men-only and mixed groups, we come to the following general conclusions:

- A women-only group settles down very quickly. Almost immediately there is an openness and sharing of life situations. In women-only groups women:
  —gain support from each other
  —recognize they are not the only ones with such problems, questions or issues
  —encourage each other
  —achieve real, in-depth work quickly
  —achieve remarkable openness, support and trust even in a group of total strangers
- A male-only group takes a long time to settle down. There is 'point scoring' off each other, and off the trainer. Jokes and games abound, and real development work is only possible after an extended period of settling down.
- A mixed group settles down more quickly than a male group and the men behave better. However, it is rather like running two courses at once—the women work quickly, and at a far deeper level, right from the beginning, while the men take time to settle, or the women hold back till they are sure of a safe environment. The women tend to support and encourage any men in the group, even if the men are in a minority. Inevitably, the men end up with more than their fair share of the time, and the women's needs and issues come second. So in mixed groups women tend to:
  —hold back
  —put men first
  —be defensive or apologetic
  —speak less
  —give more time to men's problems
  —feel that their problems are different

For example A 'training trainers' event was attended by 15 women and 1 man. The man in this case was unfamiliar with the material, and behind the women in terms of experience and quality. Everyone, including the man himself and the trainer, recognized this. The 15 women felt sorry for him, coached him and gave him particular help. He seemed happy with this and took a disproportionate amount of the 'air-time', to the women's detriment. It was enormously frustrating for the trainer, as the course ran at a speed and level to accommodate the man, and the women did not develop to their greatest potential.

For example A one-day careers workshop was attended by 38 women and 2 men. During the day, the trainer noticed that the questions raised by syndicate groups in report-back sessions were the questions which had been raised by the men in discussions, and that the two men consistently did the reporting back for the groups, aided by notes and support from the women. Halfway through, the trainer asked 'Why is George reporting back again?' and was openly told, 'None of us want to do it, and he's the man. We told him that we'd back him up'.

In both these cases, the individual men had not asked to take centre stage. The women placed them in the spotlight, and the men acquiesced. On both these occasions, the course ended up focusing on the needs of the small minority of men present.

For example A series of pilot courses was suggested as a way of helping the women in a large diverse organization to move further up the career ladder. However, in order to avoid a negative male backlash, the training department decided that a very few influential men would also be encouraged to attend, the idea being that they would become ambassadors for the course and provide support. As word got around about how valuable the courses were, managers stopped nominating women and nominated men instead. Eventually, the whole course was hijacked by men who certainly did not fulfil the criteria of being the influential opinion-forming type—some were 18 year old trainees! So, a project that was intended as a women's development initiative became mainstream, and dominated by men.

What this means to you
- You have to be convinced of the value of women-only training to do it well.
- You have to be prepared to fight to defend the all-women nature of the course, and not let it be hijacked. This becomes a particularly vulnerable spot when you are developing your strategy (see Chapter 3).
- Be ready for a possible male backlash: 'Where's the development course for men, then?' (To which the answer is: 'All the other courses we run are male development courses, as they are mostly attended by men!') There may also be a need to address men's development issues in men-only groups.
- If you are a woman trainer, you may feel pressure to deliver a women-only course, whether you personally support the idea or not.
- If you are a man, you cannot run the course. You can champion it, mentor it, set it up, design it, support it and nurture it, but you can only be there on the day as a guest speaker.
- The only men who can be involved on the actual course will attend to

deliver a specific session, e.g. 'Why the company is bothering to run this course', and then go away again—immediately!

Self-nomination

Any form of development training demands a great deal from the participant, because it is about examining oneself, and about making sometimes profound changes in both personal and work lives. It is not a series of techniques, bolted on from the outside, nor is it a skill to be practised parrot-fashion, or copied from someone else. Development comes from the inside, and grows into the external actions which the participant decides to take. You cannot force someone to develop themselves. It is impossible to do development work with someone who doesn't want to be there unless, of course, you resort to brainwashing!

For example   A four-day residential course at a luxurious venue included four women who openly expressed their resentment at being there. (The line manager had sent them to make him look good.) They refused to leave the course, as they had decided it would be a pleasant four-day holiday in a lovely place, but they injected such a high level of negativity and cynicism into the course that it was destroyed. The trainer allowed them to stay as she was trying to implement the ground rule of believing in them and not giving up on their development. With hindsight, the trainer realized that she should have insisted that they left.

For example   On a two-day personal effectiveness course, one woman said that she had been sent by her boss (an enthusiastic, well-meaning person who was sure it would do her good). The woman had doubts; she wasn't sure at all. So the trainer asked her to remain open-minded about the course and to discuss how she felt about it again at the lunch break. She did, and by lunch time was well integrated into the group and had almost forgotten she'd been sent.

What this means to you
- The participants need to be, at best, enthusiastic volunteers and, at worst, open-minded and prepared to learn (see Chapter 7 about recruitment).
- You need to devote a good deal of time and energy to making sure that the right people are on the course.
- Your communications with people responsible for nominations (personnel officers, managers, etc.) need to be very clear in this respect (see Chapter 7).
- You need to discover, right at the beginning of the course, why people are there. If you discover that someone doesn't want to be there, have a private conversation with her and explain the nature of the course—ask her to remain open-minded for a few hours.
- Do not be perturbed if people decide the course isn't for them. As long as you've had a conversation with them about it, let them go.
- Make it easy for anyone who doesn't want to be there to leave.
- Explain, encourage and persuade, but don't push anyone into attending a women's development course against her will.

- Be prepared to deal with the difficulties which arise if someone stays who actively doesn't want to be there. You cannot ignore the situation, and you may need to use your strongest assertiveness!
- You can create a really positive developmental environment knowing that each woman really wants to be there.
- The women will feel more relaxed, knowing that they have all chosen to be there.

Holistic approach

Women lead extremely complex and busy lives, constantly balancing the multi-roles of cook, mother, nurse, wife, business woman, daughter, chauffeur, etc. Women's development training accepts the whole woman. The woman who is seen at work is only one part of her, and to separate out the work aspects from her personal and domestic aspects is distorting the reality of her life, and will give you an unbalanced and mostly irrelevant course. Having a holistic approach also means that a woman can relate the course to her own specific situation, knowing that her life circumstances are seen as a valid part of the course. This is particularly important for a group of women returners.

What this means to you
- Emphasize the holistic nature of the course in your introduction.
- Encourage the women to relate all the content to their lives as a whole, e.g. applying assertiveness at home is as relevant as at work.
- Ensure that you have a wide variety of examples and anecdotes that include all aspects of women's lives.
- Stress the importance of including all the parts of their lives when you're briefing any exercise or group discussion.
- You need to work holistically on yourself too.
- Reveal a variety of different aspects of your own life.
- Help to keep the focus balanced among the many aspects of the women's lives—if it becomes too home-oriented, bring in work examples, and so on.

Confidentiality

We always agree a contract of confidentiality with women at the beginning of women's development training courses. It means that the women are able to share personal situations knowing that they will not be talked about outside the course. This enables them to talk about themselves and their real situations freely rather than discussing hypothetical situations or a mythical friend. This is especially important for women who are unfamiliar with attending courses or for a group with especially low self-confidence, such as returners. Every participant and all the tutors and speakers are included in the contract of confidentiality.

What this means to you
- Outside the course you can never talk about the situation of a specific individual.
- No reports on progress during the course or assessments of the women will be given to the organization.

- You will need to find a suitably encouraging way of agreeing the contract at the beginning of the course (see Chapter 9). The contract must be made very clearly in a light and non-judgemental way.
- Any examples you give from other courses need to be anonymous, unless you have gained permission from the women concerned.
- You'll have to resist any temptation you may have to 'show off' about how much women confide in you!
- On later courses you may meet other people who have been talked about under the contract of confidentiality. You will need to remain open-minded when meeting them.
- You will need to take action if you find the contract of confidentiality is being broken.

Demonstrate equality

Women's development training is for all women whatever their race, age, social standing, sexual preference or physical ability. Women's development training aims to help women to overcome the prejudices that they have experienced because they are women, but sexism is not the only prejudice that women have to overcome. The training offered should demonstrate all aspects of equality and encourage women from wide-ranging backgrounds to work together on their own development. Remember too that the courses are pro-women, not anti-men!

What this means to you
- Examine your own prejudices and work to eliminate them.
- Check the organization's equal opportunities policy.
- Challenge assertively any prejudices and assumptions which you perceive being applied to the women on the course or generally to other people.
- Aim to demonstrate the view that 'all human beings are capable of development', even those who seem very stuck.

Practise what you preach

You may prefer to be a low-key trainer who joins the group and takes a facilitative role, or you may like to be the up-front leader with a high profile. Wherever you fall along the spectrum of training style, your credibility is inextricably linked with your ability to demonstrate that what you are talking about works, and that you have personal experience of it.

If you are not actively pursuing your own personal and work development while urging others to do so, then you are either a coward, a hypocrite or a workaholic who's forgotten about herself! And you'll be found out!

We believe this to be a really fundamental ground rule. You do not need to have got your personal development right (who has?), but you have to be working on it.

What this means to you
- Have examples of your own struggles, successes and failures ready.
- Be prepared to demonstrate what you are teaching. For example: in

assertiveness role plays, be prepared to participate if they're getting stuck, and accept that you may get it wrong also.

- You don't have to pretend to be Superwoman; in fact, it's better if you don't even try!
- You need to recognize when you're not fit to train, either physically because of illness or emotionally because you are facing your own life crisis (see Chapter 8).

Role models

Role models give us pictures of how we might be or how we definitely don't want to be. For most women in organizations there are few role models to copy on the route ahead. So take every opportunity to introduce a wide range of women as role models on your courses—as speakers, talking about their own careers and development, or their specialist subjects, being involved as helpers or running tutorial groups. Don't forget yourself as a role model too. Role models inspire other women to action.

What this means to you
- Identify positive role models for the women in your target group.
- Include role models in the design of your programmes (see Chapter 4).
- Be aware of the kind of role model that you are.
- Include a variety of role models from different races, ages, abilities, backgrounds and current situations.
- Encourage participants from previous programmes to be role models for future ones.

No magic answers

People come on a women's development course with some form of expectation. Often the expectation is that, during the course, they will discover, or be given, some kind of magic formula which will tell them exactly how to live the rest of their lives. Some people are hungry to develop themselves and may feel cheated as they discover that there are no magic solutions which will result in the jigsaw puzzle of their lives falling neatly into place. Often people are disappointed when you tell them there are no magic answers because they have an expectation that you will provide them with a theory, materials, or guru figure that will change their lives.

What this means to you
- Make it very clear at the beginning that there are no magic answers on this course, and be prepared for their disappointment.
- Encourage group members to come up with ideas on individual problems.
- Have plenty of practical tips and examples to help people work out their own answers.
- Do not tell people what you think they should be doing—your opinion is relevant but they need to work it out for themselves. Be wary of the value attributed to the trainer's words.

- When people get stuck, offer options rather than opinions and be clear that they are just ideas.

Stretching and small steps

If a programme is truly developmental, it will involve women in 'stretching' and doing things they wouldn't have done before. 'Stretching' means achieving just a little bit more. Like stretching physically, it needs to be done gradually and in small steps. Sudden, large, physical stretches lead to muscle pain; developmental stretches that are too big lead to emotional pain. Usually nobody minds a bit of an ache if they know they are getting fitter! Small steps enable women to gain confidence and are much easier than big leaps. One small achievable step is less frightening than a big leap. Of course, as when crossing an abyss, there may be times when big leaps are needed too!

What this means to you
- Spot when the women need to be challenged.
- Do the 'stretching' activities even when they aren't popular.
- Include confidence-building activities even if they need persuasion to do them.
- Always push people a bit further, both individually and in groups.
- Beware of overstretching just to please you or to fit in your favourite exercise!
- Action plans need to have small achievable goals (see Chapter 9).
- Keep 'stretching' yourself.

Keep positive

One of the major hurdles for women to overcome is the negative attitudes they tend to have about themselves. Developing a positive self-image and a positive attitude towards their circumstances is another of the main objectives of women's development training. The material and design of your course give you the opportunity to achieve this, but only your attitude will guarantee it. At times, it will feel like a battle of wills: your determination to remain positive, matched against their negativity. For the course to succeed, your positiveness must be durable and infiltrate every aspect of the course.

What this means to you
- You need a good stock of positive anecdotes and examples to draw on.
- Be patient and determined.
- Stamp ruthlessly on any sign of cynicism (cynicism is the major enemy).
- Challenge negative examples and comments.
- Make sure you get enough personal space to keep yourself positive and energized.

Accept where people are

A trainer's life would be so easy if everyone arrived on the course at a set stage in their lives, with a common basis of understanding and co-ordinated issues. This ground rule means accepting that people's lives are not neat and tidy, and being aware that it is all too easy to slot people into categories. It is vital in women's development training to accept totally where people are in their lives, in relation to the material and ideas that you are putting across. Do not fit them into preconceived boxes or judge them in any way for being where they are.

What this means to you
- *Listen* and suspend judgement; accept that you cannot know a woman's whole life story and so you do not know or understand why she is as she is.
- Know your material well, so that when you are running the course you can speed up, slow down or go into greater depth, if someone needs you to do so.
- Really understand what the women's lives and work are like. At best, conduct an audit beforehand (see Chapter 3) and, at the very least, get out there and walk around and chat to people before the course.
- Be aware of any topical issues that may crop up.

Build people up

The main reason that women come on women's development courses is to develop their self-confidence and self-esteem. Your task is to build on existing levels of skills, determination, confidence and courage, and take them further by 'stretching' and challenging. You are not there to break people down deliberately, upset them, intimidate them, or reduce their confidence further, in order to build them back up again. We're aware that there are trainers and consultants who work on this basis, but there is no place for them in women's development training.

What this means to you
- Remember your objectives in running women's development training— you will get better results from building people up.
- Resist the temptation to make a clever comment at someone else's expense.
- Make sure that negative feedback is given constructively.
- Give lots of encouragement and praise.
- Deal assertively with cynicism and sarcasm from individuals.
- On a returners' course, explain this ground rule and stress the supportive element of the course, as returners are often especially apprehensive about the course process.

Believe in them

As women's development training is primarily concerned with developing self-confidence and self-esteem, the fact that you continue to demonstrate *your* respect is a major factor. However short the time you're with the participants, however unresponsive they are, however much they rub you up the wrong way, or however much you dislike them personally, you must always believe that they are capable of more and better and that they will change. It is your job to believe in them more than they believe in themselves, and more than others believe in them.

What this means to you
- Respect a woman's belief in herself.
- Never ever give up on someone.
- Keep faith that they will change when they are ready.
- Remain non-judgemental of someone as a person—you must use your judgement of their *behaviour* (especially when training in assertiveness), but not judge them *as a person*.
- You need a lot of patience!
- Go on working with people up to, and after, the last closing moments of the course. We've experienced the difficult sarcastic participant, who's been really negative for the whole course, but suddenly switches in the closing moments, or sometimes *after* the course.
- Accept that you'll never know! Women's development training is often like sowing seeds, except that you may never know which take root and grow and which do not. Remain open-minded—you're guaranteed some surprises!

It's their course

You are not there to provide light entertainment for a day or two. Nor are the delegates there to jump through hoops to please you. It is a partnership between you and the group, but ultimately it's their course. They must know that it's their issues that are being addressed, in a way that they can use and relate to.

What this means to you
- Use their vocabulary and jargon.
- Use their examples and credit them: 'As Fiona said on Monday . . . '.
- Use their real situations to work on in groups and individually. Keep case studies and invented scenarios to an absolute minimum.
- Be wary of telling your own favourite stories regardless of whether or not they fit in.
- Monitor the length of your inputs and check that they aren't becoming an ego trip.
- Be open to what the women have to say even though you think you've heard it all before.
- Be prepared to tackle an issue, if it's getting in the way (see Chapter 9).
- Structure your exercises so that participants give and receive feedback among themselves, and keep your comments to the end.

Practical and participative

People change their lives for themselves, by trying things out, learning from the experience, and moving on, however small the step. The emphasis of women's development training, therefore, is away from the theory and heavily weighted towards trying things out and learning through experience.

With an intellectual group of women, you will have to be particularly tough in getting them to put things into practice (for example, in role plays of assertiveness), as they will much prefer to discuss the conceptual aspects for hours! However, time and time again, we see that the real shifts that take place inside people do so through a personal experience, through *doing* and not through thinking, however satisfying the intellectual debate. It is important to make sure that people 'have a go' at new things. Often after a course women say that it was being encouraged (sometimes almost pushed!) into having a go, that enabled them to learn.

What this means to you
- Use only small amounts of theory (e.g. to introduce a new subject) and move swiftly on to the practical implications.
- Pull all discussions down to earth by asking for real examples or by trying things out in small groups.
- Refuse to discuss hypothetical situations.
- Have lots of practical exercises available up your sleeve, on a wide range of subjects.
- Keep it all very informal.
- Have lots of group work with feedback.
- Give real examples. Start to log examples that you hear which you can use on another course (ensuring that the woman's identity is protected).
- Keep the whole course action-oriented. Constantly pin generalities down to specifics. For example: 'So what this means in practice is . . .'; 'So having thought about it, what are you going to *do*?'
- Mention action points throughout the course and make sure you allow time at the end of the course for an action session which is taken seriously (see Chapter 4).

Networking

And finally, but by no means of least importance, networking. Networking is an integral part of women's development. Women need to be encouraged to network and make the best use of opportunities to build up new contacts or get to know more about the contacts they already have. Thinking in a networking way about every aspect of women's development training, from pre-course audits to post-course activities, positively increases the range and use of contacts.

What this means to you
- Use every opportunity to build up their networking skills.
- Build up your own networks and expand your horizons.
- Keep your own contact list of women's networks—produce a handout on them.
- Tell participants that you expect them to network, and encourage the swapping of telephone numbers.
- Introduce networking exercises on courses.
- Think in a networking way—'I don't know, but I know someone who does'.
- Encourage the women to set up their own network after a programme (see Chapter 11).
- Let them set their own aims and do it their way.
- Give them moral support.

Summary

In this chapter we've outlined the many ground rules of women's development training which give it its philosophy, structure, focus and common-sense approach. They interweave at all the stages of training and cannot really be separated one from the other. They combine to make women's development training successful. The main messages are:

- These ground rules establish the particular quality of women's development training.
- Familiarize yourself with the ideas behind each ground rule, so that you can implement them automatically.
- Each ground rule needs the support of the others to work well.
- These ground rules apply to all aspects of women's development training.

Sun Microsystems (UK) Ltd

Sun Microsystems (UK) Ltd is a very rapidly growing organization in a hi-tech industry. This case study shows how the development of their women's development training ground rules arose out of an audit of the general development needs of the whole organization and is an example of a women's development training programme that has grown and established itself very quickly.

Women's development at Sun Microsystems (UK) Ltd

The UK subsidiary of Sun Microsystems Inc was opened in February 1984. In the six years it has been operating, the growth of the company has been exceptional. The annual turnover of Sun UK is now £120 million. We currently employ 500 people of whom 151 are women. Of these women, 21 are in management positions.

Since the company was set up, we have provided some training and development opportunities for our staff. This is recognized as an essential part of managing and growing our business. However, in early 1990, we decided to adopt a longer-term and more structured approach to planning the company's development needs.

In May 1990 we conducted a development needs analysis in Sun (UK). From the results of our research it immediately became clear that there was a gap in our development programme. The development programmes offered for the secretarial/administrative staff were all based on technical rather than personal skills development. As with most organizations, this group is comprised mainly of women.

In order to address this deficiency we researched the needs of this group further and developed some simple but key criteria upon which our development programme should be based:

- The approach of the programme must be holistic and thus encompass both home and work situations.
- The programme should focus primarily on optimizing job performance and satisfaction within the current role.

- In order to build confidence the programme should concentrate on recognizing and developing personal strengths in terms of increasing effectiveness (rather than dwelling on weaknesses).
- Contents should include career planning, assertive communication, organizational power and politics, and stress management.
- Any development programme must be part of an ongoing process and not a one-off event.

Work and Personal Development programme

As a result, our first Work and Personal Development programme was run in July 1990. Initially, there was a degree of scepticism among some of our senior managers about the possible outcome of running such programmes. The fear was that the women, armed with new skills and highly motivated, would expect promotion opportunities immediately and would leave if these were not forthcoming.

In the event these fears proved unfounded. The programme has been a real success for the women who have attended and programmes planned for 1991 are already oversubscribed. We have experienced no attrition in the groups of women trained and their managers have been very impressed by their increased professionalism and positive attitudes. Indeed, many of the managers are now delegating far more of the interesting, challenging and higher-level tasks to their secretaries and administrators with excellent results.

Building on the success of the Work and Personal Development programme we are now looking at development needs for our women managers.

Learning libraries

Sun Microsystems (UK) Ltd provides opportunities for all employees to manage their own development and all employees are regarded as equally important. In addition to the training courses we provide we are in the process of setting up learning libraries in each Sun Microsystems (UK) Ltd office. These will contain books, audio cassettes and videos. The materials will cover a range of subjects including health and leisure, personal development, childcare, etc. All employees will be able to borrow materials from any of the libraries.

We are also running lunch-time seminars, open to all employees, on subjects such as working parents, women's health, and managing stress.

We know that to create a more balanced picture in terms of the number of women in senior positions within Sun Microsystems (UK) Ltd we have a long way to go. We will need to look at our recruitment process as well as doing further work on developing the talent and potential we already have.

However, we have recognized the need to invest in the development of women within the organization and have seen the benefits of this strategy. We are committed to ensuring that the future for women within Sun Microsystems (UK) Ltd is one of real opportunity.

Annabel Perahia
Sun Microsystems (UK) Ltd

3 Developing a strategy

Having clarified why you are embarking on women's development training and taken into account the ground rules associated with it, you can now consider taking action to implement women's development training, and for this you will need some form of overall strategy.

This chapter looks at all the aspects of developing a strategy which will work in your culture and achieve your objectives. We include the reasons for having a strategy; the influences that may affect it; how women's development training fits into women's development overall; identifying needs; defining your target group; the scale of the strategy; enlisting support; getting the timing right; and a brief look at the public relations activity (PR) needed to support your strategy.

Why have a strategy

Action that has been thought through to its eventual outcome stands a much better chance of being effective and proving durable. This is not to say that action which has not been thought through never succeeds in developing women in the organization, but it is more likely to be ineffective or even to backfire. This book has many case studies of organizations where women's development training has gone well, but there are a couple of cautionary tales:

For example A large retailing chain ran a women's development course without identifying any specific needs beforehand. The women on the course resented the implication that they 'needed to catch up' and men in the organization felt threatened by the activity. Poor feedback from the pilot course meant that women's development instantly died in this organization.

For example A multinational organization was persuaded by the enthusiasm of one woman to introduce a women's development programme into its directory of courses, without the context of a strategy and without consulting either line management or the women concerned. The course objectives and programme were published but the women who came on the course had much wider and deeper needs than those met by what was offered. Some needed in-depth career counselling, others management skills. Women came because it was the only course for women that was on offer, but several went away dissatisfied because their needs had not been met. Women's development training acquired a reputation for being superficial and the course instantly died.

The benefits of having a strategy, whether it is your own personal one, or an official one instigated by the organization, are that you will:

- minimize the risks
- be aware of what the risks are
- be able to 'sell' the whole process to the organization
- be ready for the many questions from many different parts of the organization
- gain commitment before you start any training
- demonstrate your/the organization's commitment
- be more in control

Women's development training starts in an organization with one person who begins somewhere, and often it is not that same person who is carrying the responsibility two or four years later. If the strategy is clear it can be followed through consistently even if there is a change of staff.

Your strategy can be prepared in as much depth and detail as you wish, or as briefly and quickly as you wish. Do the thinking in as much detail as you are able so that the action you take will stand the best chance of success.

Influences on your strategy

Your strategy will not exist in a vacuum, so while you may have an idea of the way forward in an ideal world, in practice you will have to bend and flex your plan to accommodate a whole host of influences, some distant and some closer to home. As these influences are themselves subject to other influences, the whole scenario is constantly changing, and your strategy will need to be flexible and responsive to these changes, without losing sight of the overall objective. Figure 3.1 illustrates the process.

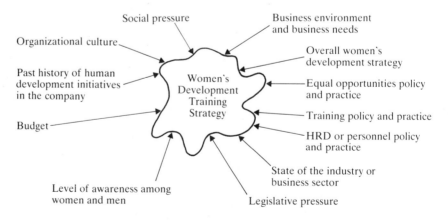

Figure 3.1 *Influences on your women's development training strategy*

Taking all these influences into account results in strategies which are unique to the organization. A good strategy is not off-the-peg but tailormade.

Depending on the objectives that you set yourself at the end of Chapter 1, and the overall culture that is operating in your organization, you will find that some of the influences shown in Figure 3.1 will have a greater impact than others. Before dismissing any of them as irrelevant to your situation, consider your understanding and the depth of your knowledge of each one.

If you are a freelance consultant, then you may be able to see overall influences clearly, but need to swot up on the culture and internal policies and practices. If you're running public courses, decide whether your strategy is for the whole employment market, or for a specific industry or geographical area, and take a general view of each of these influences.

To develop a full and detailed strategy to which the organization can be committed takes time, effort and money. Stop and think first of all about the setting in which the organization is now placed and the background against which any women's development training will take place.

Where is the organization now?
Before rushing into the detail of your strategy, think as objectively as possible about where your organization is now in relation to the employment, training and development of women. It is important to work from where the organization actually is and to accept the reality of the current situation, whether excellent or difficult. Some of the common pitfalls in developing a women's development training strategy are:

• not having all the facts
• beginning from an incorrect value judgement of the situation
• succumbing to the pressure to do something quickly
• being so fired up with what needs to be done and how it could be that some of the reality is forgotten
• not working within the culture of the organization

Do some homework around the following questions:

Where are the women in the organization?

• What are the statistics by grade, by department, by salary?
• Are there any available?
• Are they published?
• Who sees them?
• How are the statistics changing?

Is the organization an equal opportunities employer?

• How is the policy written in relation to women?
• Who sees it?
• How is it perceived?
• Which employment policies back it up?
• Who is committed to it?
• What changes in the statistics have occurred since it was written?
• What history is there of women's development training within the organization?

For advice on developing and implementing an effective equal opportunities policy, refer to *Beyond the Great Divide* by Jane Beck and Maggie Steel.[1]

How many women are using:

- in-house management courses?
- in-house skills-based courses?
- external courses?
- distance learning programmes?
- correspondence courses?
- further education opportunities?
- day release?
- women-only courses?

What is your assessment of the organizational culture in relation to women?[2]

- Which values and beliefs define 'success'?
- What do people have to do to be successful—who are the heroes and heroines?
- How are things done—rites, rituals?
- What is driving the business environment—marketing, research, production, profit, social needs?
- How does the informal communication network operate?

Women's development training as part of an overall women's development strategy

Women's development training is not something simply to be added on to existing strategies and policies. It is an integral part of any human resources strategy and shouldn't be seen as isolated from the mainstream. But where does it belong? Is it part of personnel, equal opportunities training, or general human resource development? And what are the other activities which will impinge on it, either detracting from, or supporting, women's development training?

We know of some very successful women's development training which is running inside organizations that have no other women's development activities. It is very much the exception and, because of its isolation, this training is a low-key, long-term measure being run quietly, almost subversively, and with modest objectives.

Most women's development training activity is taken in conjunction with other women's development initiatives, and is considered and promoted as part of the overall strategy. Case studies, books, articles and papers on general women's development initiatives abound, and organizations such as the Midland Bank Group, the BBC, British Telecom, Kent County Council and many of the London boroughs are well known for the broad scope of their action.

The areas for action

In their report *Women at the Top*[3] the Hansard Society Commission lists the following 29 strategies for overcoming organizational barriers for women, *in addition to* women's development training:

- equal opportunities policy
- equal opportunities training
- dual interviewing
- precise job specifications
- objective assessment criteria
- external advertising
- equal opportunity audits
- monitoring
- targeting
- job sharing
- flexitime
- working at home
- annual hours
- other flexible arrangements
- mobility requirements dropped or modified
- dual career job search
- age requirements dropped
- career-break schemes
- workplace nurseries
- childcare vouchers
- parental leave
- enhanced maternity leave
- other childcare help
- equal opportunity advertising
- headhunting
- internal promotion policies
- boardroom commitment to change
- equal opportunities training for all managers
- awareness training for all staff.

To this exhaustive list, we could also add term-time-only working, eldercare issues, networks, job evaluation and equal pay.

So, in addition to your homework on the organizational culture, give some thought to issues such as:

Childcare
- What facilities are available in the company/outside?
- What are women paying for their childcare?
- What is needed—nursery, after school, school holidays?
- How do women feel about the situation?

Career breaks
- Is there a policy?
- Is it known?
- Is it used in practice?
- If not, why not?

Returners
- How many women are returners?
- What is their experience of coming back?
- Does the company have a policy/practice of recruiting returners?
- Are any arrangements made for updating training?

Networking
- Do any networks exist?
- How do women meet and communicate with each other?

Working patterns
- Is there job sharing?
- Does flexitime exist?
- Are there variable hours?
- Are there annual hours?
- Does term-time-only working exist?

Training and development
- What programmes exist for women?
- Who attends them?
- What results do they achieve?
- How do women hear about training/development courses?
- Who decides who goes?
- How user-friendly to women are the general courses?
- What do women perceive as their needs?
- What do senior management perceive as women's needs now and in the future?
- How do women feel about women-only training?

And don't worry if you don't know the answers—yet!

Women's issues on mixed courses

Examine how women's issues are dealt with on mixed courses. Many courses in the past have been designed for men, by men, using models of management or leadership which come from male-dominated perspectives such as the armed forces. This does not mean that they are not relevant to women too, but, had they been devised by women for women working in female-dominated organizations, they might have been different.

Check the handouts and illustrative examples used on mainstream courses.

- Do they use 'he' and 'him' and relate examples from male perspectives?
- When people on courses talk about managers, do they refer to them as 'he'? (We find that even on women-only courses, women themselves often refer to managers as 'he', but then of course they usually are!)

Attitudes to women

Organizational values are seen in the 'written' and 'done' policies in human relations. Look at how your organization describes itself in human resources terms.

- Does the organization chart list the names of all its managers but just show 'secretary' or 'admin staff' as general terms?
- Are the bulk of the women lumped together in anonymous groups?
- Is it policy for the women in junior positions to answer the telephone with their own name, e.g. 'Fiona Campbell', or their boss's, e.g. 'Peter Jones's secretary'?

Organizational policies can demean or enhance the position of women. Which of your human resources development policies enhance their position and which need to be reviewed and changed to integrate the women in the organization fully as equal, respected members?

Look at the organization's recruitment and public relations literature.

- Where are the women and how are they portrayed?
- Are there 'token' women there?
- Are there women only in support functions or are women shown at all levels?

For a very detailed guide to assessing your organization's 'health check' on women's development issues, work through *No Barriers Here?*[4] if you can find a copy (at the time of writing it is temporarily out of print).

Having taken into account all the influences shown in Figure 3.1, you should have some idea of the issues that your women's development training will need to address, the likely target group and the probable response from the women themselves and the rest of the organization.

The objectives of your strategy

All this will enable you to refine your objectives so that you can make a start. One word of warning: these are only *working* objectives. Always be open, in the process of developing a strategy, to changing or refining the objectives.

Chapter 1 looked at *why* organizations embark on women's development training. At this point in developing your strategy, define *what* you are wanting to achieve, and reserve judgement on *how* you are going to achieve it.

Here are some examples of objectives stated publicly and privately by organizations:

- The need to retain quality staff and encourage quality staff to work on contract.
- To provide development opportunities for women who have remained in administration while those in other departments have fast-tracked as the company grew.
- To enable senior women to break through into top management.
- To promote more non-management women into management.
- To be part of an overall strategy to provide the workforce of the future by making the organization more attractive to women.
- To be seen to be doing something and provide internal publicity for one particular manager.

Identifying the needs

Having formed your own view of what the situation calls for, put this on one side and be prepared to listen. There is a wide spectrum of activity open to you in identifying the real needs. The scale of the action

Full audit

Mini audit

Consultations

Familiarization day

Desk research

Going in cold

Figure 3.2   *The audit spectrum*

you take will depend on the time and budget available to you. Figure 3.2 shows the stages between a full audit and going in cold.

Ideally, no piece of women's development training would ever be started without a full in-depth audit. In practice, it is often seen as a luxury, and something more hasty takes place. As we recommend the depth and breadth of thinking involved in a full audit, we outline the process in some detail below.

Full audit   A full audit involves:

- background briefing
- group consultations
- individual interviews
  —with possible target group
  —with line management
- a questionnaire
- steering group
- a report

It may take place over an extended period of time, and a possible time-table is:

Week 1
Detailed briefing of person carrying out the audit.

Conversations at policy level.
Considerable paper research—access to statistics, policies, literature.

Weeks 2–6
Group consultations: one and a half hour meetings with 10–12 of possible target group.
Individual interviews: one-hour interviews with a cross-section of line management and possible target group.

Week 4
Compilation and distribution of questionnaire, devised on the basis of responses to early consultations and interviews.

Week 6
Return of questionnaire and compilation of results.

Week 8
Presentation of draft strategy to steering group.

Here are examples of the questions asked at the briefing session in Week 1 in a large local authority:

- What is the structure of the organization?
- How is the organization referred to?
- What are the job gradings/titles in each division?
- Where are the women? Statistics?
- Where are ethnic minorities and women with disabilities?
- How do you define 'management'?
- What are the issues around graduates? Do they have a fast track of their own?
- What is a typical career pattern for a man? And for a woman? How do they differ?
- What are the key points in the organization's history?
- What other women's development initiatives are there?
- Who is responsible for an individual's access to training?
- How do women get access to training?
- What are the current buzzwords?
- What is the relationship with the trade unions?
- What key issues/questions are facing the organization now and in the future?
- What will be the effect of these on women?
- Are there any key changes in the pipeline?

Here are some examples of the questions asked in the consultation groups that followed. The same questions, suitably adapted, were also used for individual interviews:

- What is your job title?
- What is your boss's job title?
- What are the job titles of the people immediately below you?
- What is the job title of the most senior woman that you know?

- What is your ambition?
- Why do you work here?
- What do you like most about working here?
- What do you like least?
- Is the organization making the most of you? If not, what could it be doing?
- Are *you* making the most of you? If not, what could you be doing?
- What have you got going for you (i.e. skills, personal qualities, circumstances . . .)?
- What's holding you back?
- Are there any networks? If so—what?
- What opportunities are there for sideways moves?
- What are the main stresses in working here?
- What do you need to do to get on here?

Jane Beck and Maggie Steel give examples of an audit of male and female attitudes in their book *Beyond the Great Divide*.[1]

Once the questions are in draft, discuss the scope of the audit with key people to clarify:

- the scale
  —will all women be involved, or only a proportion?
  —will men be audited too?
- the process
  —questionnaire
  —individual meetings
  —group meetings
  —a mixture of all three

Giving every woman in the organization the opportunity to comment by questionnaire improves the results. At individual meetings, held in confidence, auditors are able to probe more deeply to find the real issues. Women find it easier to talk openly to an outsider, i.e. not from their department or the organization, and to another woman, when discussing questions of women's development, sexism or sexual harassment.

The implication of carrying out an audit

Audits raise expectations among the women and need to lead to action. There is no point in carrying out an audit if no action is foreseen. It's dangerous to raise expectations and not deliver any goods! Equally, if you have already decided what you are going to do, there is no point in force-fitting audit results to your plan. You need to be open-minded. Try to be realistic about what actions the organization will be prepared to carry out. What are the likely costs, who will be involved, and how long will it be before the action takes place? In some very large organizations it may be months before the personnel policy can be changed. There will be a gap of weeks or months between identifying the need and actually running the course, so be careful when you're conducting your audit not to imply any major imminent action!

Also, consider how men in the organization will relate to audits or courses exclusively for women, particularly men at non-managerial levels who may not be included in many of the other existing training and development programmes.

Feeding back results   Before conducting an audit, consider carefully how best you are going to feed back the results to:

- top management and policy makers
- managers generally
- personnel and training specialists
- the women themselves

All need to receive some form of written report, however brief, and an opportunity to raise questions in groups or meetings.

Gaining support for the audit   Gaining support for the audit also means gaining support for action to take place later, so it is essential that the supporters also have some formal authority and resources to back any plans. Some of the key people involved need to be:

Chair(man)/managing director/chief executive, because she/he:

- is the ultimate in formal authority
- needs to be convinced of the business need
- may have to 'rubber stamp' any decisions or action agreed lower down
- can free those lower down to take action

Managers generally, because they:

- need to be aware of audit process
- need to see the benefits in their own area
- will have to release staff for meetings
- may be key in distribution of questionnaires

Personnel, training and equal opportunities specialists, because they:

- will have key inputs to make
- may feel criticized by such an audit
- may be contributing from their budgets
- are often key organizers of interviews/feedback meetings

Women in the organization from all levels, because they:

- will be needed as ambassadors, speakers and participants

Women from senior levels, because they:

- can contribute as speakers, mentors and ambassadors and may be participants.

There may or may not be scope for deciding who will be seen to be sponsoring the audit. It may be that those paying for it will want the credit. The company gossip may influence it. Different messages are conveyed by whose name is associated with your audit:

- Chairman/chief executive   —   It's a business decision.
- Personnel/training   —   They're building their empire.
- Equal opportunitites   —   Well, they would, wouldn't they!
- The women themselves   —   Let them get it out of their systems.

A joint effort, with full support from the top is obviously ideal, but many organizations proceed well through the audit stage with the support of only one or two key people and with others waiting to be convinced by the results.

Steering groups   A steering group does just that: steers! It doesn't make decisions or take over, although it may feel like that sometimes. A good-sized group is between 6 and 10 people and needs to include a range of job functions, seniority, geographical bases, supporters and constructive critics, policy makers and women in the possible target group for the training.

For example   The BBC's substantial Women's Development Programme aimed at hundreds of women in a target population of 8000 was ably assisted during the audit by a steering group of women representing a variety of levels and jobs in the organization. These women were able to contribute:

- at a strategy and policy level
- from years of experience of being women in the BBC
- by those in the target group saying how the programme was for them

Final report   Includes:

- background and objectives of the audit
- method of the audit
- your conclusions
- lots of direct quotes to back up your conclusions
- your recommendations

Mini-audit   There is so much involved in a full audit that you may decide not to do one at all! The full audit is the de-luxe version, so don't stop doing something because you don't have the resources for the ideal. Many organizations have initiated excellent women's development training programmes in a small way, based on less searching investigations.

If a full audit is simply impractical, or inappropriate, then consider a mini-audit. This would consist of:

- background briefing
- group consultations of one or two days only
- the option of individual interviews
- a less formal report

The whole process is greatly speeded up and could be conducted within four weeks.

Consultations If a mini-audit is still too difficult or high-profile for your circumstances, then consider a mini-briefing, followed by consultations with small groups of women who are in the possible target group. These can be conducted very informally and would result in a brief document of your impressions. It could not be considered in any way an in-depth assessment of the organization's situation on women's development training but will generate some facts and opinions which will influence the training later on.

Familiarization days Familiarization days are purely for your benefit, to enable you to become acquainted with the organization/department/area/region/site before drawing together the threads of your women's development strategy. It simply means arranging a day when on-site staff are aware that you will be around, walking the job and stopping to ask questions. There is no written report of a familiarization day, only the notes you take for yourself.

Desk research If, for some extraordinary reason, you cannot do any of the above activities, and yet you are still required to produce a women's development training strategy, then you will be reduced to desk research. This means reading the files, organizational literature, books and statistics; talking on the telephone with on-site personnel/equal opportunities people; and drawing your conclusions in the ivory tower of your office. It is only marginally preferable to the last resort of 'going in cold'.

Going in cold This is to be heartily discouraged, and is extremely dangerous, as it can do more harm than good. It basically means inventing a strategy out of thin air, without any reference to the organization's or women's needs. Do not even consider it!

Redefining the objectives Having provisionally set your objectives prior to the audit, you are now in a position to review the objectives and decide whether to:

- confirm them as they are
- change them entirely
- change them partially
- define them more specifically
- widen their remit

Having gathered so much information about the situation for women in the organization you are now also well placed to define the target group for your training.

The target group

From your audit you can identify exactly which group of women you are aiming your women's development training at. Consider the following possibilities.

Targeting non-management or management women

Where does the break occur between management and non-management? Is it by grade, job title, or a general recognition? Could someone quite low in the grading system be a manager, while a senior specialist is regarded as non-management because she has only half a secretary reporting to her? Are the systems clear or is there generally an agreed 'feeling' about where the changeover from management to non-management takes place? 'It's usually Grade 6 or Band 3'—whatever is appropriate to your organization.

Targeting all women

If there is a wide range of women in the target group you need to consider how they might feel about working on their personal development with more junior or more senior women present. One golden rule is to avoid having a woman and her boss in the same programme. At least give them space by putting them in different groups. Just asking them if they would mind working together isn't good enough, as it only needs one of them to be non-assertive in her reply and a development opportunity is lost.

If the women's development training is pitched generally, to meet the development needs at all levels, it is likely that some of the women who have reached the top will have thought through most of the basic issues. However, they may have specific situations and questions of their own which they wish to work on.

Targeting specific jobs

Women's development training is often assumed to be about training secretaries. If your audit reveals that there are specific needs in a particular sector, such as in engineering, secretarial, production, etc., then it is a valid criterion in identifying your target group. However, unless you are proposing to look very specifically at issues around their job, one of the strengths of women's development training is to mix women in different jobs together.

Women returning to work

If you are targeting women returning to work, the most important factors to bear in mind are that their confidence is likely to be low and that they will need encouragement to work on transferring to the world of work those skills and talents they have in running a home and caring for a family. As their needs are so specific, it is helpful to run training for groups composed exclusively of returners.

Self-nomination

This is absolutely essential and one of the ground rules of women's development training. We'll look at the implications of this in more detail in Chapter 7.

Attendance at a previous course

Very occasionally, a course will be designed to build on work done on a previous course, so your target group will be restricted. This may appear élitist or exclusive to people outside the group; however, it enables work to be dovetailed into the previous experience and provides a deeper and more effective experience.

For example   In order for women to be trained as trainers for the Women's Development Programme in the BBC, they must have attended either the Programme itself or the management equivalent, Women in Management. Similarly, when piloting Women and Leadership in Kent County Council, it was important that women had experienced the general development-based career development programme. This meant they could focus on leadership questions and build on work already done on the previous course.

The danger of tight criteria, such as these, is that they can prevent some women from volunteering. A mother with childcare or eldercare problems may not be able to attend the residential Women in Management programme but could still be an excellent trainer for the Women's Development Programme. Every time you make a rule like this, be prepared to break it.

Knowing each other

Part of the challenging and growing nature of a women's development course is in meeting and working with new people. However, occasionally we are presented with a group who all know each other very well and may even work together day to day. This isn't a disaster, but it goes against the spirit of women's development training, and ideally it would never crop up, as you would have had conversations with the course organizer weeks beforehand and encouraged her/him to recruit a wider group of women.

If all this fails and you are presented with a group who know each other very well, be aware of the differences. The course will still work but it will be a different type of course and, in our judgement, one of less quality and depth.

Here are the advantages and disadvantages of everyone knowing each other:

Advantages	*Disadvantages*
• All group members understand the situations each of them is dealing with at work.	• Everyone comes with already established relationships and patterns within those relationships.
• Joint difficulties can be discussed and joint action decided upon (e.g. on sexual harassment).	• People tend to fall back into habit patterns of behaviour with each other.
• If the group works well together, there is a greater sense of support.	• There is a risk of hidden agendas which can distort your course material without your being aware of it.
• You can tailor your material to specific issues of their culture.	• Risk of 'in-jokes' and trainer being alienated.
• Can be boost to morale for an overlooked and overworked group and provide a team-building opportunity.	• Danger of group being led by established leader: 'You don't know *our* boss', etc.

Advantages	*Disadvantages*

	• Too comfortable.
	• Individuals' greater reluctance to discuss difficult work or personal issues with people they have to work with every day.
	• Lack of privacy and respect for the individual.
	• Danger of a hierarchical conflict.

Starting at the top   Starting at the top of the organization and involving the most senior women has many advantages. The women at the top are role models for other women lower down, so if they are seen as competent, effective, whole women, other women may be inspired by their example. Sometimes very senior women want to be the first to experience women's development training because they may have had very few opportunities to be involved in development with other women.

For example   'I'm a capable strategist and at all the courses, conferences and meetings that I attend I'm usually the only woman. I was suspicious of women-only training to start with, but soon realized that I could be more open and relaxed with other women and I was relieved and heartened to find I wasn't alone with the problems I face. I've been knocking on the "glass ceiling" for some years now and gaining the support from the other women on this course has made me realize that I'm capable, I'm a bit too aggressive, and I can make the next step up. Even if I don't, I'm going to make damned certain some other woman does. I don't feel so alone now.'

Another reason for the women at the top to experience women's development training first is to check out the training, make sure it's appropriate and gain experience of it so they can promote it to the women in their departments.

For example   'As the most senior woman in the company, people thought that I wouldn't need assertiveness training. I think I do. The higher I've climbed, the less confident I feel, so I thought it was important for me to get myself on this women-only assertiveness course. I would find it difficult to talk about certain issues with my male colleagues because I think some of my issues have to do with my being a woman. Some of the more junior women were suspicious at first that I was there to spy on them, but they soon settled down when I shared some of my difficulties. These women have helped and encouraged me a great deal. The role plays have shown me how to change. Now I'm off to try it out!'

A final good reason for starting with women at the top is to show the commitment and support of the women in the organization for women's development training. Against this are the reasons that some organizations give for starting elsewhere in the hierarchy, such as:

- The women at the top have made it, anyway.
- They have had access to other forms of training.
- The women themselves sometimes do not wish to be singled out or exposed in this way.
- There may not be enough women for a whole course at this level.

Women in the middle

Many organizations start women's development training in the middle, i.e. junior-middle management levels, which has the advantages that:

- There are sufficient numbers of women at those levels so there could be several courses to evaluate.
- The women have broken into management and are keen to keep going.
- Most of the women have several years of work experience to draw on.
- They are accessible role models for women lower down.
- There are other women as role models above them in the organization.
- It is relatively easy to monitor their progress.

The disadvantage of starting in the middle is that, in many organizations, the majority of women are not in these positions so only a relatively small number are able to take advantage of the training. In Kent County Council, for instance, after a few years, the career development course for women in junior management positions had reached most of them and the women who were then attending were from non-management levels. These women's needs were different to the original target group, and so the course became inappropriate and was reviewed and revised (see Case Study Three Kent County Council).

Women at the bottom

Most women are at the bottom of organizations so it might seem the logical place to start. Our experience shows that very few organizations do this. Those that do, have taken quite a radical step. When taken overtly it has been a success because:

- The majority of women in the organization are in the target group.
- There is a large number of women who can receive development training and the effects can be monitored on a substantial scale.
- In some organizations it is seen as less threatening than developing women higher up.
- The women themselves represent a large cross-section of ages and stages of careers.
- Those women are the managers of the future and the workforce of the next decade.
- There are role models higher up the organization.

The disadvantages are that:

- Development can be seen as unimportant if it is aimed at the lowest grades.
- Women higher up may feel disadvantaged as their staff return from development programmes with ideas that the managers have not benefited from themselves.

There needs to be support from the women higher up the organization and this support is most effectively given when the more senior women have experienced similar women's development training themselves.

The scale of your strategy

The scale of your strategy will depend on the needs identified, budgets available, the importance that the organization places on the results and the degree to which the culture supports women's development activities.

For example   In one organization employing about 3000 people, women's development work is being done quietly, without any publicity, and in parallel with some courses for men. The scale is small—one or two courses per year—and, because the culture would not accept overt women's development training, the progress is slow but steady.

For example   The BBC, on the other hand, has 8000 women in non-managerial grades, so when it launched its Women's Development Programme in 1989 it aimed for big numbers (at least 400 participants per year) and to be running all the programmes with internal resources within two years—ambitious objectives which have been achieved.

Consider the scale of your strategy:

- How many women do you want to reach?
- How quickly do you want to reach half of them?
- What size of budget is available?
- Who holds the budget?
- Do you charge out training to other parts of the organization?
- When will you breakeven/make a profit on the women's development training?
- What is the opportunity cost of women's development programmes (what else will not receive funding)?
- What benefits do you expect to receive as an organization from the training?
- By when do you need the benefits?
- What development/set-up costs are there to be recovered?
- What depth and breadth of activity do you want to achieve?
- Are you aiming to influence many people lightly or a few people deeply?

For example   One large public organization which was faced with having to make drastic cuts in terms of its numbers chose to run in-depth biography courses (a biography programme is shown in Appendix 1), aimed specifically at women who were older, black or disabled, because it was recognized that these women would find it more difficult to find work elsewhere. Over five days plus one follow-up day, the biography work enabled the women to make a comprehensive study of where they were in their lives, what patterns and themes there were and what questions they had in their present uncertain circumstances. The work was done in depth in small groups with a facilitator.

Once the analysis of the past was done the groups moved on into the options facing them for the future and the choices and consequences of the choices they might make. A follow-up day six weeks later assessed progress and built up skills to face the future situations. A support network was formed and for two years the women met regularly to continue working on their own development and supporting each other. In total, seventy-five women went through the process and the network meetings regularly attracted more than twenty members. After two years they decided they had achieved their task and formally closed.

For example   A financial organization began its women's development work with a one-day workshop on career development. The women attending found the work helpful but not sufficient to meet their needs. More in-depth work was developed but the one-day workshops continued as a taster, serving to whet appetites for further work.

Enlisting support

Who owns the women's development activities in the organization? Support needs to come from the top, from at least the equivalent of board level, if not from the chief executive/chair.

From undertaking many audits it is obvious that there are very many different categories of support and opposition. Here is the range we've met in most organizations:

The champions who

- really own the programme
- say all the right things
- mean them
- demonstrate support by speaking out
- release women from her/his department/division to attend meetings and courses
- tell you what the issues are
- put money into it
- put time into it

The ambassadors who

- spread the word in the organization
- get women's development on the agendas of management meetings
- often identify the champion at the top
- speak about it outside the organization
- know how to handle the politics
- face up to the opponents

The kudos seekers who

- do it for the status
- want to be noticed
- pay lip service
- say a lot of the right things
- may trip themselves up and reveal their true colours
- are often patronizing

	• will easily go the other way if the boss does
	• need reassurance of success
The opponents who	• openly challenge
	• ask lots of questions
	• have a lot of 'what ifs' and 'yes buts'
	• are easier to deal with than kudos seekers because opponents are in the open
	• if they change their minds are great allies
	• need to be listened to
The subversives who	• get on and do it quietly
	• need a strategy
	• can fail because of lack of support
	• can be turned into real allies
	• may be scared to go public
	• can help or wreck an overall strategy under the guise of being helpful
	• can provide lots of useful information
The blockers who	• never declare war
	• may be playing a political game
	• may overtly declare support and quietly do nothing
	• will do something about it when the boss says so
	• are often heard to say, 'I support it, but my boss/staff/colleagues make it difficult'.
The allies who	• include ambassadors and champions
	• are open to ideas
	• want change to happen
	• do things that support
	• check their actions with the strategy

In one large organization operating a Springboard women's development programme (see Appendix 2), the head of one of the major departments became the champion and a group of senior women became the key ambassadors, together with a senior male development consultant. The kudos seeker was the key project organizer. The financial director, a woman in her late fifties, became one of the greatest allies by arranging lots of extra meetings and activities, but checked them first to make sure they fitted with the strategy.

The subversives had no public relationship to the programme, but kept us informed about rumours and threats, and the blocker nearly wrecked the work in one whole large department. Meanwhile, the key opponent tested out severely our assertiveness and eventually warmed (but only just) to the idea of women's development training.

Getting the timing right

What does your organization's culture like and thrive on?

• a small start and a gradual build-up?
• a big splash?

What may seem like a big splash to one organization may appear like a drop in the ocean to another, so make sure that your strategy fits your culture. Taking approaches and timescales from someone else's successful activities may not cross the culture gap. Notice if the culture is changing and there is a need to do something different. Check your support at the top and get a measure of what is needed. Figure 3.3 shows three examples of different strategies and timescales.

	Organization A	Organization B	Organization C
Year 1	Commissioned audit	Audit	No action
Year 2	Women in Management programme	Career development course for women	No action
Year 3	Women in Management and commissioned non-managerial women's programme	As above	Senior women's consultative work
Year 4	Launched non-managerial programme alongside Women in Management programme	As above	Big splash women's development programme I
Year 5	Pilot Women and Leadership	As above	Programme II

Figure 3.3 *Three different timescales for implementing training*

It often takes a long time between having the original idea of introducing women's development training and the idea becoming reality. It can be a year or eighteen months between the initial conversation and the first piece of women's development training taking place. Equally, it does occasionally happen quickly: a conversation in July can lead to a course being run in September.

High profile/ low profile

The public relations (PR) profile of women's development training needs more consideration than that of less controversial forms of training, especially if the course is a pilot event. This is because:

- Women's development training is often misunderstood.
- Men and women often feel threatened by it.
- It is vulnerable to stereotyping and jokes.
- It is vulnerable to manipulation by PR activities.
- It is still relatively unusual inside organizations.

The details of your PR 'campaign' will be dealt with in detail in Chapter 6. Meanwhile, give some thought to your overall PR objectives as part of your strategy.

Is your women's development strategy:

- going to be publicized in the in-house magazine?
- discussed at high-level meetings?
- announced by the PR department?
- going to be quietly implemented within one part of the organization?
- going to be hidden away in the course directory or launched with posters and drinks parties?

What are your PR objectives? Refer back to your overall objectives. How can internal/external PR support these objectives?

Here are two examples from opposite extremes. Both are equally valid, and both supported equally the objectives of their women's development training. The actual form and content of the training was more or less identical.

Organization A

- The full audit report was published.
- Reports of the consultative meetings were circulated.
- Special leaflets and posters in full colour were printed and circulated throughout the organization.
- Customized pens were produced for participants.
- A photographer was present at the pilot workshop and extensive coverage appeared in the in-house newspaper.
- Women involved in the pilot programme spoke at a national conference.

Organization B

- Overall women's development training strategy was unwritten and not often spoken of.
- The course was held off-site and had an ambiguous title.
- The only public printed information about the course was included in details of mainstream courses, so it got 'lost' among the others.

Here are the advantages and disadvantages of high-profile and low-profile strategies.

High profile—Advantages

- increased chance of reaching the 'rest of the world'
- gives your course security if it's seen to be supported by senior people and influencers
- increased chance of target group hearing about it
- gives the course respectability
- makes you more visible

High profile—Disadvantages

- could be seen as provocative
- gives you less flexibility
- makes you more visible
- higher risk

Low profile—Advantages

- can be initiated quietly and without fuss
- allows the course to become established without having the spotlight on it
- gives you more scope for manoeuvre
- minimizes the chance of a backlash

Low profile—Disadvantages

- course can be dropped without too much fuss
- you don't get recognition for your achievement
- target group doesn't get to know about it
- could be seen as subversive
- course could be misunderstood
- increased chance of rumours
- very little chance of organization getting good PR through outside visibility of course

In this chapter, we've looked at all the ingredients of a women's development training strategy and why a strategy is so important. The danger of such information is that you may become so self-conscious about what you're trying to do, or that the detail becomes so overwhelming, that you never get around to actually initiating anything!

Having put your strategy in place (courses, audits, network meetings)—whatever it is—now action is needed. Where there has been no women's development training before, your priority is to get something going, to set a precedent.

For example   Following a short audit in a computer company, it was decided to offer, in a quiet, understated manner, a career development course for women. The pilot course was entered in the company's brochure of courses, and provoked a ripple of comment at the time, which soon faded. Four years on, the course is recognized and well established.

You may have to put your ideal strategy aside, just so that some action takes place. Large and ambitious projects often frighten organizations and take a long time for committees, layers of management, personnel specialists and others to discuss, approve and initiate action. So start somewhere—anywhere. You will find that action:

- sets a precedent
- encourages the women
- lets people see the benefits
- can be developed further
- can be monitored for business results
- enables people to talk about actual development rather than hypothetical situations
- often reduces fears
- builds links with existing programmes
- builds courage for further stages

Wherever you can start, have a go, do it well, and use that as a foundation stone to build on.

Summary

In this chapter we've looked at all the different aspects of a women's development training strategy, and how it fits in with overall women's development, personnel and training strategies. The main points from this chapter are:

- It's vital to have some sort of strategy, however minimal.
- Time and effort you devote to your strategy is time and effort well spent.
- Be clear about what you're planning to do.
- You can't do it on your own—find your support.
- Timing is important.
- The PR profile of women's development training has a huge impact and needs careful consideration.

References

1. Jane Beck and Maggie Steel, *Beyond the Great Divide* (Pitman, 1989).
2. Valerie Hammond and Dr Margaret Ryan, *Power and Influence in Organisations* (The Training Agency).
3. Report of the Hansard Society Commission, *Women at the Top*, 1990.
4. *No Barriers Here?*—A guide to career development issues in the employment of women (The Training Agency).

BBC Scotland

BBC Scotland is of particular interest as it is an organization with one of the most comprehensive range of women's development training in the UK. The case study that follows illustrates how organic a women's development training strategy can be, with the whole process constantly under review and the organization responding creatively and quickly to newly defined needs. It also demonstrates the power of a formal audit and report. Before 1985 the BBC had no women's development training, but the presentation of the Sims Report in 1985 demanded immediate action which was rapidly and positively taken.

This is also an excellent example of how networks grow out of women's development training; in BBC Scotland, the original network has spawned sister networks, which have positive links with the personnel department and which continue to work to everyone's mutual benefit.

Background

In November 1987, as part of its equal opportunities programme, BBC Scotland held its first women-only training course in conjunction with BBC Northern Ireland.

Women-only courses were one of the recommendations of the Sims Report, an internal inquiry on women and top jobs in the BBC, carried out by Monica Sims at the request of the BBC's board of governors because there was concern that few women were reaching the top of the Corporation. Figures showed that in 1985, out of the top 165 jobs, 159 were held by men and 6 by women, and this ratio had been much the same in 1975, even though women, during the intervening 10 years, were entering the BBC's training schemes in larger numbers than ever before.

In her report, published in 1985, Monica Sims made a number of crucial recommendations which, together, provided the basis for the BBC's equal opportunities policy. The report recognized the need for a full range of practical initiatives and policies which included the appointment of a women's employment officer, improvements to maternity leave, an audit to monitor the progress of women, more flexible ways of working (e.g. job sharing, career breaks), improvements to the recruitment policy, more career development and the determination by managers to interpret the spirit as well as the letter of equal opportunities policies. This report was a milestone for women in the BBC and the last five years have seen the implementation and development of almost all her recommendations. Most recently, the BBC has introduced gender targets for its three most senior grades of staff.

Crucially, the present Director General, Michael Checkland, has given a firm active commitment to equal opportunities, as has Patrick Chalmers, Controller, BBC Scotland.

Training

Prior to 1985 the BBC had resisted initiating courses for women in the belief that it would reinforce a 'ghetto' mentality; instead they had felt it more important to concentrate on increasing the number of women on mixed courses.

However, some women had found their way onto women-only courses then run by the Industrial Society's Pepperell Unit and other external agencies. Their view, conveyed to Monica Sims, was that these courses gave women confidence, helped them to realize their own potential, to be assertive rather than aggressive, and also gave women a forum in which to discuss the dual nature of career and home. Senior women in the BBC also stressed the need to talk to other women at their own level because they felt isolated and they emphasized their awareness of often being the only woman at meetings.

These views were supported by the reactions of women attending the first BBC-wide courses which began in May 1986. They were run by the management training department in conjunction with Liz Willis, an external consultant. Since then five or six courses have been run each year nationwide and in Scotland we have run one course each year.

This initial course was, and still is, entitled 'Women in Management'. It is a three-day residential course for women managers and team leaders, including radio and television producers. It is a personal development programme intended to 'provide an opportunity for women managers to assess where they are in their careers and to equip themselves with some of the skills and determination to achieve their future career goals'. The subjects covered include current career assessment, power and influence in organizations, listening skills, using personal influence, personal presentation, assertiveness skills and career/life planning. It is not a programme intended to develop managerial skills, but it is intended to develop individual women for more senior jobs in the Corporation. It is self-nominating, with applications supported by line managers and personnel officers and there are 12 places per course. Since November 1987, 56 women in Scotland have been through this programme.

The Scottish women who attended our first course formed themselves into a support and action group. In 1987 the BBC was only offering courses for women in management grades and these women believed that such courses should be run for all women. They secured the agreement of the Head of Administration, Scotland, Steve Ansell, and he obtained funding from the central equal opportunities budget. A course was then devised for BBC Scotland, entitled 'Personal Effectiveness'. It is a two and a half day non-residential course covering the same subjects as the Women in Management course, though tailored to suit. It is aimed at women at any level in BBC Scotland not already in a managerial job. It is again self-nominating with applications supported by the line manager and personnel officer. We run 3 courses each year with 12 places per course and so far 70 women in Scotland have attended this programme.

Women's Development Programme

Until recently Scotland's Personal Effectiveness course was the only such programme available for non-management women in the BBC. Then, in late 1988, Liz Willis started work with the BBC's management training department in London on a similar course for the whole BBC. However, the BBC estimated that there were 8000 non-management women and it was obvious that a revolutionary new type of programme was required. The Women's Development Programme was born, developed by Liz with Jenny Daisley. This is a private study programme over three months, using a specially developed journal and supported by three one-day workshops spaced at the beginning, middle and end of the event.

It is aimed, as I have said, at women at any level in the BBC not already in a managerial job 'who have a personal commitment to developing themselves in their lives and in their work'. Again, this course is self-nominating with line management and personnel approval required. Each course takes 100 delegates. The first programme was held in May 1989, and since then there have been four programmes each year. In the last 18 months 65 women from Scotland have attended this programme. The consultants we use have now handed this programme over to the BBC and in 1991 we will be running a programme in Scotland as well as sending women on the national courses. BBC Scotland employs 580 women and so far 191 women have attended women-only courses, so there is some way to go.

As resources are limited we have decided to discontinue the Personal Effectiveness course. We plan instead to devote these resources to a new course which was piloted in October 1990, called 'Women in Leadership' and again developed in conjunction with Liz and Jenny. This is a five-day residential programme for 'graduates' of the Women in Management programme to enable senior women in BBC Scotland to develop a management style which increases their effectiveness and fits their own personalities and values. The course is very participative; some theory is introduced, but the main process is experiential. The pilot course was successful and we plan to run more. This again is a first for BBC Scotland. The pilot course taught us that we need to have a mixture of women from all parts of the BBC and we are therefore discussing the running of such joint courses with other areas including Network Television.

We have discovered that women's development training is not a 'quick fix' but is a developmental process. These courses have had a real impact in BBC Scotland. Changing the culture of an organization is a fundamental and sometimes difficult process. It requires support from the top and from the women themselves.

The small action and support group formed in 1987 has now grown into 'Action for Women', a much larger umbrella group for women in BBC Scotland which has contacts with women in other Scottish organizations. Also, these courses have a greater impact by being one of a range of equal opportunities policies and initiatives aimed at encouraging women to realize their full potential.

The figures so far (see Table 3.1) demonstrate the success of the initiatives taken. There has been a steady increase in the number of women in senior grades, but there is still work to be done. It is a continuing developmental process.

Isobel Macdonald, Personnel Manager
BBC Scotland

Table 3.1 *The movement of women through salary grades in the BBC 1987–1990*

Nov 1987	M	F	% of women	% increase
AMP grades	5	–	0	
Band 5	19	–	0	
Band 4	105	22	17	
Band 3	181	65	26	
Band 2	216	134	38	
Band 1	19	78	80	

Nov 1989	M	F	% of women	% increase
AMP grades	5	–	0	0
Band 5	24	4	14	+14
Band 4	100	22	18	+1
Band 3	175	72	29	+3
Band 2	214	158	42	+4
Band 1	18	82	82	+2

Nov 1990	M	F	% of women	% increase
AMP grades	4	–	0	0
Band 5	29	5	15	+1
Band 4	96	23	19	+1
Band 3	175	72	29	No change
Band 2	200	163	45	+3
Band 1	22	82	79	−4

Key:

AMP grades	=	Senior Management
Band 5	=	Heads of Department, Editors, Executive Producers TV
Band 4	=	Heads of Department, Senior Producers, Radio, TV Producers
Band 3	=	Film Editors, Personnel Officers, Radio Producers, Camera People, etc.
Band 2	=	Studio Managers, Production Assistants, Researchers
Band 1	=	Radio Production Assistants, Administration Assistants

4 Designing the course

Design of women's development training needs to take account of all the usual factors of training design plus specific additional features or emphasis because the training is women-only. In this chapter we will look at setting the course objectives, the material to be included, delivering the material, profile speakers, open learning, the course size, the length of the course and the choice of venue.

Course design is a very delicate and skilled activity. Ill-advised or inexperienced course design enables organizations to declare that women-only training is of no value. Good design needs you to take time to think, plan and review. Designs need to be tested. Pilot courses are invaluable in giving opportunities to test, monitor and evaluate, and revise the design.

Good design pays off by ensuring that objectives are met and that the time is best spent. Overall, good design needs:

- clarity of objectives
- rhythm or patterns in the days, so that participants can settle and know where they are
- good links from subject to subject
- a good balance between different types of activity to address different learning styles

Setting the course objectives

You will set your course objectives, keeping in mind four elements which could agree or conflict:

- what the women in the target group say they need
- what line management say they need
- what key organizational people say the organization needs
- what you as the professional women's development specialist trainer believe they need

You will have discovered the first three when conducting your audit and consultations. To this you will add or subtract what you feel is important. This means they won't necessarily get the course they think they want!

Women in the target group will be able to identify their own needs depending on:

1 *Their maturity as learners* Many of the women we meet on women's development training courses have never previously attended any courses apart from perhaps induction training. This means that they don't know what to expect, are generally quite passive about what they need, and have little or no experience of anyone encouraging them to think about what they need. So they require help to articulate what their real needs are, and this leads into the second aspect.

2 *Their level of confidence* Extreme arrogance will lead some people to declare that they have no need for a particular form of training or even to declare that they are developed enough. Low confidence levels result in vague and general statements about development needs, usually because of embarrassment at the lack of confidence or attempts to cover it up.

For example At the beginning of a recent women's development programme one woman working in a small group who were discussing what they wanted to get out of the programme declared: 'I'm going to be really brave and come right out with it. Maybe you lot will think I'm silly, but really my problem is I have no confidence in myself.' To her amazement, more than half the group said they felt the same and she went on, 'In fact, I was almost too frightened even to come here.'

Even women higher up in organizations talk about their lack of confidence and the feeling that one day they will be found out—'The Imposter Syndrome'![1]

In a survey of women managers, reported by the MSC,[2] the women identified their own needs as shown in Table 4.1.

Table 4.1 *Needs of women managers*

	Percentage of total sample
Confidence building	50
Assertion	42
Interpersonal skills	12
General management skills including delegation, disciplining, negotiating	10
Learning to cope with men, including sex-role stereotyping, imposition of roles	8
Political awareness	7
Training for men to cope with women	6
Desocialisation re sex stereotyping*	5
Leadership	5
Retraining women for entering workforce	3
Personal presentation	3
Power of speech and public speaking	3
Resilience	2
How to do well at interviews	2

* i.e. changing the conditioning received in traditional social processes

And these needs persist into senior levels, as Jane Beck and Maggie Steel[3] point out:

Although interpersonal skills training may be perceived as necessary for both sexes in early management development, for women this need seems to persist at more senior levels. This may be due to their increasing isolation at the upper levels where women have identified difficulties in being taken seriously as a woman and in dealing with men.

At more senior levels, in managerial posts, many women are still battling as one of the few women at the top of their organization. Being a pioneer can be tiring and uncomfortable even if rewarding when they succeed. Women at these levels often identify the need to balance work and home and the need to survive the stress at senior levels as their key needs. Bearing all this in mind the objectives set for women's development training need to meet the following criteria:

- achievable
- measurable
- positive and developmental
- action-oriented

Here are some examples of course aims.

For a one-day career workshop
   To enable members to assess where they are in their lives and careers, consider where they want to be in the future and draw up action points to enable it all to happen in practice.

For a three-day course
   To enable delegates to become more effective at work through the development of skills and self-confidence.

For a three-day women and leadership course
   To equip participants with the personal and professional skills to increase their effectiveness at work and home in a way which fits their own personality and strengths.

For a five-day senior management course
   To enable senior women to develop a management style which increases their effectiveness and fits their own personalities and values.

For a follow-up day
   - To draw out positive points from the successes and failures of the last 6 months
   - To learn from each other's successes and failures
   - To identify goals for the future
   - To draw up positive action points for the next 6 months

For a one-day assertiveness workshop
   - To understand the background to assertiveness and why it is so helpful
   - To practise the basic techniques
   - To learn some additional techniques
   - To try it out with some real work situations

Another approach is to detail the achievements that the women can expect to achieve during the course. Here is an example of objectives set by a small company for its first women's development course for women in secretarial and administrative jobs.

Self-development programme: Objectives
On completion of this programme, participants will have:

- Identified strengths, weaknesses and values at work and in personal life
- Practised assertiveness for work and personal situations
- Become aware of their career and personal development
- Recognized the importance of 'image' and the positive approach
- Produced personal action plans

And another from a women and leadership programme run in the television industry:

Women and leadership: Objectives
At the end of the programme the delegates will have:

- Tried out models of leadership and developed their own effective style as a woman
- Practised and experimented with their own style during the programme
- Developed healthy life management strategies to prevent/reduce stress
- Practised four key stress-reduction techniques
- Made action plans to transfer their learning to their day-to-day working lives

The first example demonstrates a broad perspective on women's development while the second shows the specific application to women and their role as leaders.

These are the visible, publicly stated course objectives. In addition, you will have your own objectives which could include any of the following:

- provoke action
- provide support and encouragement
- build skills
- build confidence
- inspire
- encourage networking
- provide examples
- raise awareness

The material

Having set the overall objective, you now have the task of deciding what you're going to include in your course. Some women's development courses are single subject, especially if they are short, one-day or half-day workshops. Some examples are assertiveness skills, career planning, and presentation skills. Most women's development courses include more than one subject, and here your task is more difficult, judging the blend and getting the emphasis and balance right.

Deciding on the priorities

Following on from setting your objectives, think intensively and compile a chart of priorities. This is for your own use and will:

- enable you to design the course
- keep you on track while running the course
- enable you to evaluate your own performance

Think about what the participants need simply to know about, what they need to understand in greater depth, and what they need experience of, in order to take action. Then prioritize it in terms of what you must cover in the course, what you should cover, and the optional extras that you could cover if you had time. Use the layout shown in Figure 4.1.

Deciding on the content

There is no set content for women's development training. As with the objectives, you will decide on a delicate balance between what the target group, line management and key organizational people identify and what your own judgement indicates they need.

When developing an extensive women's development programme, we were faced with an enormous list of subjects, identified as follows:

The target group wanted to include:

- career/life planning
- assertiveness
- supervisory skills
- changing men's attitudes
- time management
- getting a sense of direction
- management skills
- goal setting
- coping with interviews

The line management wanted to include:

- being more confident
- being more positive

The key organizational people wanted to include:

- equal opportunities issues
- organizational policy material
- coping with change
- issues around changing business environment

And in addition, we identified a need to include:

- putting yourself across more positively
- developing a positive image
- gaining information
- networking
- organizational culture
- stress management

	KNOW	UNDERSTAND	DO
MUST	• What assertiveness is • What it isn't	• Definitions of assertive, aggressive and passive • The five basic ingredients	• Role plays • Work on real situations • Get feedback • Practise basic ingredients
SHOULD	• Books available on assertiveness • When to be assertive	• Relevance of body language • Own inclinations and habit patterns	• Some additional techniques • Listening exercises • Giving and receiving criticism/compliments
COULD	• Background to assertiveness • Other relevant theories	• How assertiveness relates to other theories • Research relating to assertiveness	• Some starter scenarios

Figure 4.1 Priorities for a two-day assertiveness course

A conscious decision was made not to include any skills material which was already on offer on mainstream courses, so the ultimate list of material included was:

- dealing with change
- understanding organizational/industry culture
- knowing yourself
- assessing what you've got going for you (i.e. skills, personal qualities, circumstances . . .)
- finding support
- setting goals
- getting information
- assertiveness
- stress management
- managing your image
- blowing your own trumpet
- making it happen
- action sessions

Some of the women were initially antagonistic to the inclusion of material on image building as they did not feel they needed it and some didn't want it. However, by the end of the programme, they recognized that it is an important element. In your choice of material you are treading a narrow path between offering a cosy course of the women's own choosing where their assumptions and views of themselves are not challenged, and a course which they cannot identify as addressing their needs at all!

The content can be anything developmental. There's a lot of common ground among the many women's development courses that are currently running. Some of the most likely subjects are annotated below.

Career planning   Establishing where a woman is in her career, how she got there, who and what helped, what skills and qualifications she has, how they can work for her now, what her options are for the future and how she can achieve them.

Life planning/biography work   Looking at the whole life of a woman either in general terms or in considerable depth (the latter is biography work). The whole life includes the interrelationship of herself, her work, her relationships and the world (see Figure 4.2).

Life planning and biography work encourage her to look at the past, to see the significant events or turning points, the patterns and themes; to consider the relationships and current questions in the present; and to think about the options and consequences of the choices she makes in the future. Simple life planning can be undertaken by trainers with some skill and training whereas in-depth biography work should be handled only by those with considerable skill and training in the biographical field (for a biography work programme, see Appendix 1).

Values   It is often difficult to balance values between relationships, work, yourself and the world at large. In single-sex groups women are

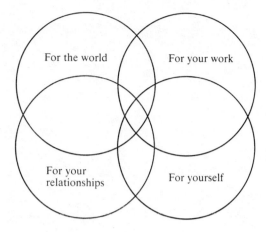

Figure 4.2 *The whole life concept*

usually quick to share quite deeply held values and work with each other to prioritize their values. This gives a sure, personal foundation for work on goal setting or image building and raising their profiles later.

Strengths and weaknesses   We take the view that there are no weaknesses, just strengths that are out of balance because they are either being overdone or underdone. This enables women who have focused on their weaknesses in the past to view themselves in a more positive light.

Performance, image and exposure   This work comes directly from the research of Harvey Coleman (ex-IBM) who investigated a large number of organizations and identified three factors that determine whether or not someone is promoted (see Figure 4.3):

1 *Performance*—the reality of how good your work actually is.
2 *Image*—the impression you create about yourself and your work. We all know of people who were overlooked for promotion, even though their work was actually good, because they gave the impression of being confused, or unable to cope, or not interested in promotion.
3 *Exposure*—whether people know of you. This means raising your profile, becoming more visible and building your contacts. You may do a great job, have a great image, but if the right people don't know that you exist, you won't get promoted.

We include the work on performance, image and exposure in women's development programmes because we believe it is important for women to know the reality of situations and not continue to believe that, if they do a good job, this alone will bring them promotion. Many women dislike these statistics, but when they come to terms with them they realize their relevance.

Luck   When we ask women on courses how they've achieved things in

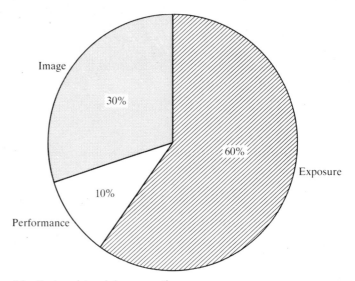

Figure 4.3 *Factors determining promotion*

their lives, they often say: 'I was lucky' or 'It was just luck really'. We believe that this is mostly rubbish! When we ask for anecdotal evidence, we then hear wonderful and inspiring stories of women who:

- set themselves goals
- plucked up courage
- picked brains
- kept going despite many difficulties
- made contacts
- volunteered
- told people what they wanted
- made opportunities for themselves
- refused to give up
- responded positively to failure

They had developed the right attitude, and taken the right steps to place themselves in the right place at the right time. So we feel it is important to dispel any sense of waiting for a lucky break. Women need to start making their own luck, their own opportunities, and prepare for any other opportunities that may come along.

Setting goals   Women need to be encouraged to set goals and not just to wait for someone to come along and offer them the next job. Women at more senior levels have often learned how to do this and do it well, but need to reset their goals when they have achieved earlier ones. At more junior levels they have difficulty and often declare they can't. If they haven't a goal then their goal needs to be: 'to find out what my goals are'.

Failure/success   Women's attitudes to these two words vary enormously, but the general trend is that more junior women in organizations tend not to value their successes and therefore tend to focus on their failures. Women at the top also tell how their failures, plus deter-mination to succeed, got them to where they are now. There are great lessons to be learned from creative ways of looking at success and failure, and from defining personal definitions of 'success'.

Networking   The 'old-boy network' has a bad reputation and often taints women's views of networking as a whole. Challenging assump-tions head-on gives women an opportunity to find their own ways of networking so that they gain support and boost their confidence, share problems and information, think in a networking way and help others, particularly those coming up behind them.

Listening   This needs to be done in a wide range of situations—and lis-tening not only to words but to the feelings and intentions that underlie the words.

Putting yourself across positively   Women need to learn to put them-selves across with energy, enthusiasm, conviction and confidence; not always a popular subject but one which boosts confidence.

There are also the more skills-based subject areas such as:

Assertiveness   Most women's development programmes include some assertiveness training. Our definition of assertiveness is based on real respect for yourself and the other person, which is as much about expressing feelings as about end results. This means that training in it isn't easy and requires many ingredients. We have moved away from the 'bolt-on' techniques base of the 1980s into an approach which requires the women to develop assertiveness from the inside out. This results in a greater depth of understanding and enables each woman to develop a style of assertiveness which fits her own values and personality. When including assertiveness in women's development programmes, it is essential to build up confidence and skill based on solid foundations.

Presentation skills   Some organizations include presentation skills in their women's development courses because women need these skills for their work or careers. They can also be included as a confidence builder. For some women it may be the first time they have stood up and spoken to a group. Even for experienced speakers, it can be a testing experience if they are asked to talk about themselves.

This is often the part of the course that participants find the most nerve-wracking. Include in it an element of image building and 'blowing your own trumpet' and it is also often the part of the course that they find most helpful and confidence-building.

Leadership/management skills   John Naisbitt in his book *Megatrends 2000*[4] predicts that the 1990s will be a decade of women's leadership. There is little evidence of this at the beginning of the 1990s. Women display the many qualities of management and leadership that organ-izations are predicting they will need, and there is growing talk of the switch from what we call old-order management to new-order manage-ment. Some of the key features are shown in Table 4.2.

Table 4.2 *Key features of changing management styles*

Old order	New order
Efficiency culture	Enterprise culture
Production-oriented	Market-oriented
Optimizing status quo	Managing fast-moving changes
Authority	Leadership
Conformity	Initiating
Following procedures	Flexible—juggling many things at once
Be logical	Tolerate ambiguity
Tell others what to do	Listen to groups and individuals (ideas and concerns)
Follow company training schemes	Be responsible for own development

Many would say that women have the qualities and abilities required by 'new-order' leaders and therefore will be well placed to take advantage of the new requirements. That's exactly what was said about women and computers in the 1960s and yet today computer companies, with one notable exception, are dominated by men. In leadership and management skills development, the training needs to focus on:

- accepting that women's ways of managing/leading are valid
- women seeing themselves as successful in these roles
- experimenting with extending their styles to be more effective
- gaining feedback based on real events, real feelings and results
- linking their skills to implementation back at work

Action   It may seem obvious that there should be an action session, in which participants translate their good intentions into specific actions they are going to take. It's particularly important on women's development courses because:

- Women need to be 'stretched' to set challenging goals.
- Women need to think practically about small steps.
- Small steps are easier to take than big leaps. They build confidence, make for small failures or successes, are not so frightening and can usually be achieved quite soon.
- Sharing action points helps commitment.
- Hearing others' action points provokes ideas.
- Women take action more readily with support and encouragement.

Company visits   Include these in courses for returners to familiarize them with the world of work.

Time with a personal coach/tutor   Make space on returners' courses and in-depth or long-term development programmes for coaching and review time with one of the trainers.

Audio-visual aids   There are very few bought-in course materials for women's development training. This is because the whole emphasis is to work from the inside out, so that the raw material for the course is the women's own situations and issues. Appendix 4 gives some potential suppliers of materials.

Pre-prepared films/ videotapes/audio cassettes

We do not use any films or videos in women's development training as we feel that the women's own issues are more important than any decided on by a film maker. Also, we haven't ever come across any materials that are sufficiently sensitive or non-sexist to consider using. However, we are open-minded to the possibility of some being produced, so it's always worth keeping an eye and an ear open, and decide for yourself.

In any form of distance or open learning, films, videos and/or cassettes are valuable for presenting the 'role-model' ingredient of the course, and to overcome a potential sense of isolation, but they run the risk of being irrelevant to the group and may even become negative role models.

For example The Open University course, Women into Management, contains an audio cassette with a variety of women talking about themselves and their lives, which is very successful as a motivator.

Unless you are setting up a distance learning pack, we'd strongly recommend that you work with issues that come up on your course.

Videos/camcorders

Women consistently devalue their own worth and their own performance, so providing an unbiased video recording of their performance can enable them to see for themselves how well they're doing, and enable them to ask for specific feedback from you and their course colleagues.

Video recordings can be used, with great care, towards the end of a longer course of four or five days. Used in the second half of a course, once the participants have settled down and are feeling more confident and secure in the group, a video recording can be a huge confidence boost. It is by no means essential, so can be considered a very optional extra. We suggest you restrict its use to filming exercises about:

- leadership/management
- public speaking
- 'blowing your own trumpet'
- image building

If the budget will run to it, have one cassette per participant, which she can then take away and ponder over, afterwards.

Advantages of video recordings

- They enable individuals to continue learning after the course.
- They enable participants to ask for feedback on a specific piece of behaviour.
- They enable each woman to see herself in comparison with other course participants.
- Women always come across better than they thought they did and the video provides proof of this.

Disadvantages

- The video camera can become the centre of attention.
- It can be very threatening and stressful.
- There is the possibility of technical hitches which divert attention.
- The technology gets in the way of the human interaction, i.e. how people believe you come across is more valid than your own interpretation of a video.
- It takes up too much time to play it all back. On the very rare occasions when we use video recordings, we do not play all the cassettes back during the course; each participant is given her cassette to look at in her own time, or we just play back selected 'highlights'.
- It's expensive.

Overhead projector slides These are only to be used with a large group when a flipchart can't be seen by everyone. They can be used in two ways:

- prepared slides with brief statements or short punchy bits of information, e.g. a definition of assertiveness, a few statistics on the place of women in the organization
- blank slides for the women to record the results of group brainstorming sessions—these can then be used for large report-backs (see Chapter 9).

Handouts There are two types of handouts in women's development training: the ones you prepare beforehand and take with you, and the ones you develop on the course. Whatever handouts you take with you, check that they are non-sexist in their assumptions and vocabulary. It is not good enough to use, for example, management material, which is written virtually exclusively for men, with the use of 'him', 'he' and 'his' and lots of sporting and/or military analogies, and ask the women to 'translate' as they read. This is tantamount to telling them they are second-class citizens.

Either rewrite the handout beforehand or, better still, develop a new handout on the course. Many of our now standard handouts were developed from brainstorms and flipchart checklists developed by women on courses. Be prepared to get flipcharts typed up and circulated to everyone after the course.

Whatever materials, OHP slides, films, videos, cassettes or handouts you decide to use, do look at them closely. There is some good non-sexist material about, but most of the mainstream material is still depressingly insensitive to issues of gender, race, disability and age. By being concerned with this issue, you may be seen by your personnel and training colleagues as obsessive or super-sensitive, but it is essential in order to support your women's development training.

Delivering the material

Having decided *what* the content of your women's development training consists of, now consider *how* you're going to deliver it. The menu of ingredients and range of decisions includes:

- course size
- input
- group role plays/discussions/brainstorming sessions
- report-backs
- individual exercises
- profile speakers
- other guest speakers
- 'me' time
- open learning

In deciding the quantity and mix of these ingredients, bear in mind:

- the overall objectives of the course
- your chart of 'must include', 'coulds' and 'shoulds'
- learning styles

Use the learning styles questionnaire devised by Peter Honey and Alan Mumford,[5] which outlines four learning styles:

Activist—learns from action and needs to try things out.
Pragmatist—learns by seeing the practical application and needs real examples.
Reflector—learns from thinking about it and needs time to think.
Theorist—learns from concepts and theories and needs structure and input.

A predominance of activists and pragmatists attend courses. In their research of 174 women managers, Honey and Mumford found more activists but fewer pragmatists than among male participants. When in doubt aim for a balance of the styles. Leaning towards practical work is usually most effective. As you won't know the learning styles of your participants before you start, you need to build in enough of a range of activities to accommodate all four learning styles.

Input Input is usually used sparingly to introduce a new topic or generate discussion. The ground rules of women's development training dictate that the course emphasis is on the practical and participative, using the real issues that the women raise. Straight lecture-type input will particularly help the theorists and input with lots of anecdotes and examples will help the pragmatists.

Exercises Lots of practical exercises usually achieve greater developmental change than lots of theoretical input. Generally, exercises fall into three categories:

- group discussions/brainstorming sessions
- role plays
- individual work

Group discussion/
brainstorming sessions One of the most frequently heard comments at the end of women's development courses is: 'It's been marvellous to discover that I'm not the only one who feels like this', or 'I now feel I can go and have a go, knowing that I'm not the only one'.

When they lack confidence, women's experiences and feelings about their world and the role of work within it seem to result in a sense of isolation and worthlessness. 'It must be my fault that I feel like this.' As a result, they tend to keep quiet about their real feelings about their work and thus reinforce the sense of isolation. Whatever the material you decide to include in your course, it's vital that your course design includes lots of swapping experiences in small, safe groups. This means that the whole course is run out of *their* experience and not yours, tackling their real issues, not your carefully constructed ones.

Note the smiles of relief and recognition that sweep the room when the old chestnuts emerge: the assumption that the woman will make/pour the coffee; coping with the decision about arrangements for the family Christmas; or feeling guilty about wanting even a little time to herself. The shared experience of these common situations creates a support network which may well carry on long after the course. The more the ideas come from the participants, and not from you, the better. So use a lot of group discussions and brainstorming sessions in women's development training, but facilitate the process closely. Group discussions and brainstorming sessions enable the women to swap experiences and realize that their experience is valid, and in this way they build confidence.

In brainstorming sessions every idea is accepted as valid in the initial collection of thoughts. This means that contradictory statements can be made and all are collected, usually on a piece of flip-chart paper, so that everyone in the group can see them. It is a quick way of getting a lot of ideas out in a non-threatening way.

Here are some examples of questions that can be put to a group to provoke proactive discussion or lists of ideas:

- How have you got to where you are today, and who and what helped you?
- What are the hurdles to your further progress?
- Who are you and are you using your present strengths to your future advantage?
- What have you achieved since last meeting?
- On the spot compile a checklist for dealing with sexual harassment.
- What have you got to offer to help the other women in this room?

Activists and pragmatists find group discussions particularly helpful.

Role plays   Role plays deserve a special mention. On the whole we find them one of the most effective ways to develop skills and confidence, particularly in assertiveness. As a generalization, we find women need to be encouraged to do the role plays. So often they would prefer just to discuss the situations and not actually tackle them. The discussions seldom turn the situation round, but role plays do, particularly reversed role plays where a woman plays the person she's trying to deal with and someone else plays her. That way she is convinced that the role has been well played because, after all, she knows this person better than any of the others in the group. She also feels what it is like to be on the receiving end of someone being assertive! On how to run a role play exercise, see Chapter 9.

It has been known for women to refuse to come on courses because they know there will be role plays. Never force anyone—sell them the benefits and encourage them. Activists and pragmatists will learn from doing the role play, while reflectors will learn from being in the observer role.

Individual exercises   To counteract the public nature of discussions and brainstorming sessions, include some exercises that people do as individuals. This gives them time to think, helps the reflectors and provides a different tempo for the course.

Reporting back   Allow space in the design to hear examples and anecdotes from the women themselves. Their examples are often better and more relevant to the group and the organization than those chosen by the trainers. Using their own examples:

- validates their experiences
- relates development to real life situations
- widens their pictures by hearing others' views
- helps them to relate to each other's situation (usually helps to end the 'I'm the only one with these problems' situations)
- consolidates learning by working with their own experiences

Particularly useful for reflectors and pragmatists. For how to take a report-back, see Chapter 9.

Profile speakers   A gift to the pragmatists, profile speakers are the living examples which bring the material of your course to life (see below). Always include them, unless the course is specifically focused on one skill such as assertiveness. If your course lasts only one day, include a session with a short input from a profile speaker. If you have more than a day, include two profile speakers if possible and, if residential, consider an after-dinner profile speaker. Profiles provide examples of:

- behaviour
- career paths
- life and work situations
- ideas

They enable the women to relate their situations to others and compare and contrast. Profiles help women to believe that they too can do something, even if not in the same way as the speaker. Profile speakers need to give a broad spectrum of life and work experiences, such as:

- different racial and cultural backgrounds
- working mothers, single parents

- single women, those with partners, divorced, widowed
- those who've had career breaks
- all ages
- with and without disabilities
- graduates, non-graduates
- qualifications, no qualifications
- top management
- middle management
- junior management
- moving sideways or taken a step back
- talking about their failures
- demonstrated determination to succeed
- overcame illness
- relating to the environment the women work in

Above all, they must fit in with the women on the programme that you are running.

Profile speakers on courses need to tell their own stories of how they got to where they are, and who and what helped them, and give hints and tips to other women who are following them. They are usually more senior women, either from the same or other companies. The level of seniority needs to be chosen carefully because, if they are too senior, their post may be seen as unattainable to more junior women and if they are too junior, they may not be inspiring enough. Speakers who are role models need a clear brief and need above all to bring:

- energy
- inspiration
- enthusiasm
- encouragement

Groups can switch on very easily if they hear enough to relate what the speaker is saying to their own circumstances. They can just as easily switch off. Imagine the reaction of a room full of women who are predominantly non-graduates to a woman who begins, 'I graduated with an honours degree in . . . ' in contrast to the same group listening to a woman who begins, 'When I left school I had no qualifications, so I've had to pick them up on the way . . . '. Selecting speakers with compatible backgrounds is important; so too is briefing them so they will highlight the right points in their own background and in the programme you are running. Speakers appreciate briefs. It helps their preparation. For how to introduce and sum up a profile speaker, see Chapter 9.

Meanwhile, here is an example of a brief for a profile speaker:

Profile speaker's brief for Springboard[6] workshops

Setting   Three-month programme consisting of a workbook and three one-day workshops. Your session in this workshop is the only session with a speaker, the rest of the day is spent working in groups and trying out some of the exercises in the workbook.

Aim   To inspire and encourage the participants by providing them with an example of what another woman (you!) has done.

Timing   Please prepare a 10–15 minute talk and be prepared to take questions.

Approach   Enthusiastic; encouraging—'You can do it'; practical; down to earth.

Content   These profile sessions bring the issues raised in the rest of the programme to life, and often have a considerable impact on the participants. Your objective is simply to tell the story of what has happened to you, in as down-to-earth a way as possible. Start off briefly with what happened when you left school, as this is a point which everyone can relate to. Then take us rapidly through your career up to the present, pausing to explain occasions that were major turning points, or people who had major influence. Please don't bother to give too many dates as you are not reading your CV! It may be that several years passed without anything significant happening, or it may be that one year was particularly important and needs explanation. It is important to include personal aspects, especially children, as participants are often very concerned at the impact on their career of having children. The other factors which speakers mention include:

- the role of a mentor or helpful boss
- a major failure which forced a re-assessment
- ways of being able to pick yourself up and have another go
- knowing someone, who knew someone!
- networking and finding support
- ways of coping with stress and looking after yourself
- taking professional qualifications in the evenings and weekends and passing the exams against all expectations
- negative events such as divorce, as a motivator, forcing a rethink.

Please use your own examples to illustrate the points that you make. It is helpful to finish your talk with some pointers or tips such as: 'Things I wish I'd known when I started out' or 'Five tips for success'. Whatever makes sense.

The most important thing to remember is that they want to hear about you, so let your personality come through and please do not think that there is a definitive talk. These notes are simply for your guidance. The golden rule is to make it as real as possible.

Other guest speakers

Other guest speakers may fill whatever gaps you feel there are in your design. They tend to fall into two categories:

- Senior people, often men, whose attendance is important in order to demonstrate visible support. Asking them to be a guest speaker is simply an excuse to get them involved in the course.
- You need specialists to impart specific information, e.g training

opportunities, the new career-break scheme, the proposed women's network, etc.

If you are running a public course, you might also use a 'big name' guest speaker as a draw and part of the PR strategy.

'Me' time   This is a course ingredient which is peculiar to women's development training and which you need to include, particularly on residential courses. Most women spend most of their lives doing things for work, the house, the children, their families and friends. Their lives are full of duties to others. As a result, women have significantly less time for themselves than men.[7] Even when they find themselves with a bit of spare time, their low self-esteem makes it difficult for them to spend the time on themselves. 'Me' time can be a course subject, but you also need to include it as part of your course design. Allow chunks of time and designate them as 'me' time.

The Springboard[6] suggestion for the use of 'me' time is:

In your 'me' time we want you to give yourself treats. When was the last time you did something that was just for you? It's not self-indulgent, it gives you time to recover and re-energise. If you're out of the habit of treating yourself— try it. We all need it. For example: lock the bathroom door next time you have a bath, and get the kids used to the idea of you having some time to yourself! Add an especially nice bath oil and you're getting the idea!

It's also valuable time for the reflectors to reflect and digest the business of the day.

Open learning   Open learning opportunities in women's development training are increasing all the time (see Appendix 4 for material). The advantages to women are:

- They can fit the learning around child/elder care commitments, shifts or flexitime.
- It can be very low-key, avoiding a backlash from colleagues.
- It is very cost effective, so is often more easily available to women than a full residential course.
- It may not be seen as so threatening or controversial.
- It enables large numbers of women to train at a time.

The disadvantages are:

- There are no opportunities for swapping notes and experiences.
- Participants are isolated from other women and therefore have no support.
- Networking is more difficult or impossible.
- There are no opportunities for raising visibility.
- There is less sense of occasion and fun.

However, for many women with complex domestic commitments or work patterns, open learning may be the only opportunity available to them.

The Midland Bank Group's LEAP programme has specific modules for women entitled:

- *Confident Me*—assesses skills and demonstrates that many skills developed at home are easily transferable to the workplace.
- *Clear Communication*—investigates the way women communicate and how communication can be improved.
- *Happy Children*—examines childcare options, problems and coping with guilt.
- *Good Organization*—deals with prioritizing, delegating and saving time.
- *Wellbeing*—covers assertiveness and making time for yourself.

Each unit consists of an audio tape and an instruction booklet which are available separately from the LEAP library, on loan for several weeks.

The Springboard women's development programme also contains an element of open learning, together with workshops and networking (see Appendix 2). Increasing numbers of courses offered through the Open University and Open College are specifically women's development training.

Open learning is particularly suited to reflectors who can reflect and look back over the material.

Course size   The ground rules outlined in Chapter 2 have implications for the size of the course. Part of your responsibility is to create a safe and secure environment, to enable real issues to be raised and to provide encouragement and support. There is no prescription for the size of the group but general guidelines are:

- Smaller groups are more suited to in-depth and longer-term courses.
- Really large groups (50–100 or more) are marvellous for networking and for generating enthusiasm and support, but need very clear design and organization to work well. They can be broken into smaller groups for exercises.
- Medium-sized groups can be neither one thing nor the other. Trainers don't get to know everyone and the group may be too large for in-depth work.

Deciding how many trainers you need for a course will depend on:

- numbers of participants
- in-depth nature of the work
- the amount of coaching/practical work to be facilitated
- the complexity of the practical work

Here are some examples which have worked:

- One trainer running Work and Personal Development course with 12 participants over 2 days with trainer able to coach 3 groups of 4 in assertiveness role plays.
- Three trainers running in-depth Biography Workshop with 12 partici-

pants over 5 days—each day intensive small-group work with 4 participants.
- Two trainers running Women in Management course for 16 participants over 3 days with coaching in role plays.
- Three trainers running Springboard programme for 100 participants over 3 one-day workshops with participants in self-managing groups for discussions and exercises.
- Two trainers running a women returners programme for 12 participants, one day per week for 12 weeks.

The importance of getting the group size and ratio of trainers to participants right is illustrated by this cautionary tale.

For example A company with a well established and respected women's development course suddenly experienced a mysterious drop in numbers. The course had been designed for 12–15 women and 2 trainers had been engaged for the whole of the 4 days. The numbers dropped to 5 but the decision was made to run the course as designed.

The trainers experienced difficulties all through the 4 days, with the participants being unforthcoming, negative and apathetic. Following the course, a complaint was received from one participant about the intrusive nature of the course. Having a trainer:participant ratio of 1:2½ had been seen by the trainers as a luxury—an opportunity for real in-depth development work—but in practice the 5 participants had felt overwhelmed by having 2 trainers there all the time and were uncomfortable with the amount of 'airtime' they were forced into taking.

The course design was excellent for 12–15, but totally inappropriate for five. Unless you are planning an extraordinarily in-depth course, cancel or postpone a course which falls to less than eight.

The use of time

For women, particularly those with childcare or eldercare responsibilities, it is vital to consider carefully the use of time in relation to this availability. Make the length of the course and the length of the days as appropriate as possible to the needs of your target group of women.

Length of the course

Obviously the length of the course will depend on:

- the budget
- content and objectives
- organizational culture
- availability of staff
- mobility
- the design itself

Think about what can be achieved in different periods of time.

One day Usually just an introduction or a specific focus on one subject. A series of one-day workshops can be successful where the same group goes through a longer programme broken into one-day sections spread out over a period of time.

Two days   More helpful, as the women have the opportunity to sleep on the ideas from the first day and come back to build on them. This is helpful to the reflectors who learn most when they have had time to digest material. There is also more opportunity to build a group.

Three days   Many personal effectiveness, women's development and career development courses run very successfully over a period of three days, particularly where there is an element of skill development, such as assertiveness, as well.

Four days   This is more usual for more skills-based development programmes, allowing time for practice and time to build on skills and link one skill to another.

Five days   Used mainly for in-depth programmes such as biography work and for major change programmes such as women and leadership or management skills for women.

More than five days   Not so easy to gain release or budgets. You need to be really clear about the level of skills you are developing and the range of subjects. Well designed and managed courses can be very effective but there are dangers of overload and other hygiene factors in terms of people's ability to keep growing in a healthy developmental way. A long-term programme has a different group dynamic, so unless you're used to running programmes of this length, get advice on your design and proceed with caution!

Follow-up days   These are designed to re-energize, revitalize and re-encourage, and need to be a mini-course in their own right. To be successful they need to include:

- reviewing progress and celebrating success
- building on work done in the course and since
- moving into the future

Follow-up days that consist simply of a review tend to discourage those who feel they haven't achieved much, so they don't turn up. Knowing that there will be new material encourages people to come. Once they're there, it's your job to help them find the successes in what they have done!

The dangers and disadvantages of follow-ups are that they are often perceived as social reunions and not taken seriously in terms of their work content. Equally they can be feared by those women who feel they haven't achieved very much. Publicize them with the three aims and make it clear that new work is to be done. There is sometimes a drop-out factor between the course and the follow-up—the reasons why need to be monitored.

The advantage of follow-ups is that they do enable progress to be monitored and, if there is a point where energy flags, they can be revivers. Timing is crucial. A one-day follow up to a two-day course needs to come after about six weeks and certainly not more than four months after the original course. A five-day course could have its follow-up three to six months later and a three-month programme could be followed up a year later.

There can be no set programme for follow-ups, not even for the same course which is run several times. Basic content may be the same but the emphasis needs to be related to:

- the specific needs of that group of women
- their performance on the original course
- the challenges they need to be faced with
- the support they require
- whether they take action easily or reluctantly
- whether they need to focus on specifics or see the wider picture
- the balance they need between reviewing the past and moving on to new things for the future

The programme shown below is typical of a one-day follow-up event which might come after a course of 2–4 days duration. The women need to be sold the idea on the original course that the follow-up is an integral part of the course to be treated seriously, to enable them to re-energize and go forward into the future. The trainer's role is to step back and leave the direction to the women themselves.

Typical follow-up programme

Session 1
What has gone well, and why? What could have gone better, and why? (usually done as group brainstorming sessions with lots of coaching and encouragement from the tutor, as women often forget or belittle their achievements). Celebrate successes.

Session 2
Learning styles—if learning is to continue beyond development prog-rammes, what is your preferred style and how can you develop in other ways?

Session 3
What blocks are there now: • in your thinking?
                                     • in your feelings?
                                     • in your will?
Self-assessment and exercises to overcome the blocks.

Session 4
Problem solving—groupwork to make constructive, supportive sugges-tions to each woman on her current question or task.

Session 5
Timing—going with the flow of time, getting it right for yourself.

Session 6
Action plans—small steps, timescale.

Split courses
Split courses need to be closer in timescale than follow-ups for people to make the link. In most organizations it is difficult, if not impossible, to ensure that the same group will meet again because of business pressures, illness and other personal reasons. In addition, if any participants have found that Part I of the programme has not lived up to their expectations, they may absent themselves from Part II, even if it contains the learning that they really need.

In an experiment in the late 1980s individual and career development for women's programmes were run on three days one week and two the following week. The women reported:

- The break lost the flow—for some.
- For some it allowed digestion of material.
- The first three days were mainly about past and present issues so it was tempting for those very future-oriented women to give up (they didn't!).
- It offered the temptation for some women to drop out so they would not have to face the future (one did!).

The trainers reported:

- Initially it felt good to be giving participants a break; they had worked hard and deserved a rest.
- But some had to go back to work in the break.
- All went home at the weekend and were engulfed by family needs and issues.
- On the second week we had to build up the group again and it took extra time to get out of the weekend's activities and into their own development again.
- It was all the organization could allow because of pressure on training rooms and pressure from departments for the women not to be away for a week at a time.
- Development opportunities were lost, but if we hadn't done it this way it wouldn't have happened at all.

On balance we'd rather cover most of the learning and development on a main course and then hold a follow-up day. Then if there is any drop-out, most women have had most of the material.

Length of the days
The decision about the length of the working days will be determined by:

- whether the course is residential or not
- the participants' usual working day
- travel arrangements

The expense of a residential course puts pressure on you to pack a lot into a working day. This can be counter-productive to the effectiveness of the course, as people get overloaded and tired. On a residential course, you have the choice of having an early dinner plus an after-dinner session, or working on into the evening and having dinner later. Given the choice, most course participants prefer to work late and then have a later dinner, so that they can relax over their meal.

For example   An assertiveness course for a group of women returners was designed to be delivered over two full consecutive days. The women found arrangements difficult for two full days and asked for the course to be run in six two-hour sessions. The course was successfully redesigned into six self-contained modules, with 'homework' for the women to do between modules.

Course venue

If you have no say in the course venue then you will have to design your course around the constraints of the venue. The most perfect course design will flounder when you turn up to find yourself in a cramped basement room with no space for the role plays and no privacy for syndicate discussions.

If you choose or voice an opinion on the choice of venue, then your course design will be influenced by whether the course is run on-site or off-site, residentially or non-residentially. Our strong preference is for off-site training, and preferably residential. This is for the important reason that it gives an individual woman time to herself in a neutral space—literally; a breathing space where she won't be interrupted by the day-to-day demands of work or personal life, and will be able to concentrate on herself and her own development. Of course, this is not always a practical possibility, and it has drawbacks of its own. Here are some of the arguments both ways on the options:

On-site and non-residential

This is often used for one-day workshops. It's cheap and easy to organize, but there is a danger of messages and interruptions on days such as these. It sometimes seems that the indispensability of the person to their place of work is measured in inverse relation to their place in the hierarchy, i.e. the more junior they are, the more likely it is that their department can't manage without them for a few hours!

Advantages
- cheap
- familiar ground
- familiar journey
- high visibility
- easy to organize
- child/elder care arrangements as usual
- most easily accessible for most women

Disadvantages
- easy to be interrupted
- tempting to pop back to work in breaks
- difficult to be different
- difficult to 'lower the barriers'
- familiar ground can be threatening or too cosy
- difficult for the day to be different from usual

Off-site and non-residential

This is also often used for one-day events where it can emphasize that the organization is taking the training seriously—otherwise why would they spend all this money? It's also often used for two or three day events where you're trying to create the atmosphere of a fully residential course but the budget won't stretch to it!

Advantages
- gets people away from work
- dramatically reduces opportunities for interruptions
- keeps group together
- increases the chances of people speaking openly
- demonstrates the organization's commitment
- raises the level of expectation
- makes the point that it's different from an ordinary day

Disadvantages
- you lose time by having to allow for departures and arrivals
- people find it difficult to 'switch' back into the course when they arrive from home
- partners often feel threatened by course material and the woman is not fully equipped to deal with difficult conversations at home until the end of the course
- you run the risk of them not turning up
- more expensive than on-site
- more difficult to organize
- unfamiliar journey
- could create child/elder care difficulties
- could be too frightening
- distractions in the evenings

On-site and residential
This is an unusual combination and can be the worst of both worlds, but does crop up occasionally when working in the hotel industry, or if an organization has its own training centre on site.

Advantages
- cheaper than conventional hotel
- possibly easier to organize than conventional hotel
- often have easy access to admin facilities such as typing and photocopying
- familiar surroundings
- no domestic responsibilities

Disadvantages
- difficult to cut yourself off from work
- participants are easily accessible to others
- interruptions
- distractions of talking to colleagues in the evenings and over meal breaks
- familiar surroundings

Off-site and residential
For a course of more than one working day, this is by far our preference, with the one huge drawback that it can create enormous problems for women with child/elder care responsibilities and can therefore rule out the course for some women.

Advantages
- enables real concentration over an uninterrupted time
- no domestic responsibilities
- gives time for the individual to settle and grow
- gives a real breathing space
- demonstrates the organization's support
- more of a treat
- more able to put herself first
- much greater opportunities for informal networking and pooling of experiences over breaks and in evenings
- people are more able to relax and be themselves
- unfamiliar setting makes it special
- may not have been away on her own before; sees it as an achievement
- for a public course a good venue can be a selling point

Disadvantages
- can be exhausting if poor course design
- expensive
- if the venue is inappropriate you're stuck with it
- will rule out some women from attending through other responsibilities
- unfamiliar setting can be unsettling
- may not have been away on her own before and sees it as a threat

All these elements will contribute to your course design. It may now appear impossibly complex and be tempting to overlook! Remember that your course design is the foundation of your course. A good design will give you support and confidence, and enhance the developmental process. Lots of examples of course programmes appear in Appendix 1.

No design at all, or a poor design, will fight against your efforts and, however sparkling your delivery on the day, will reduce the effectiveness of your course. Time spent on course design is time well spent and will contribute to your seemingly effortless success!

Summary

In this chapter we have looked at all the different aspects of designing women's development training. The main points are:

- Good design takes time and thought.
- The course design puts the ground rules into practice.
- Decisions about venues, course numbers and ratios of trainers to participants are crucial.
- Prioritizing 'musts', 'shoulds' and 'coulds' of what participants need to know, understand and do gives you the key content.
- There is an enormous range of subject matter which can be used in women's development training.
- A good course design gives your course a solid foundation.

References

1. 'The Imposter Syndrome', *Management Solutions* August 1986.
2. Manpower Services Commission, 'Women Managers: their problems and what can be done to help them'.
3. Jane Beck and Maggie Steel, *Beyond the Great Divide* (Pitman, 1989).
4. John Naisbitt and Patricia Aburdene, *Megatrends 2000* (Sidgwick and Jackson, London, 1990).
5. Peter Honey and Alan Mumford, *The Manual of Learning Styles* (Peter Honey, 1984).
6. Liz Willis and Jenny Daisley, *Springboard: Women's Development Workbook* (Hawthorn Press, 1990). See Appendix 2 for further details.
7. Social Trends 1987, HMSO.

Kent County Council

Kent County Council has a comprehensive women's development training programme, and has had for some years. This case study has many interesting points to make, but two specific aspects are especially interesting:

- It is an example of how an ongoing programme needs to be constantly monitored, the design reviewed and changed to fit the changing culture of the organization and the changing needs of women attending.
- It describes the creation of a formal women's network, LINK, with financial backing from the organization. Usually, women form informal low-profile networks themselves, so LINK is an exciting and unusual example.

Context Kent County Council is a large organization, employing 50 000 people (two-thirds of whom are women), with an annual budget approaching £1 billion. It is divided into 19 departments ranging in size from Education which employs 30 000 people to Personnel which employs less than 50. Although some staff work in large central offices, many work in small geographically scattered units (e.g. schools, old people's homes and daycare centres). The total training budget, excluding special funds for teacher and uniformed police training, is about £3 million. This is double the figure for three years ago, but is still small compared with some other organizations of comparable size, e.g. Marks and Spencer or the Midland Bank.

Local authorities are going through a period of unprecendented change, driven both by external pressures such as new legislation and rising customer expectations and an internal desire to improve the service that we offer. One feature of this is a move to devolve responsibility nearer to the point of contact. This in turn calls for new skills at a time when such skills are in short supply in the marketplace. Put simply, we expect more out of less.

So Kent County Council's interest in developing its female workforce is therefore based on business needs. Women employees are in the majority, particularly at the service delivery end of the business (e.g. social workers, school secretaries). However, we have not approached this in the classic way by producing a board level policy on women's development and translating this into an action plan. Rather, we have tried to create a climate in which good ideas can flourish and risks be shared and supported. This is not to say that recruitment, retention and training are not board level issues or that we do not have policies in these fields. But, like all good strategies, they follow the entrepreneurs in the organization who discover new ways of doing things which take off. As an American business commentator said, 'Be successful first and then worry about your strategy'.

Women's issues

An interest in women's issues was first recognized in 1987 when a Career Development for Women working party was set up. Some of its outcomes included: the launch of a maternity pack, the appointment of an employee services officer, and notes of guidance on non-discriminatory interviewing and selection practice. More recently, initiatives such as a career-break scheme (for women and men), increased access to nursery provision, and the development of flexible employment practices such as homeworking have been introduced.

At the same time a pilot three-day programme on Career Development for Women was set up. The course was intended for women who were seen as having management potential and it covered practical areas such as assertiveness and presentation skills as well as identifying barriers to development and strategies to overcome them. This proved very popular and 11 more courses were run between 1987 and 1990. However, towards the end of this time, it was recognized that in some ways the courses were missing their mark. Some women were put off by the word 'career' as they did not see themselves as having or wanting a career. Also, as women who had been on the course went back to the workplace, they encouraged other women to attend and we then started to attract women who wanted to be 'developed' but who did not necessarily see themselves as having management potential. It was also a very slow process; although we ran 12 programmes, this reached only 200 women.

During this period, Kent was also looking at new approaches to learning which aimed at greater accessibility and appeal, such as open learning methods and self-development techniques. We also recognized that information on training was not always reaching staff, so we looked at other ways of publicizing initiatives, such as sending out information with payslips.

Springboard

These ideas were combined in the introduction of the Springboard initiative in 1990. Springboard (see Appendix 2) is a three-month self-development programme for women, which consists of two workshops, an open-learning workbook and tutorial support provided by women managers within Kent. Unlike management programmes, it aims to develop the whole person, not just the bit we see at work. Each programme takes 100 women at one time and we have run two programmes already with another two fully subscribed. This method enables us to reach a large group of staff whose talent and skills have never before been collectively recognized by the organization. It is also very cost and time effective. The interest from both within and outside the organization has been enormous.

One of the underpinning philosophies of Springboard is the importance of networking. Kent County Council has given financial support to set up a women's network known as 'LINK' and 18 groups have been established throughout the County. Such initiatives must be owned by the employees themselves; a too heavy management involvement could be counter-productive. The aim is to create the right climate to enable networking to happen.

As a counterpoint to Springboard, we are also planning to pilot a three-day senior management course for women. The objective is to enable women managers to develop a management style which increases their effectiveness and fits their own personality and values.

Individual departments are also introducing initiatives. For example, staff in the Police force who have a grievance concerning discrimination are now able to raise it directly with their equal opportunities officer without going through their line manager. Police are also reviewing height and age restrictions in order to make their recruitment practice fairer.

Social Services runs a programme of training including assertiveness, career planning, and six-day Women in Management courses. Women who have attended these courses are given the opportunity to network afterwards. The department has also set percentage recruitment targets at senior management level.

Outcomes One of the measurable outcomes of these initiatives has been increasing numbers of women appointed to management posts. The ratios are still small but the situation is improving. Following a recent staff survey, we now have a measure of the perceived sex discrimination in the organization, and will be able to compare this with future data.

However, although some outcomes are quantifiable, some of the most important results are not, although they are likely to have a greater impact on the organization in the longer term. The initiatives have started to change the attitudes of some managers to women in the organization but, more importantly, are leading to a change in the women themselves. Some quotations from Springboard participants illustrate the point:

- 'I feel more able to deal with problems than I did; I let them go over my head.'
- 'Springboard gave me confidence to go ahead with my career.'
- 'It was a chance to meet the other "you".'

The important message about women's development is that it is not just about providing increased career opportunities. In order for organizations to tap the potential of all their staff, they must enable women to develop themselves while providing a supportive climate in which this can happen.

Rita Bryant, Area Training Co-ordinator
Education Department
Kent County Council

5 Getting the arrangements right

You've identified the needs, designed your course and communicated with your target group. So it's just a matter of all the detailed administrative decisions now.

Don't skip on—even if you have years of experience of running courses—because what you do regularly and with good results for every other course you run may have different results or implications for women's development training. In this chapter we'll look at why logistics are important, consider the hours and timing of courses, the setting, the room and layout, getting there, childcare and facilities for women with disabilities, food and breaks, and all the other paraphernalia needed to make the course run smoothly.

What on earth can be special about the implications for women's development training of logistical decisions about such things as venue and lunch? Surely any place will do? Well, actually, no—because the objectives of women's development training usually include building confidence, and giving encouragement and support, so decisions such as venue, date, handouts and lunch all have an enormous impact on the effectiveness of the training.

Why logistics are important

There are two main reasons for getting the arrangements right:

- to make them appropriate for a wide range of different life situations which women have to cope with
- to ensure that the message of the course, and the message that the practical arrangements give, are in tune with each other

This applies to public courses as well as those in-house. This chapter covers all these practical aspects of setting up the course. All are common sense, but this is an area where attention to detail and thorough thinking will really pay off and ensure that your course gets off to a good start—before you've even opened your mouth!

Getting the times right

The dates and hours that you decide upon send out strong messages about the course and your attitude to women's issues. The likelihood is that a proportion of your potential participants will have school-age or under school-age children to consider, or elderly people. So a residential course on strategies for working mums run during half-term could be viewed with some cynicism! Running a women's development course is usually intended to send out a message of support to the women targeted, so choose dates and set the working hours with their circumstances in mind and without putting additional hurdles in the way of their participation.

Sometimes it is impossible to avoid difficult dates and times, and if it means the difference between running the course or not, then we hope you will still go ahead. However, in these circumstances, find a way to acknowledge the potential difficulty through the joining instructions, and consider any concessions that you can make. *For example*, you may be able to keep to the work pattern of the usual working day or, if your budget will stretch to it, offer a crèche facility.

An on-site non-residential course within usual working hours should present the least difficulties, although those women working shifts, job sharing or working part-time could still be affected. You need to be sensitive to these difficulties, plan for them and talk to line management about alternatives. One of the greatest enemies of the success of women's development training is the supervisor or line manager who can smugly say 'I'd love her to attend your course, but she can't be available on that day/at that time'.

It's important too not to make assumptions, e.g. that a woman with two small children will not be able to attend a residential course. Ask the women and find out what is feasible for them.

As with many of these issues, your decision on the dates, times and length of your course will be a balancing act. In this case, it is between the needs of the course and the day-to-day running needs of the organization. The needs of the women come first—that's what your course is all about—and, while the difficulty of releasing them has to be considered, it is also important for the organization to be seen to be supporting your initiative, even if it is inconvenient in the short term.

It is interesting to observe that there seems to be significantly less fuss about a male high-flyer being released for a high-status two-week management course than there is for a junior level female clerk to be released for a day for a women's development workshop. Perhaps this says something about how dispensable the individual is to the running of the organization!

Finding the right setting

The criteria for the right setting will be determined by your course objectives, course design and budget. The advantages and disadvantages of on-site versus off-site and residential versus non-residential have been discussed in Chapter 4. Two other aspects to consider are the quality of the setting, the course room itself and the layout.

Quality and status: The Savoy or the Church Hall?

When choosing the venue, consider your objectives and budget and decide what level of luxury is appropriate to support your objectives. As we've said in earlier chapters, women's work is undervalued and underpaid and so is women's training, so if you can, go upmarket! This is particularly relevant with residential venues for in-house courses; if one of the course objectives is to help the women feel of greater value, then treat them as though they matter.

If, however, they are paying for themselves, or are returners, an up-market venue can be counter-productive. Women paying for themselves may resent having to scrape together money for a luxury venue and so not enrol, and returners are easily intimidated by traditional venues such as hotels, or even colleges. Choose your venue with sensitivity, and consider a local church hall or community centre for returners.

For example A women's development course for highly stressed senior women executives was held at a particularly luxurious hotel with wonderful leisure facilities. One of the course objectives was to remotivate these women who were a vital part of the senior management team. 'Oh, I feel better already!' was the comment of several of the women *on arrival!* What may seem like an indulgence can be part of the course.

At the other end of the budget scale, a bit of a treat doesn't have to cost a fortune—it may take some ingenuity instead.

For example A public women's development course was run on a shoe-string with very basic facilities: no private bathrooms, little heating except a log fire, and no bar facilities, but set in breath-taking countryside. Everyone agreed that the lack of facilities paled into insignificance, as the greatest treat of all was five days among natural beauty, clean air and peace and quiet.

There are some practical arrangements to consider. Which of these will you provide, and what do participants have to pay for?

- all meals, tea, coffee, etc.
- set meals or 'à la carte'
- ensuite bathrooms
- wine with meals
- leisure facilities such as swimming pool, sauna, etc.
- a bar
- course materials
- travel to and from venue
- newspapers and bar bills
- telephone calls

Consider what would be the comparable quality for a group of men of equivalent grade/status? Are you giving the women 'second best'? Curious discriminations can creep in here.

The course room

The actual course room is best described by listing what it should *not* be, i.e.:

- not too big, not too small, for the size of the group
- not too hot, not too cold
- not too formal, not too relaxed

We have only three golden rules:

- total privacy
- daylight
- movable furniture

It is possible to run women's development courses almost anywhere if you stick to these golden rules. We have reluctantly run workshops with fixed, tiered seating and without daylight, but it is not possible to run women's development training without ensuring total privacy. One of the main points of women's development training is to provide a safe and secure environment for women to raise and discuss any issue at all—personal and professional; and having the ground rule of total confidentiality also means not being overheard either.

The ideal room is a comfortable empty space with daylight, in which you place chairs, a table or two to put books and notes on, a flip-chart stand with paper, an OHP if you're using one and any video equipment, the participants and yourself! Here are some examples of unusual rooms which have still worked well:

- A group of about 20 women squeezed into someone's sitting room for a 2-hour workshop. Some people had to sit on the floor, and the trainer had to alter her style drastically, but it worked.
- A group of 12 women gathered in a coffee area with fixed kidney-shaped settees and large potted plants for a one-day Saturday career development workshop. The problem for the trainer was knowing where to stand, but it worked.
- A group of 100 women met in a big formal boardroom, theatre-style, for a one-day workshop. The key here was to get them working in small groups for most of the day and moving the chairs around, which overcame the formality of the setting.
- A library with kitchen and meeting rooms was used, on a day when the library was not in use. It had been laid up with tables and chairs and had a distinctive 'schoolroom' air about it. Getting rid of the tables and encouraging the use of the kitchen for making coffee made it quite cosy!
- A bar of a hotel had plenty of daylight but only subdued lighting after 4 p.m. on a winter's day—pleas for extra light brought just enough to make the flip-chart visible!

As cautionary tales, here are some examples of rooms which resulted in courses that didn't work as well as they could. The courses were still successful, but operated at a much more superficial level than they could have done:

- A group of seven women worked in a bar area for three days, with interruptions from phone calls, people delivering drinks and people peering through glass doors at them. This broke the privacy rule and hampered the course process.

- A group of 15 women attended a women's management course for 3 days in a dark, overdecorated room with a hard wooden floor. The hard floor resulted in a lot of noise from chairs scraping, and the dark heavy decorations were oppressive. The atmosphere made a great impact and syndicate discussions were notably better when groups moved into adjacent syndicate rooms.
- A large lecture theatre with formal, fixed, raked seating (for 100 women) and a fixed lecturer console was the venue for a one-day workshop. This was overcome by having lots of syndicate areas close by and by only using the lecture room for plenary sessions. A great deal of time was lost by people moving from one room to another.

Layout   Tables kill development courses, so avoid any layouts with tables. If you need a table to put your own bits and pieces on, put it behind you or to one side. Your objective in the layout is to reduce the number of barriers between the participants and you and between each other. Formal layouts with straight rows of chairs are also killers. Here are some popular layouts and what you can do to turn them to your advantage.

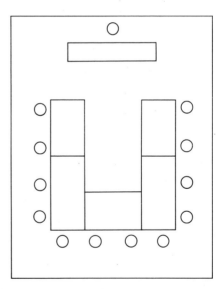

Figure 5.1   *A popular but unhelpful layout: U-shaped with tables*

Figure 5.1 shows a popular but unhelpful layout, a U-shape with tables. If your arrive too late to change this, you can minimize its deadening effect by pushing your table back and sitting in front of it. You will also need to walk up and down in the centre of the horseshoe. However, the tables are still a problem, so either ask the hotel to move them out overnight, or get the participants to push them to the sides during the day.

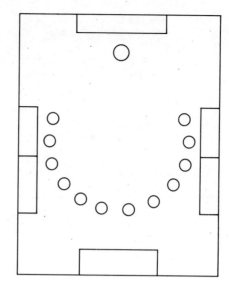

Figure 5.2 *A successful adaptation of the layout in Figure 5.1: U-shaped without tables*

Do not attempt to do role plays with this set-up. Instead, turn it into the U-shaped arrangement of chairs shown in Figure 5.2.

A conventional theatre style is shown in Figure 5.3. If you arrive too late to change it, again, push the top table behind you and walk around a lot! If you arrive in time to get it changed, move the room through 90° to minimize the distance between you and the back row. Also, curve the rows. This means you'll have to take special care with your eye contact at the ends of the rows but it creates a much more informal

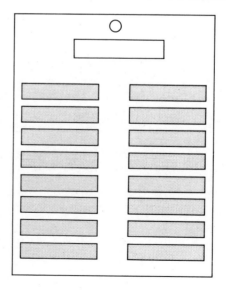

Figure 5.3 *Conventional theatre style*

feel to the room—less like a lecture room. Turn it into the arrangement shown in Figure 5.4.

Sometimes you cannot move the top table—they are increasingly often fixed to the floor, with audiovisual controls wired in—so minimize the formality of the room by positioning yourself in front of it. The same goes for a lectern. If you decide that you don't need microphone support, then do not feel intimidated into using a wired-up lectern; stand beside it or in front of it. Remember too that most lecterns are designed to be the right height for men, so if you're not very tall, not much of you will show above it!

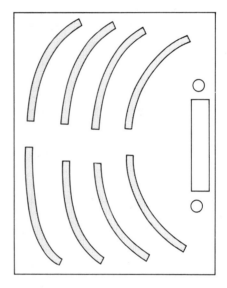

Figure 5.4   *Adapted theatre style*

If you are doing anything in this formal set-up, other than a straight talk, organize delegates into discussion groups as soon as possible to help people not to feel overwhelmed by the sheer size of the group. Hence the need for movable chairs. Within moments, your room layout can resemble the circular arrangement in Figure 5.5.

When you're addressing the whole group, ask those with their backs to you to turn round; otherwise you run the risk of losing half the room!

As you will usually be asked or consulted about the room layout, the ideal layout for up to 18 people is shown in Figure 5.6. This gives you the ultimate in flexibility and the minimum of barriers. For syndicate exercises or role plays, form smaller groups in the room, as shown in Figure 5.7.

If the room isn't big enough for syndicate discussions to be held in the room itself or if more privacy is needed for discussions, then you will need smaller rooms to adjourn to. These need to be nearby, laid out

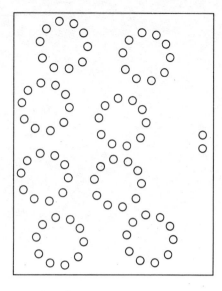

Figure 5.5 *Circular seating arrangement*

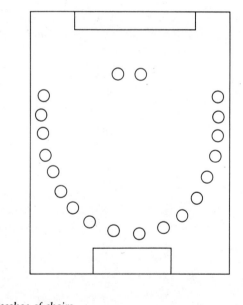

Figure 5.6 *Horseshoe of chairs*

without tables as in the main room, and private. It is very important that the rooms are nearby. You can lose the whole atmosphere of the course if participants have to trudge for 10 minutes across a hotel complex or along corridors in order to get to their room. Also, you will need to be able to drop in on their discussion several times during the time allocation to keep them on track and give encouragement, and to keep the atmosphere of the course intact. Many venues have a habit of providing

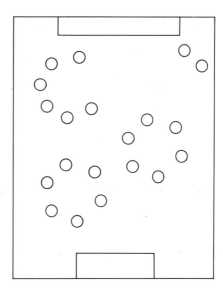

Figure 5.7 *Group discussion layout*

rooms which are a long way off or are difficult to find. If in doubt, ask for less fancy rooms nearby, or consider keeping all the participants in the main room.

In addition, there are several other aspects about the setting to be considered, such as:

- getting there
- access for women with disabilities
- childcare facilities

Getting there   The issues of geography and travelling arrangements are related to the length of the course. If you're running a five-day residential course in a luxurious hotel, the fact that it's set in the middle of nowhere could be seen as part of its attraction, whereas a Saturday morning workshop on assertiveness needs to be centrally placed and served well by public transport. Public transport is a women's issue because it is quite common for women to:

- have less money than men
- have less access to cars

Women are mostly in the lower grades in organizations and women's earnings (for non-manual workers) are only 62.2 per cent of their male equivalents (1988).[1] In addition, in most homes where there is one car, men have first access to it. So, unless you are running a course for women with company cars, you need to consider public transport arrangements, hiring a minibus, or arranging for lifts or taxis.

The extent of your consideration of this seemingly unimportant aspect can have a remarkable effect. We were dramatically reminded of this when running a one-day women's development workshop in central London. A middle-aged woman came up to us before we'd even started and thanked us for running the day. She was a part-time worker from a far-flung outpost of the organization and said, 'I've been working part-time for this organization for 20 years and no one has ever taken any notice of me. This morning they paid for me to have a taxi to the airport and paid for me to fly on the shuttle to Heathrow! I feel marvellous; my confidence is much higher now and I feel that I matter. Thank you!' And so the objective of the day had been achieved—and without us opening our mouths!

If you're organizing a public course, you need to be especially sensitive to accessibility, particularly if people are paying for the course out of their own pockets. A women's network, with the best of intentions, organized a Saturday workshop for local women, on a shoestring budget. To keep the costs down, they decided to use a member's particularly large and pleasant sitting room as a venue. They were disappointed at the low turnout and subsequently discovered that, while many women had been able to find the money for the workshop fee, they couldn't stretch to the additional £5 for the taxi fare to the inaccessible venue.

Again, for a public course, consider seeking sponsorship 'in kind' from organizations who are centrally placed and who may have large rooms sitting idle in the evenings or weekends. It's a cheap and easy form of publicity for them, although you'll have to offer a guaranteed level of publicity. Many of the women's networks operate in this way and, in return for a prominent use of their logo, some companies include coffee and sandwiches too.

Facilities for women with disabilities

When viewing a potential venue, have in mind the needs of women with disabilities, not just the obvious need for ramps for wheelchairs, but also for women with the less visible disabilities such as hearing or sight difficulties. Many disabilities may not be obvious, in which case you will need to create an environment in which the women feel comfortable enough to come and tell you of their special needs.

For example There was a deaf woman who asked to sit in the middle of the front row of a workshop of 100 women, to enable her to lipread our words. These considerations also have implications for your presentation style, such as keeping your lips in view, not distorting your lip movements and repeating questions or comments from other women not in her view.

The Royal National Institute for the Deaf (see Appendix 5) will always be prepared to give you the address of your nearest interpreter for the deaf. Ask for a woman and brief her about the nature of the course.

For example On a five-day biography workshop attended by three deaf women, the RNID advised on the choice of an interpreter and we were able to make sure that the same interpreter attended the whole workshop and the follow-up day. She was briefed on the nature and confidentiality of the course and quickly became part of the group. The tutor explained the interpreter's role and kept an eye open for the times when things were happening between the interpreter and deaf participants that blind women attending the course needed to be kept informed of. That course was the only exception to the 'no males' rule— Bracken the guide dog, whose only interference was raiding handbags left unsuspectingly open!

For example One of the best organized courses (on which one of us was a tutor), and one which encouraged women with disabilities, was run by the Women's Therapy Centre in London. They thought of just about everything and laid on extra staff to help with the practical arrangements. Severely disabled women were encouraged to bring their helpers, ambulances and taxis were organized to bring the women to the centre and a great variety of chairs and cushions were provided to make the women as comfortable as possible. Where small parts of the arrangements weren't perfect, everyone knew it was because of lack of funds to change the building rather than lack of care. This experience really brought home the careful and imaginative thinking that is needed to make sure that women with disabilities do not become second-class citizens on women's development courses.

For women in wheelchairs, or with standing/walking difficulties, consider:

- access between the course room and the lunch room/nearest disabled toilet/outside/bedrooms
- door frame widths and narrow corridors for wheelchair access
- the location of the nearest toilet to the course room which can accommodate a wheelchair
- if residential, whether there are any bedrooms on the ground floor or close to the course room
- whether there are any specially trained staff or volunteers available to help
- the availability of chairs at buffet meals
- the provision of a variety of chairs for different means of sitting
- lifts
- portable ramp
- ambulance, taxi/car access to the building

Childcare facilities

This is an aspect of choosing a venue that is being considered more often and is most usually offered for non-residential courses. Very occasionally we've encountered residential childcare, but in almost every case it's been organized in advance by the woman herself. Very occasionally, women have asked if their partners also could stay in the hotel or conference centre to look after the child while the woman is on the course. We have some concerns about this as it destroys one of the advantages of a residential course, i.e. getting away and having space, but we also accept that it may be the only way that the woman can attend. Some women have reported that it is unsettling for the woman herself, or for other women attending, to have a partner and small child on the periphery of the course. The effect on the course depends a great deal on the individual woman and how she handles the situation.

Childcare facilities are more often offered on non-residential courses where they can be:

- part of the venue's usual activities
- part of the organization's workplace nursery
- a special facility set up for the course

If you're thinking of setting up a special facility for the course, we advise that you:

- contact a specialist organization for advice (see Appendix 5)
- consider having a qualified child minder, nanny or nursery nurse
- get some mothers to advise on the facilities needed first
- do a special check for health and safety
- make sure mothers bring plenty of toys/games for their children
- locate it far enough away from the course room for the noise not to distract

Paraphernalia

Paraphernalia are all the bits and pieces that need to be considered before the course. Some of these are optional extras which the venue may provide, while others are essential and you may need to provide yourself. Here are some to consider, especially for women:

Name badges   a must to help people get to know each other quickly and to speed up conversations. Most of these badges are very women-*un*friendly, as they use hefty safety pins or clips which have obviously been designed for men's suits and are totally unsuitable for lighter materials. Take care with the type of clip or consider the fabric stick-on type. Get the names written large to help those with poor sight and also so that you can read them across the room.

Books to refer to   not essential, but highly recommended. For many of the participants, this will be the first training course they've ever attended and may be the first formal learning they've done since school, so providing books with further or associated learning encourages them to take the process further. Also, not everyone learns best on a course: the 'reflectors' and the 'theorists'[2] may need to mull things over and read around a subject further before they can really accept what you're putting across.

We nearly always take a selection of books with us from our own bookshelves for people to borrow and browse through for the duration of the course, even if it's only a one-day workshop. For non-management women this is important as they may not have come across books on women's development before; and for the management women this is important because most books on management are written by and for men, so they may not be aware of those books on management specifically relevant to women (see p. 232).

Some of these books we have listed on pp. 232–233 of *Useful Books* (Appendix 6). If you are able to invest in a mini travelling library, start with those in the strongly recommended section.

Swap-shop table   only relevant for an ongoing programme, so this is an optional extra. On a programme which carries over a period of weeks or months, we always set aside a table on which participants can put anything that they've come across which may be of use or interest to the others on the course. This usually comprises newspaper and magazine articles, but also books and even vitamin pills which people recommended, or the address of a clothes consultant. It makes the point to the participants that they are there to help each other, and that the advice and information isn't always going to come from you.

Display of relevant leaflets and information   another optional extra, dependent on where you are running the course. Some in-house courses find it useful to supply updates on the latest on career-break schemes, workplace nursery provision, further training opportunities, etc. and it is an opportunity for the organization to talk directly to women, without line management censorship.

Here is a checklist of paraphernalia to take with you—or make sure it is supplied there. The women's development trainer's basic 'first aid kit' of useful bits and pieces includes:

- A4 notepaper
- pens and/or pencils
- thick felt pens (enough for one per participant if a small group, or one per group if dealing with hundreds)
- blutack or masking tape
- badges, including one for yourself
- your own notes
- your travelling library of books
- name plates
- drinking water/juices

Food and breaks

As with any course, you can produce the very best in the way of ambience, course material, wonderful discussions and life-shattering learning, and the comment that appears on the evaluation form will be 'Pity about the lunch'. Breaks and meals contribute to or detract from your course in a fiendishly out-of-proportion way, so consider what is special about breaks and meals to a *women's* course and how you can ensure that they work in harmony with all your other well-laid plans. There are two special aspects of breaks and meals in relation to women's development training.

Remember, first, that encouraging networking and facilitating the swapping of ideas and experiences is one of the ground rules of women's development training. This makes breaks and meals as important a part of the course as the work in the course room.

Secondly, as women are generally still responsible for thinking about, buying and cooking food at home, having meals placed in front of them is liberating and a treat in itself. As with the choice of venue, many women say 'It's wonderful not to have to think about getting meals for other people for a day or two'; or even on a one-day workshop, 'This makes a change from sandwiches'. In our experience of working with mixed groups we've noticed that the men tend to take the food for granted—it's never commented on unless it's very poor—while for the women it is a really important part of the day and again conveys a message which says 'You're important'.

You don't have to have a lavish budget; any special effort will be noted and appreciated. If your budget is non-existent, then you may have to ask participants to bring their own food and if it's that or not run the course, then so be it. You can still make the meal fun and a bit special, depending on the way you set it up.

Having looked at food and breaks in principle, here are some guidelines about breaks specifically for women's development training:

- Keep everyone together.
- Remember that breaks are a valuable opportunity for networking and informal discussion.
- Keep an eye on the time—an overlong coffee break will lose the momentum of the course.
- Discourage participants from drifting off to make phone calls or, even worse, checking in to the office.
- Encourage people to open windows, get fresh air and walk about a bit.
- Do stick to the time you've announced, so that people know where they are with you.
- Do remind them of the books and information literature that's available—sometimes people need to be reassured that it's OK to look at them during breaks.
- Ask for a light buffet lunch, which can be eaten easily standing up, to encourage networking. Some caterers include hot soup and elaborate desserts in a buffet, which can get very complicated with lots of different plates and bits of cutlery to balance!
- Have lunch served in a private room if possible.
- Ask for a different menu every day.
- Remember people on different diets and ask about their requirements in advance. When a vegetarian recently complained that the buffet lunch was the same every day (different cold meats and lettuce) she was given the hurt reply that the caterers had made a special effort for her—there were three different sorts of lettuce to give her a variety!
- Tell participants that you expect them to network over lunch.
- If residential, make one dinner a special occasion, possibly in a private room with an after-dinner speaker.
- Allow at least 30 minutes between the close of the course and arranging to meet for dinner; this allows participants a chance to freshen up and 'phone home.

For example   An active women's group ran a series of four one-day workshops, two on assertiveness, and two on reducing stress. The local community hall allowed free use of the kitchens and small cafeteria so the women decided to organize a 'bring and share' lunch. As several had experienced this kind of lunch before, they knew it was essential to have it well organized. For each meeting two women took responsibility for telephoning or visiting everyone else to get their agreement on whether they were bringing salads, bread, cheese, main dishes, puddings or fruit juices—all on a low budget. It was a great success; everyone helped clear away and wash up and much good networking was done at the kitchen sink.

For example   A small organization, which regularly runs on-site women's development courses, has a permanent crisis with lack of space. On one notable occasion, the entire five-day course was held in what appeared to be an extended cupboard, with lunch wheeled in a good hour before the lunch break, and the remnants of lunch lingering for a good hour into the afternoon. The food was good, but its presence created a rather run-down feeling in the room, which became oppressive. Just moving to a different room for lunch would have made all the difference and enabled a fresh start to the afternoon.

Summary

Some of the major points from this chapter are:

- Make sure the practical arrangements help the women to attend the course.
- Ensure the needs of women with disabilities are met.
- Make the arrangements for meals/breaks enhance the opportunities for and practice in networking.
- Back up the quality of the message of the course with the quality of arrangements.

References

1. Equal Opportunities Commission, *Women and Men in Britain 1990* (HMSO, 1990).
2. Peter Honey and Alan Mumford, *The Manual of Learning Styles* (Peter Honey, 1984).

Oxford Women in Publishing

Good women's development training doesn't have to have a huge budget.
Here is a case study of an excellent women's network which is running
high-quality public women's development training courses with nationally
recognized consultants, at a local level, and on Saturdays. We know of
very few groups of women who are so well organized in terms of
women's development training, so this is an inspiring example. (See
Appendix 5 for a contact address for OxWIP.)

Personal effectiveness

Oxford Women in Publishing is the Oxford branch of the support and
networking group for women working in publishing, printing and allied
professions. One of its aims has always been to provide training for
members and other women. The group started by providing one course,
Personal Effectiveness—Improving Managerial Performance, in 1985.
The course was so popular that the group decided to compile a whole
programme of publishing courses and women's management and development training. In the first year, after failing to obtain sponsorship, the
group launched the programme with a nil balance and a carefully
worked-out cash flow forecast. Fortunately, courses were always booked
well ahead.

Training

At the time of the formation of Oxford Women in Publishing in 1983
there was a great need for training in the publishing industry. Few
companies provided more than job-specific training for their junior
employees and external management courses for a very few (usually
male) top executives. It was difficult for women in the lower and middle
ranks to get the sort of training that would help them develop the confidence and managerial skills to move into more responsible positions.

The situation has improved since then. Publishing companies do seem
to be taking training more seriously, but women's development training
is still not seen as a separate issue by most managers.

For the last five years the group has provided a programme of ten courses a year, mostly one-day or two-day courses run on Saturdays on a shoestring budget and administrated and serviced by volunteers. A cheap, central location for the courses and the willingness of committee members to order and collect sandwiches and make tea and coffee has been a vital ingredient of the group's ability to run the programme at fees individual women can afford.

The programme varies from year to year but courses on career/life planning, leadership and delegation, and handling increased responsibility have earned regular places. The courses on publishing topics such as an introduction to publishing, and copy-editing, tend to be taken by those with more junior jobs. Speaking with Confidence, and Moving into Commissioning, attract more experienced women who are unsure about their ability, desire or confidence to move higher up the career ladder.

The personal effectiveness course is still part of OxWIP's programme and runs twice a year. It consists of a mixture of assertiveness training and confidence-boosting exercises and remains the most popular course.

The women-only context has provided support for women who lack the confidence to speak about their anxieties in a mixed group and has enabled women to explore ways of handling work and personal issues which particularly suit them.

Tutors are either drawn from the Oxford Women in Publishing group itself or hired from outside. Only one male tutor has ever been hired—when no suitable woman could be found. The group believes that tutors should also be role models.

Many women have returned to their companies with new ideas and a notable increase in confidence. Over the years more companies have sponsored their employees to take the courses. It is difficult to assess how many of these women would not otherwise have received similar training and how many would have been sent on more comprehensive, more expensive courses. The latter would not necessarily be better, of course!

Valerie Fawcett
Oxford Women in Publishing

6 Publicity and PR

Having developed your strategy and designed your course, you now need to decide what you're going to say about the course, and to whom and when. This chapter deals with the publicity and PR considerations of women's development training, whether you're running an in-house or public course. However, the main emphasis in the chapter is on in-house courses.

The public relations aspects are particularly crucial for women's development training, as it is always seen as controversial and will attract comment and attention in a way which simply doesn't happen for most other forms of training. The launching of a radical new mainstream management course can pass without comment, while a tentative one-day women's development workshop will attract the limelight!

This chapter emphasizes the importance of being pro-active in your PR and ensuring that the messages being communicated about the course are positive and clearly understood. It is better that you send out the messages you wish people to receive rather than allow others to guess what you want to say. We discuss who you need to communicate to, whether to be high or low profile, when you need to communicate, what to say and how to say it before, during and after the course.

Women's development training is exciting and innovative. It challenges assumptions about women, about organizations and about women's role at work and in society. It offers a different way of developing people. For all these reasons, it demands a conscious publicity and PR strategy, to ensure that these positive messages are communicated effectively and to pre-empt a backlash.

Your target audience

You need to communicate to four main categories of people.

1 The influencers

These include:

Opinion formers—the people who influence opinion in the organization/industry/sector, and who are respected, trusted or feared.

Line management—who will have a substantial influence on whether an individual woman will hear about the course and be released to attend.

Influential professional groups—such as personnel managers, training officers, equal opportunities officers.

Trade union officials—as part of the network of influence.

For a public course, also add professional organizations such as the British Institute of Management and the Institute of Personnel Management, and women's networks such as Women in Management and the European Women's Management Development Network.

2 The target group
Your potential participants, as defined in your strategy.

3 The rest of the organization
Everyone else in the organization—people who don't have any direct or indirect involvement in the course, but who will contribute to the overall atmosphere and climate of opinion. This category does not apply for a public course.

4 The rest of the world
This can be as big or as small a group as you like and will be influenced by your decision on how high-profile you want to be. For a public course it is important, as you will be spreading your message wide. For an in-house course it is an optional extra.

Consider reaching:

- other organizations in the same sector
- professional groups
- geographical areas
- women's groups and networks
- trade organizations
- the local and national press

High profile/ low profile

You will have decided in Chapter 3 how high or low profile you want your women's development training to be, as part of your overall strategy. If you are running a public course, you will seize the high-profile approach. Unless a group of women ask you to run a course privately for them, you will inevitably be operating in the glare of the spotlight!

When you need to communicate

The emphasis of your message will change depending on when it has to be delivered. Broadly, you need to consider what you're going to say, and to whom:

- before the training
- during the training
- after the training

Getting the timing right is essential to effective communication.

Before the training
To the influencers: to gain support and credibility; to spread the word; to encourage recruitment.
To the target group: to recruit.
To the rest of the organization: to create understanding and involve them.
To the rest of the world: to create a good image.

During the training
To the influencers: to maintain support.
To the target group: to give encouragement and support; to encourage networking.
To the rest of the organization: to create understanding and support.
To the rest of the world: to create a good image.

After the training
To the influencers: to give feedback; to consolidate support for future courses.
To the target group: to celebrate; to reinforce a sense of achievement; to inspire, encourage and support; to generate interest in future courses.
To the rest of the organization: to change attitudes; to change the organizational culture.
To the rest of the world: to create a good image; to get the credit for what you've done.

What to say

What the message consists of will depend on all the previously mentioned influences: who you're communicating to, when, and how high/low the profile you want your women's development training to have. What this means in practice follows in Figures 6.1 and 6.2. The high-profile strategy is described in detail. If you want to adopt a low-profile strategy, or adapt the high-profile strategy to something in between, simply leave out whatever is inappropriate. You will need to do many of these things more diligently if you are launching a pilot course, whereas an established course will provoke its own publicity through word of mouth.

Before the training

This period begins right from the moment that you think you might take some positive action. It is always a delicate point when an organization first considers women's development training. What image will it have? How will the men react? It is seldom introduced without a few ruffled feathers or sarcastic remarks somewhere in the organization, so it's best to be prepared.

Communicating with the influencers

Identify the influencers who may be supportive and go to talk to them about it. Discuss with them how you will communicate with other influencers and ask them to be ambassadors for your women's development training. At this point you may set up a steering group, to give visible support. Lobby as many influencers as you can, individually.

Having gauged the level of support, arrange to brief:

- senior management meetings/committees
- line management
- the personnel function
- equal opportunities networks
- trade union networks/committees

	Influencers	Target group	Rest of Organization	Rest of World
Before the training	Talk to them one-to-one Formal presentations to: • groups • committees • steering groups Letters Reports Leaflets	Talk to groups Posters Leaflets 'Open house' meetings Advert in in-house magazine Through line management	Article in in-house magazine Through line management	Press release Word of mouth
During the training	Keep informed Invite as speakers Invite to join for lunch/drinks	Monitor how they heard about it	Invite as speakers Invite others to join for lunch/drinks afterwards	Invite journalist to interview participants Feature article
After the training	Keep informed Evaluation report Thank them	Get them to spread the word! Encourage them to write articles	Explain what has happened and what happens next Article in in-house magazine and photos of course	Press release that course has happened, case studies of success Speak at national events/conferences Write articles, case studies for publication Enter course for award

Figure 6.1 High-profile PR strategy

	Influencers	Target group	Rest of Organization	Rest of world
Before the training	Lobby individually Formal presentations to groups	Talk to groups Leaflet or one-page informal sheet	Rely on line management to brief	
During the training	Keep informed			
After the training	Thanks Keep informed Circulate Evaluation	Get them to spread the word!		

Figure 6.2 *Low-profile PR strategy*

Make use of letters, proposals and promotional material and, most importantly, give presentations at their meetings. This enables them to ask questions, voice their support-concern and suggest help and ideas. It also gives the opportunity for them to collect information so that they can answer the questions of those to whom they communicate. Briefing these key groups first is crucial in getting their support, in ensuring that the message passed on to the rest of the organization is positive, and in setting the recruitment process going.

Consider what your message is going to be:

- 'We're committed to positive action for women and are working out how to do it.'
- 'Women's development is going to happen and you are needed to . . . .'
- 'Women's development training is going to happen and this is what is proposed.'

It's almost impossible to monitor how the message is interpreted. We've experienced the whole spectrum from:

- 'The organization is creating a new and positive approach to the training and development of its human resources—particularly women.'

to:

- 'Now we've been told, we'll have to do something to help the girls catch up with us.' (ugh!)

and

- Not saying anything at all.

Make sure that all these key groups and influencers are fully informed before talking to your target group. As with any course, it's common to hear of line managers who block women from attending a course because they didn't know about it first.

The *course title* depends entirely on your strategy. If it is high-profile and direct you may be able to give a title that describes exactly what you are doing, e.g.

- Career Development for Women
- Women's Development Programme
- Women in Management
- Women and Leadership
- Work and Personal Development for Women
- Personal Effectiveness for Women

If your strategy has to be more low-profile, you may need to use a general title, e.g.

- Assertiveness for Secretaries
- Developing your Potential
- Career Development

As much as possible, the title needs to say what the course does and also needs to fit in with your organization's culture and existing course range. So the same Springboard programme (see Appendix 2) in several different organizations is called variously:

- Springboard—a programme for non-management women·
- Springboard—Women's Self-Development
- Springboard—Women's Development Programme
- Women's Development Programme
- Springboard
- Springboard for Women

The title may in the end need to be a political decision.

At this point you can refine your publicity message and go public!

Communicating with the target group

How many women are you trying to reach? Your organization may have 30 or 30 000 women, so logistically you could have quite a challenge.

To reach your target group, put posters, notices, advertisements and leaflets where they will see them. Putting them on noticeboards which traditionally have been covered with notices about the darts match and the cricket team won't work! Clearing a space for a well designed poster or placing posters on special stands by entrances will be much more effective.

Put articles and 'adverts' in in-house publications. This makes it official, lets everyone know at once and offers a fair chance to all. But, of course, not everyone reads the in-house magazine. Organizations find that advertisements for development courses do well when put on the 'Situations Vacant' pages of in-house publications, as these are the pages more carefully read by people who are uncomfortable with their present situation.

Leaflets sent in wodges to offices get wasted, and leaflets sent via line management and/or personnel run the risk of being filtered. Use your creativity and ingenuity to think of ways to reach the target group *direct*. Kent County Council achieved this very successfully by attaching a full colour leaflet to every woman's pay packet or pay advice. They also went to a lot of trouble to ensure that the illustrations on the leaflet included women who were:

- black and white
- able-bodied and with disabilities
- older and younger
- fatter and thinner
- with glasses and without
- fashionable and not-so-fashionable

This reinforced the message that the course really was for *any* woman in Kent.

Fill a pilot programme by issuing personal invitations. This has the advantage of getting the course under way quickly but the disadvantage that it appears élitist and leaves other women out. It may work for a course of 12, but becomes more difficult for a workshop with 100 participants.

On pages 117–120 are examples of advertising literature used by various organizations. Leaflets can be anything from a photocopied A4 sheet to a glossy full-colour brochure. Make sure it is at least as good as the other training literature in the organization. All the examples that follow are of organizations that took care in the presentation of the message and were successful in achieving their aims.

Example 1   Figure 6.3 shows the one-page advertisement used by Sun Microsystems to introduce its new women's development training programme (see Case Study One). It went on electronic mail (the organization's company-wide computer mail system). This was a low-profile start. It said nothing about being specifically for women because all the secretarial and administrative staff are women.

Example 2   Figure 6.4 shows the cover of the Oxford Women in Publishing's directory of public courses (see Case Study Four).

Example 3   Grand Metropolitan Foods Europe produced their specially printed leaflet to fit in with their corporate initiative called the 'Learning Edge' (see Case Study Five). Their Springboard women's self-development literature was the same size, style and quality of design, reproduced here in black and white and reduced in size (see Figure 6.5).

Example 4   In the Midland Bank Group an element for women returners was introduced into their LEAP open learning programme, and publicised with the leaflet shown in Figure 6.6.

Meet in small groups with the women who are the target of your course to give opportunities for them to ask questions, voice concerns, size you up, find out more about it, begin to meet each other and to be encouraged to attend. Either go to them, and meet with small groups arranged by on-site line or personnel management, or let them come to you, and organize 'open day' type meetings at lunch time or immediately after work.

In attempting to reach all the women, you will find there are many deliberate and unintentional filters that act to prevent them receiving the material, so care needs to be taken either to beat the system or to join it. Here are some common hiccups:

- all notices to departments about women's development courses filed in the bin
- women being told that the course is not for their grades
- information being circulated to women after the closing date
- managers in large departments giving the impression that they are only allowed one place per course, per year, etc.

Work and Personal Development Programme

Intended for

Secretarial and administrative staff at all levels.

Objectives

On completion of this programme, participants will have:

- recognized the importance of 'image' and presenting yourself positively
- examined strengths, weaknesses, and values in an organizational and personal context
- practised the use of assertiveness and its role in the resolution of conflict
- gained an awareness of individual responsibility for career and personal development
- developed personal action plans

Contents and method

The course will be run with a mixture of tutor input and group and individual exercises. The approach is highly practical and will be directed towards action to be taken back in the working environment. At the end of the course, participants will produce personal action plans to transfer the learning to work and personal lives.

Subjects covered will include

- What is assertiveness?
- Strengths, weaknesses and values
- Recognizing and managing aggression and passivity
- Winning, losing, influencing and gaining respect
- Assertiveness in groups
- Action planning

Duration/dates

2 days—residential 1 night   23–24 July 1990

Number of participants

Maximum 12—minimum 6

Figure 6.3 *Advertisement for Sun Microsystems' initiative in women's development training*

- courses for non-management women being advertised by the management training department, so women didn't read the notice as they assumed it didn't apply to them
- only one notice being provided per department for an already crowded noticeboard
- women being told that courses were full when spaces were available

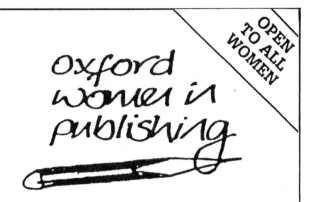

Training Programme 1991

Our training programme for 1991 includes some courses which continue to be popular from previous years and some new courses.

Training can help you to increase your effectiveness in your job, give you confidence and increase your chances of promotion. Take advantage of these very reasonably priced courses and ask for sponsorship from your employers*. They will benefit from the skills you learn. There is a minimum of 8 and a maximum of 12 places on each course.

Courses are open to all women, whether or not they are members of Women in Publishing, although members pay a lower rate. All courses take place at the Clarendon Press Centre in Walton Street.

Courses fill up quite quickly—book early to be sure of a place.

We regret that we are unable to give refunds on places cancelled less than four weeks before the course.

* A reduction in price may be possible on some courses for those who are unemployed, students or those unable to get sponsorship from their companies.

Figure 6.4 *The cover of the Oxford Women in Publishing's directory of public courses*

WOMEN'S SELF DEVELOPMENT

As you may already be aware, the Learning Edge is a new approach to training and development for Grand Metropolitan Foods Europe. Its aim is to promote the development of individuals and at the same time achieve the business objectives of the Company. We believe that if we can help individuals to realise their full potential and provide them with greater job satisfaction, that will help us to develop and maintain a competitive edge and therefore continue to be successful as a Company.

We have already introduced one programme – the Certificate of Management – and another, relating to Supervisory Management, is in the process of being launched. Springboard is an exciting new development which will continue the process of extending the Learning Edge throughout the Company.

What is Springboard?

Springboard is a new training and development programme specifically devised for women. More particularly, it is aimed primarily at women in GMFE employed in non management positions.

As the name suggests, the purpose of the programme is partly to act as a career springboard for women who want to improve their position within the Company. In addition, Springboard is also about personal development and gaining a better understanding of yourself. As a result, we anticipate that you will enjoy your job more and gain greater satisfaction out of being at work.

Springboard is new but it has been tried and tested and found to be successful. The first organisation to use the programme was the BBC, who have 8,000 non management women. It received a very enthusiastic response from everyone who participated and has now become an integral part of corporate training and development within the BBC.

We have taken the Springboard programme and tailored it specifically to the needs of women within GMFE.

EXPRESS FOODS GROUP (INTERNATIONAL) LIMITED

Figure 6.5 *Extract from Grand Metropolitan Foods Europe training leaflet*

WHY IS THIS PROGRAMME NEEDED?

The facts

- women will consitute 50% of the workforce by 1990
- the fastest growing group of workers are women with pre-school age children
- 63% of women in the 25–49 age bracket work
- in the 15–19 age bracket there will be 28% less workers in 1994 than in 1984

It is generally accepted that women returners will be needed in the future to fill the skills gap, especially in the light of the figures concerning the drop in the numbers of school leavers. Competition to attract women back to the workplace will be fierce, and the companies who provide support in the transition period will undoubtedly have a competitive edge.

So . . . Midland Bank will need to:

1. Attract women returners
2. Retain women returners
3. Retain existing staff

WHY DO WOMEN RETURNERS NEED A SPECIAL PROGRAMME?

Specific problems

On re-entering the workplace some women lack confidence because:

- they feel out of touch:
  recent changes in technology and practice mean that women may be returning to a largely unfamiliar job and environment.
- society undervalues mothering:
  time spent at home—and skills learned—are undervalued by society at large and often by the women themselves.
- good childcare is hard to find:
  problems with inadequate childcare anxieties, absenteeism, loss of productivity and perhaps even having to give up the job.
- managing a home and a job is difficult:
  women may feel unsure about their capacity to manage home, family and career. Struggling to deal adequately with all three means that they often neglect themselves and become tired and stressed.
- managing a home and a job causes guilt:
  there are still pressures—both external and internal—for women with children to remain at home. These can lead to feelings of guilt and inadequacy, both as mothers and as workers.

WHAT DOES THE PROGRAMME CONSIST OF?

Pack contents
LEAP Forward programme

5 self instructional units, each consisting of information and instruction accompanied by a 30 mins audio tape. The five units are independent:

1. Confident Me
2. Happy Children
3. Clear Communications
4. Good Organisation
5. Well-Being

LEAP Forward workbook
to be used for activities in all five units with a how to use section explaining how the programme works. These elements . . . . .

LEAP BACK TO WORK

This pack is given to *all women returners* to *Midland* and consists of:

Welcome back audio tape and A5 leaflet-checklist to introduce the Leap Back to work pack and explain the Leap Forward programme.

Friendly guide
For the returner to give to the person who will be supporting her through the training programme.

Ten keycards
to reinforce the keypoints and information that each woman needs.

Figure 6.6 Midland Bank's leaflet for the LEAP women returners programme

Communicating with the rest of the organization

Line managers can help or hinder your reaching the target group. Women at the bottom of the organization have not traditionally had access to or demanded training and development, so it is easy for a line manager, on hearing about the course, to assume that it is not intended for the women in his/her department. Equally, a manager who supports and encourages the women in his/her department sets a precedent and causes questions to be raised about other departments.

For example A Self-development in Careers course for women was consistently well attended by women from one particular department. The (male) manager of this department was particularly open to issues around women's development in the organization and actively suggested that the women attended the course. Women who attended then encouraged their colleagues, and women's development training became an accepted part of the culture of this particular department.

Line management are also likely to be asked about the course and may have to deal with questions from people both in and outside the target group, so it is important they understand your objectives.

Give some thought to other ways of explaining what you are doing to the rest of the organization. Posters and notices about women's development training are often the victims of sexist graffiti, but an article or interview in the in-house magazine should put your point of view across, preferably reinforced by an endorsement from a senior influencer.

You may need to remind the men in the organization of all the developmental training that is already open to them and explain why the organization is taking positive action. As with any training, there will always be a group of both men and women who will feel threatened and antagonistic.

Telling the rest of the world

If you want the rest of the world to know your plans, use a formal press release to the trade and personnel and training press.

During the training

During the training you will consolidate the positive PR and set the wheels in motion for good publicity and PR afterwards. Keep the influencers informed about what is happening, how effective the recruitment has been and how the training is progressing.

Involve them and other key people (e.g. more senior women) by asking them to attend as guest speaker, or to launch the training or join the participants for a chat over coffee/drinks immediately after the training. This way they can hear the success of the training from the participants themselves, build links and visibly demonstrate their support.

While the training is taking place, you have an opportunity to monitor the effectiveness of your pre-training PR, by asking the women what they had heard about it, and also by carrying out a formal monitoring process such as analysing the bookings by department.

For example   A large local authority undertook a monitoring exercise on the first 300 nominations for a big women's development training programme, which identified departments who were releasing a lot or very few women. Action was then taken to make sure that women in the under-represented departments knew about it and were not being blocked from attending.

The best time to tell the rest of the world will be after the training, when you have more of a story to tell. However, during the training, you could consider inviting a woman journalist to interview participants. The ground rule of confidentiality means that you will not have *anyone* sitting in on the training as an observer, so journalists can come only during breaks or at the end of the day, and talk only to women who have volunteered to talk with her. This also applies to the taking of photographs.

You would only ever depart from this practice with the participants' full permission and then only for a very short space of time, and for a plenary session.

After the training

This is the time to give feedback to the influencers. You may write a full-blown evaluation report sometime later but, meanwhile, informal feedback—verbally, in a letter, or in a very short report—needs to circulate fast.

Also, give your thanks and appreciation to the influencers for their help and support. You may choose to disband the steering group at this point, unless you've decided to move on to another initiative which could benefit from their support.

The best source of PR for women's development programmes are the women who have attended the programme. Encourage them to go back and spread the word. Our experience shows that more than half the participants on courses come because they have:

- been encouraged by ex-participants
- seen the changes in other women who have attended

Re-issue successful literature and update it when changes are made or when you feel you need to give the training a new boost. Articles in in-house publications can give the official view, or the ex-delegates' view, both of which are needed, so write or encourage the participants to write articles about the programme and its success for the in-house publication.

The following are extracts from an article in *Ariel* by Janet Graves[1] about her experience of a women's development course:

. . . Rarely does one have the chance to spend a day being inspired, and on the firm's time at that. The first day of the Women's Development programme was just such an opportunity.

The chance to visit the Council Chamber at Broadcasting House—oak lined, with art deco lamps—was almost worth the trek from Manchester alone. Until you noticed them. Six oil paintings dominating the room. Six Director-Generals. Six men. Then it all fell into place . . .

. . . The task is enormous. Women are 52 per cent of the population, 48 per cent of the working population, and 0.00 per cent recurring of the BBC's Board of Management. That's why those men look so smug. A blush, I hope, came to their cheeks as 70 women spoke up about their experiences.

Pledged to secrecy, I can't reveal the stories of daily sexism, ageism, discrimination, condescension of all of us bar none . . .

. . . The course is self-nominating, and if your building will pay for three trips to London, you can go. The third course has begun and new graduates from the first two are helping the new recruits. But we won't create an 'old boys' network that excludes everyone but the élite. The 'new girls' network will help and support each other, be generous and kind with their experience.

For me, returning to BBC Manchester with renewed determination to be noticed and appreciated, it's full marks for the development course.

For the rest of the organization, articles in in-house publications will explain what has happened and what is planned for the future. If it's all going well, shout about it! It will encourage other women to nominate themselves and silence the sceptics.

If you want the rest of the world to know what you've been doing, after the training is your busiest time and, for a public course where more are planned, a crucial part of your ongoing recruitment drive.

Women's development training is news. The late 1980s and early 1990s have seen an increase in media criticism of organizations which do not appear to be doing anything for women. So when you are doing something positive it's worth blowing your own trumpet! It's even more worth shouting about when you've actually completed your pilot programme and have more of a story to tell.

Issue press releases
- Let your trade press know—you may be leading the field in your industry.
- Tell the specialist personnel and training press—women's development is still newsworthy.
- Talk to national and local press; everything you do to help develop women enhances your image as an employer and supports the organization's ability to recruit and retain women.

Write articles and case studies
- Put your view across in the way you wish to be represented.

Enter for awards
- Choose particularly the National Training Awards and the Lady Platt Award for equal opportunities training (see Appendix 3 for more details).

Make sure that all the appropriate internal messages have gone out first *before* your external messages. People, and especially key influencers, don't like discovering about their own organizational practice in the general, trade or professional press.

Speak at national/international/trade conferences
Human resource development, personnel, and women's conferences welcome case studies of good practice. Write and volunteer your services and, if possible, involve one or two ex-participants in your presentation.

Summary

In this chapter we've looked at all the messages that you send out about your women's development training and highlighted ways of using internal and external publicity and PR to support your women's development training strategy. The main messages from this chapter are:

- Women's development training attracts publicity in a way that other training doesn't.
- Use this visibility positively.
- Women's development training is something that everyone seems to have views about, so you need to consider how you communicate to everyone in the organization.
- Women's development training provides the whole organization with a PR opportunity. It can be a key factor in the organization's face to the world.

Reference

1. Janet Graves, 'Beware—the Super-flossies are Coming', *Ariel* 31 October 1989.

Grand Metropolitan Foods Europe

Grand Metropolitan Foods Europe is an organization which has tackled the situation of communicating with staff on a large number of sites. They have placed their women's self-development programme in the context of a major initiative, the 'Learning Edge', with its high-quality publicity material and image.

Introduction

We are a large food manufacturing organization with many of our employees at sites throughout the UK. We are constantly reviewing our personnel, equal opportunities, and training and development policies and practice in the light of our business needs. As a result, we have recently introduced a new initiative called 'Learning Edge' which aims to promote individual self-development as well as achieving business objectives. This is done in the light of our belief that the knowledge, skill and commitment of people are key deciding factors in our organization's success. The future demands of our business will require all employees to make the most of their skills, potential and talents, to ensure that the company continues to prosper.

With this as a background, we examined all the ways in which we can make the best use of our resources to match our future business needs, and in 1989 decided to look specifically at the development of women within the organization, as we were aware that they were a very underutilised resource, mainly at the bottom of the organization.

Thinking about policy

We were very aware that it would be unwise to rush quickly into any development specifically targeted at women without thinking through our strategy very clearly, and without considering the consequences for the rest of the organization. So in 1989 we decided to organize a meeting of eight senior women in the organization to review and discuss women's development in the light of our current business needs, company culture, and the expectations that this might raise as far as women were concerned.

It was decided, in conjunction with an external consultant who facilitated the meeting, that these senior women would experience women's development training for themselves, as well as holding the policy discussions. So the first two and a half days of the three-day residential meeting involved them in a developmental process so that they would have a clear understanding of the type of activities they might be asking other women within the organization to engage in, and would be able to see the kind of results that might emerge from such developmental training.

Attending a developmental workshop with women only was a new experience for most of the senior women concerned. Managerial and developmental courses are attended almost exclusively by men because they constitute the target population, so it was with some interest and perhaps even a little trepidation that the women entered into the developmental process. The benefits from being able to talk as a group of women quickly emerged as they were able to realize the common problems faced by most of them in very different jobs and in different parts of the organization. By the end of the two and a half days they clearly saw the potential benefits for other women in the organization, particularly those lower down.

They then looked at the policy and strategy for developing women in the organization, and realized that women's development training was only a small part of this, and that more changes would need to take place in the culture of the organization and the personnel policies and procedures in order to facilitate the development of women. A career-break scheme for family responsibility for both men and women has since been introduced, which was really needed in terms of policy.

It was also decided to collect precise statistical evidence about where the women are in the organization to back any future development plans.

Parallel initiative

At the same time as the meeting with senior women was taking place, the director of employment policy (who is responsible for equal opportunities within the organization) was also considering an initiative that would be specific for women. His initiative came from an attitude survey conducted in the organization, asking women for their views of the organization as an employer, and for ideas about what could be done to improve employment conditions for women within the organization. It was decided that women's development training would take place for the bulk of the women who are not in management positions, and who are at the bottom of the grading structure. A mini audit of the needs of these women in relation to their own development was commissioned and the decision taken to pilot a Springboard programme.

Communicating within the company

Because we are an organization of very many subsidiary companies, each with their own personnel and training functions, it was essential that we communicated our intentions well. This was not an easy job. Our Personnel Policy Committee is the vehicle for discussing new policies for all the companies, and the implications in terms of results, budgets and staffing for the training needed to be discussed with them first. The decision to go ahead was not taken quickly, and it involved many meetings with the different people concerned before contributions to a central budget were agreed, and we were able to go ahead.

This whole process took some months and a lot of commitment and energy on the part of the central staff who were masterminding the whole operation.

Getting the programme started

We decided to launch the programme within our 'Learning Edge' series and so we produced literature which matched the existing brochures. We then had the task of actually trying to reach the women, and convince them that these brochures were actually for them and not part of any management training scheme.

Managers and personnel staff were briefed at line meetings and the information was sent out to all parts of the company. We were overwhelmed with the response, and had no trouble at all in filling our first programme of 60 places; even before the pilot was run, we had people wanting places on the second programme.

The response from the women to the pilot programme has been very good and the results that they have achieved have included:

- promotions
- job interviews
- rewriting CVs
- being more assertive
- being more confident
- taking on extra responsibility
- arranging visits to other departments, sites or factories
- finding out about more training and development courses
- deciding to undertake the 'Learning Edge' Certificate of Management
- making sure appraisals were taken
- undertaking further education
- rewriting an administrative manual
- making a presentation to people at head office
- taking on new roles
- being more active in meetings

There were the main work-type achievements and there were also a whole host of personal achievements which related to their lives outside work.

What now?

We are developing other women as trainers to run the Springboard programme and we are now open to the possibilities of developmental work for women at other levels within the organization. The company is committed to changing its culture, policies and procedures in such a way that it will enable women to progress as easily as men within the organization.

Helen Loughlin, Group Training and Development Manager
Grand Metropolitan Foods Europe

7 Recruitment

You can have the best course design in the world, and the full support of the organization, hire the best women's development trainer, and the best venue, but if you don't have the right people on the course, it will fail.

Getting the right people onto your women's development training course is absolutely crucial. You will have identified your target group as part of your strategy in Chapter 3. This chapter looks at how you ensure that they turn up, and in the right frame of mind. Much of Chapter 6, which looked at the publicity for your training, fits in with this chapter, which will deal specifically with the implications of self-nomination, the nomination procedure, joining instructions, and monitoring the recruitment pattern.

All these issues are especially important for a pilot programme, because it sets the precedent and thereby either helps or hinders the longer-term prospects of the training.

Self-nomination

However brilliant your training technique, you cannot force people to work on their own development. The most important results come from those changes in behaviour and attitude that the woman makes for herself. A level of commitment is needed from the individual, which is why one of the fundamental ground rules of women's development training is self-nomination. Women's development training involves an individual woman in taking responsibility for her own life and future. This means that the decision to attend must also be her responsibility. Self-nomination does not necessarily mean volunteering. Some women will volunteer, others will need encouragement, support and persuasion. Self-nomination simply means that it is the woman herself who makes the decision to enrol on the course, and not her line management or personnel officer, however well meaning they may be. This has a range of advantages and disadvantages:

Advantages
- When the course starts, you know they all want to be there.
- You can assume a level of support, however passive, when you start the course.
- The women are being given an opportunity to choose for themselves.

Disadvantages

- You can't force anyone to attend. If any woman is forced to attend she may have different objectives if she has any at all, and her feelings about the course may be quite strong.
- You can't even force someone whom you feel sure would enjoy it once she gets there!
- You can't pack your course with renta-crowd to make yourself look good!
- You run the risk that no one enrols.
- You can't rely on line managers or the personnel department to fill your course for you.
- Other people can easily block a nomination simply by withholding information.
- You cannot assume that the self-nominating ground rule has been observed—the trainer will have to check at the beginning of the course how people were nominated.
- Your publicity has to be very effective in order to reach individuals who traditionally have difficulty in gaining access to training.
- You will have to pay more attention to recruitment than the more usual procedure of personnel or line management nomination.
- You have to give greater thought to reaching the target group direct.

As you can see, most of the disadvantages of self-nomination occur at the recruitment stage, while the advantages appear when the course comes to be run. So time taken to recruit the right people in the right way is time well spent.

Self-nomination makes the process and the course vulnerable to people who don't want it to succeed. Consider your strategy to deal with some of the blocks that might occur, such as:

- managers giving false information
- women being verbally harassed for having an interest in the course
- your publicity material mysteriously disappearing
- managers actively discouraging attendance
- managers openly blocking attendance: 'I'm not letting any of *my* staff attend'

Can you tackle these yourself, or are you going to need senior management to take action? This is where you may need help.

The nomination procedure

The nomination procedure needs to be kept as simple as possible, not because women are stupid, but because you need to reduce any hurdles as much as possible between the initial decision to enrol and actual attendance at the course.

This is especially true when you are recruiting women with low self-confidence levels, which can include women at the bottom of the organization and women returners. For these women in particular, the nomination process needs to be as friendly and reassuring as possible. For women returners, it is particularly important that they are not asked to nominate themselves too far in advance of the course. Four to six weeks is long enough. The nomination procedure should also include an opportunity to meet before the course for the trainer to explain the course content, discuss their expectations and deal with any initial concerns. Otherwise, keep the logistics to a minimum, and consider what you actually need to know at this point:

- the woman's name
- how and where you can contact her
- which course she is enrolling for
- agreement from her line manager to release her for the training

You may also want to make clear that there is a source of help for women who have difficulties with gaining line management agreement, and encourage anyone who encounters this to contact you direct.

Grand Metropolitan Foods Europe (see Case Study Five) have a good nomination form for their self-development programme (see Figure 7.1).

Joining instructions

Having received a completed nomination form, it is up to you to respond. Most women attend women's development training to build self-confidence, so whatever you send must be sensitive to this. For many women, this may be the first training they've ever attended, so you also need to address this. There isn't any pre-course work needed for women's development training but your communication with the participants beforehand should:

- reassure
- set the tone
- give an outline or programme of the course
- give information on how to get there and a map
- give information about what, if anything, they'll have to pay for

These pieces of paper assume enormous importance, as they will be the only contact that the participants have with you before the course. We've heard of women cancelling their places on courses because of insensitive or frightening joining instructions, while, on the positive side, we've also heard of women who were relieved and reassured by the tone of the joining instructions.

If you're a freelance trainer, it is likely that you won't have any say in what is sent out beforehand, as most organizations have a set formula. In this case, make sure that you get a copy of everything sent, so that you can attempt to influence it and anticipate the mood in which the women arrive at the venue. If you do have a say in the content and style then bear in mind the objectives and ground rules of women's development training and make sure it:

- is informal, friendly and informative
- stresses the non-hierarchical nature of the course

NOMINATION FORM

The next series of Springboard workshops will take place at the Heathrow
Holiday Inn in West Drayton on the 12th September, the 26th October and
the 29th November. You need to discuss the programme with your manager
and if you decide that it is of definite interest, please fill in the details below
and send this form to Lynda Tuff, Block I, South Ruislip (ext 5034).

SURNAME _____

FIRST NAME _____

SITE LOCATION _____

EXTENSION NUMBER _____

YOUR SIGNATURE _____

YOUR MANAGER'S NAME _____

YOUR MANAGER'S SIGNATURE _____

The Learning Edge

Figure 7.1   Sample nomination form (Grand Metropolitan Foods Europe)

- gives enough information about the course to be non-threatening
- avoids potentially frightening terms such as 'role plays', 'intensive group work', 'personal situations'
- uses positive phrases such as 'working together', 'your course', 'wonderful opportunity', 'getting the most out of it'

There will also be additional information that you need from them at this point: any special facilities required for women with disabilities, dietary preferences and requirements, and travelling arrangements.

Monitoring the recruitment

It is important to monitor where and who the nominations are coming from, for four specific reasons:

- A self-nomination procedure makes it easy for nominations to get blocked or discouraged.
- Women have traditionally had less access to training, so they may assume that training isn't for them.
- A good mixture of participants enriches the course.
- Women who lack self-confidence may not nominate themselves. Ironically, it is often these women for whom the course is designed.

As the nominations arrive, check whether you are receiving nominations from:

- your target group
- women right at the bottom of the organization, if your target group encompasses this level. Often a course aimed at 'non-management women' will attract graduate trainees, senior secretaries and other non-management professionals, while other non-management women will assume that it is not accessible to them.
- women from ethnic minorities
- women with disabilities
- women who have never been on a training course before
- part-timers
- women on flexible working patterns
- women from different geographical areas
- women from different departments and functions in the organization
- women of all ages. Development training is often assumed to be just for young women starting out. Check that you are recruiting women right across the age bands.

Of course, your target group may have deliberately excluded some of these categories. If not, and some of these categories are missing, take action first by going to talk to the women you are concerned about. Find out from them direct why they are not nominating themselves for the training. It may be that they are genuinely not interested. It may be because:

- They didn't know about it.
- They were given false information.
- They need extra encouragement and explanation.

- They want a course of their own.
- Their manager won't release them.
- They're being teased/harassed about it.
- The venue/times/date is impossible for them.

Information you gain at this stage enables you to take last-minute action to refine your course design, the course logistics, the publicity, the nomination procedure. It may even cause you to question and revise your overall strategy and to take different action in the long term.

Summary

Getting your publicity material to your target group is one thing. Finding that they nominate themselves is the first sign of your strategy working. In this chapter we've seen how recruitment and nomination link in closely with your overall strategy and the publicity and PR considerations of your training. The main messages are:

- Self-nomination is essential.
- Keep the process as straightforward as possible.
- Give careful thought to the tone and content of the pre-course communications to the participants.
- Monitor the recruitment pattern—it is the first way of evaluating how effective your strategy is and enables fine-tuning.

Royal Insurance (UK) Ltd

This case study is a good example of the power of the pilot programme; in this case, 25 courses were run in one year, following the pilot. It also illustrates how important it is to devolve ownership of the programme out from the centre, and how valuable it was to take trouble in getting the message across to line managers and potential participants before the training.

Personal development programme for women

In 1986 Royal Insurance (UK) Ltd undertook a survey of attitudes towards the employment of women within the company. This survey formed part of the 'Women in Insurance' project carried out by the Pepperell Unit of the Industrial Society. Eight of the major insurance companies took part in this project and the findings were published in a report entitled 'Developing Your Womanpower'.

The report highlighted the traditional attitudes prevailing towards women employed in the insurance industry and identified a number of potential barriers to women wishing to advance in their careers. Child bearing and child rearing were the greatest single barriers to women's career development. These affected women not only when they had children, but throughout their career. Expectations that a woman would leave to have a family affected her job opportunities early in her career; and if she left to have a family it was difficult for her to return.

Why the training programme was implemented

In response to the survey findings, as well as other organizational changes, Royal Insurance (UK) Ltd introduced a number of measures designed to encourage more women into senior and other responsible positions. Structural barriers (such as mobility requirements) were addressed and schemes such as enhanced maternity leave and career breaks were introduced. The number of women in first-line management positions increased significantly.

However, in overall terms, the number of women in management remained low and it was felt that encouragement should be given to women to develop their potential, without necessarily focusing on management. It was envisaged that by building confidence and increasing personal effectiveness those attending the course would be encouraged to review their careers, set goals for career development and take action to achieve those goals.

Setting up the programme

At the time that the training programme was running, responsibility for personnel and training was devolved to regional areas. The corporate training manager had responsibility for overall training and development, but the final decision on whether or not to introduce a training programme rested with the area managers.

The decision to introduce a personal development programme for women was made corporately and the initial programme was funded by the corporate training budget. It was made clear to each area manager that they would be expected to run one course in their area. If any further courses were run, those would be paid for by the area concerned.

The process of introducing the programme was important. There was some resistance to the concept of women-only training among the managers and some of the course participants. This needed to be addressed and was dealt with in two ways.

Firstly, training and personnel managers were briefed by the course leader at one of their regular meetings at Head Office. The background to the programme, the objectives and the reasons for running women-only courses were explained. The managers were able to express their views and discuss the issues involved. By the end of the session there was a general acceptance that there may be a case for women-only training even if individually they did not agree with it. They were prepared to support the programme within their own areas.

Secondly, the issue was discussed at the outset of every course. The course leader addressed this by asking how many of the women attending had been reluctant to go on a women-only course. She then explained the background to the programme and why the decision had been taken to run the courses for women. She also explained in detail the content of the course and method of working. Finally, she asked those who had expressed their reluctance to reserve judgement until the end of the course. The evaluations and follow-up showed that, by and large, the concerns had disappeared by the end of the course and that participants felt they had benefited by being in a single-sex group.

The programme ran over the period of one year and some twenty-five courses were held. In addition, a number of areas held half-day or one-day follow-ups three to six months after the course. In the majority of areas more than one course was run. Some areas ran up to four, representing considerable investment on the part of the areas concerned.

The course participants

Participants were nominated by their managers. A majority of the women attending were in non-management positions. In some areas it was decided to focus on women with little or no supervisory experience, while in others nominations were extended to include women with considerable supervisory experience.

This created differences between the various courses. The women with little or no supervisory experience were used to working in largely female groups and many had little awareness or understanding of difficulties that they might face as they moved into more responsible positions. This contrasted with the more senior groups who were already in positions in which women were the minority.

Programme aims and content

The course aimed to help participants to:

- develop a greater sense of career direction and self-confidence
- be equipped with self-development skills to enable them to be more effective in their work
- identify and commit themselves to a personal plan of action to achieve their goals

The programme ran over two days and was highly participative, with a mix of specialist tutor input and small group work involving practical exercises, role play, discussion and feedback. The topics covered included career/life planning, personal effectiveness (assertiveness), time and stress management, presentation skills, and power and influence in organizations.

Ideally, the course was residential, although this was not always the case. A course dinner was held in the evening and attended by senior management. In most instances, the area manager gave the after-dinner speech and underlined the importance they attached to the programme.

An important element of the programme was the talks given by senior women about their careers and how they had progressed to their present positions. These women acted as role models for the participants and their contribution was highly valued.

Outcomes

The course evaluations and follow-ups indicated that on an individual level the programme was successful. Each participant was asked to commit herself to an action plan at the end of the course and when they returned to the follow-up most had achieved what they had set out to do. A number had been promoted and everyone felt the course had helped them to clarify their goals and set priorities.

The organization hoped that the women attending would gain confidence and recognize their potential, and that they would take greater responsibility for their own career development. It also wished to demonstrate its commitment to encouraging more women into responsible jobs and its recognition that, unless women were given this opportunity and encouragement, the organization would lose valuable resources.

The personal development programme for women was part of a much larger package of measures designed to encourage women and give them the opportunity to advance their careers. It is therefore difficult to separate out the effectiveness of one part of the total picture. Overall, the proportion of women in management has risen and is continuing to rise. This programme has contributed to that picture.

Liz Bargh, Director
The Domino Consultancy Ltd

8 The trainer, her role and development

The final decision to be made before the course begins is about the person delivering the course—the trainer. In this chapter we shall clarify what the trainer's role is and is not, and look at the selection of your trainer or trainers, co-training, developing new trainers and some of the common pitfalls for trainers.

The trainer's role

From our joint experience of running an enormous range of training, including women's development training, from health and safety programmes to sexism awareness events, from till operation workshops to senior management development programmes, and from public speaking workshops to in-depth women's development programmes, we find that women's development training in particular demands a great deal from you as a person.

You are not there just as the person running the course, you are also there as another working woman, a role model, so that your own values, attitudes and circumstances become valid to the course in an unusual way. So, for example, a trainer running a returners course needs to be sensitive to, and understand, the fears and doubts that returners experience. It is better still if she's been a returner herself. The line between you the trainer, and you the individual, still needs to be defined, but will be different from, say, skills-based training.

The trainer's role has been defined by many women's development trainers and a summary of qualities is shown here:

What it is	What it isn't
positive	cynical
optimistic	negative
honest	solving problems
in control	timid
motivating	sarcastic
responsible	waffly
supporting	an ego trip
enabling	academic

What it is	What it isn't
entertaining	patronizing
inspiring	magic answers
missionary zeal	prescriptive
energetic	judgemental
energizing	superior
challenging	scoring points
empathizing	dogmatic
confident	in a hurry
informal	prejudiced
relaxed	personal
clear	putting down
assertive	distracting
open	holding hands
practical	bored
equal	sympathizing
encouraging	being a joker
approachable	
flexible	
organized	
charismatic	
providing a balance	

The trainer's task

Having outlined your role, what are you expected to do to demonstrate all this? The four crucial things are to:

- **energize**
- **encourage**
- **empower**
- **enthuse**

This is because many women think negatively about themselves, their potential and their achievements. It is this negativity that you are about to tackle in running this course. It's your job over the duration of the course to help the participants to:

- change their attitude to themselves and their potential
- develop the skills to develop themselves more positively
- gain support and encouragement
- grow in self-esteem and determination
- build their confidence
- take small steps in their development

Some of this will be achieved through the course material and course design. Some of it will be achieved through the interaction with the other participants. Some of it will be achieved simply by running the course. Some of it—a good proportion—will be achieved through *your* ability to enthuse, energize, encourage and empower.

Marjo van Boeschoten developed a model for leadership and counselling styles which we have adapted to relate to the tasks that people

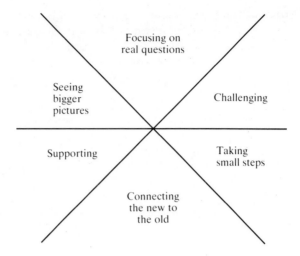

Focusing on
real questions

Seeing
bigger
pictures

Challenging

Supporting

Taking
small steps

Connecting
the new to
the old

Figure 8.1 *The trainer's task*

perform in their role as trainer (see Figure 8.1). This model shows how, in your role as trainer, your task lies in balancing the opposite polarities. We have already said that women need support, but if what you give is all support and no challenge, there may be little movement. Women's development programmes are holistic, so in that sense they aim to take account of the bigger picture, but you could become so engaged with the big vision that the participants don't take the small steps that are needed to achieve it. If time is spent focusing on detail, it is equally likely that the whole may not be reflected, and ideas for the future may not be linked to the solid ground of the past.

This is oversimplifying this excellent model because, of course, the movement will not always be in the opposite polarity. A woman who is, for instance, stuck in a particular situation may respond to a challenge which will then help her to take some small steps.

So your task is to keep yourself and your group moving into the situations where development is most likely to happen.

Selecting trainers

The key criteria for selecting trainers for women's development programmes are their commitment to the development of women and their ability to work with the ground rules, particularly in respecting where the women are and building them up, not knocking them down. The options open to you are:

- women professional trainers
- women line managers and other professional women
- ex-participants of the programme
- men

Professionals   Professional trainers are likely to be the backbone in initiating, developing, designing, piloting and evaluating women's development training in any organization. Their professional expertise combines with their commitment and their own experiences as women. The main choice here is between internal and external trainers.

So why bother with expensive external trainers? There are advantages and disadvantages in using either internal or external trainers, and much of your decision will depend on the culture and circumstances of the training.

Internal trainer   *Advantages*
- cheaper
- can tailor the material more easily to the culture
- relevant role model
- can be involved in other women's development initiatives and therefore provide links/bridges
- can provide support after the course
- knows about the individuals who may be causing difficulties to the participants
- may know the participants and can build on existing good relationships

Disadvantages
- may be less experienced in women's development
- can't provide examples of other organizations so easily
- may not be relevant role model because of her specialist job
- can be restrained by the organization culture
- greater danger of getting too involved or not challenging enough
- participants come along with a set of assumptions about the trainer
- danger of being pressurized by participants' seniors
- may know the participants and make assumptions about them

External trainer   *Advantages*
- in-depth knowledge and experience of specialist subject
- width of experience
- able to provide comparisons with other organizations
- greater variety of anecdotes
- can put the situation for women in the organization into perspective
- no employment overheads
- bring a breath of fresh air
- can spread good PR about the organization

Disadvantages
- expensive
- no continuity—they go away again
- may need familiarization days prior to the course
- may be insensitive to the organizational culture
- could be out of touch with what's happening in the business/industry
- could deliver a standard 'package' course and not take account of your special needs
- may not live up to all she promises

While high-level training specialists and outside consultants bring professional expertise they are not essential in the longer term. It is our policy, wherever possible, to develop other women to take on and run programmes: women with little training experience, or none, women managers and women from non-management grades, women who have participated in the course and women who have not. This approach:

- frees training specialists to develop new programmes
- provides development opportunities for many more women
- usually costs less after an initial course to develop trainers
- practises what we preach about wanting to maximize the development opportunities for women
- builds up a pool of women who are able to run the training

Line managers Women line managers make excellent role models, usually know the organization well and can pass on their practical experience of moving around in the organization. They are able to encourage women more junior to them by believing in them, challenging them and supporting them. It is helpful to find women volunteers from a range of professions, e.g. personnel, marketing, finance. All these women can draw on their own experiences to contribute to the women's development programme.

Ex-participants Ex-participants make ideal trainers because they can relate easily to the situation that the participants are in and their experience of their own development is often what makes them volunteer. The woman who can open a course by saying, 'A year ago I was sitting where you are now, and if anyone had said to me then that in a year's time I would be up here doing this, I'd have laughed and said that I'd never have had the confidence' is delivering many of the messages of the course.

As another said: 'My experience of the programme was that it made me realize that sitting on the fence had become uncomfortable and I'd better get on and do the things I wanted to do, so here I am'. She was able to encourage a lot of other women to get off the fence too.

Opening the doors to the variety of experiences that a wide range of women can bring to specific development programmes contributes to the personal and professional development of the trainers themselves as well as providing a wider range of role models.

The most important aspect of all the selection criteria is the extent to which they believe in women's development training. When selecting trainers, it is more effective to take a woman who has had no training experience but who has a natural enthusiasm and a commitment to women's development training, and teach her how to deliver a course, than it is to use a highly skilled, but ambivalent or cynical professional trainer. However skilled and experienced she is, her own personal lack of commitment will affect the whole course.

Male trainers Obviously, if one man is present, it means that it is no longer a women-only course and this will affect the way in which women behave. Only once did we hear of an occasion when it was helpful to have a man as co-trainer on a development course for women and that was where the man concerned had developed a very specific way of enabling people to look at their lives, i.e. through biography work. Several such courses had been run by men and attended mainly by male managers. The experience of the woman trainer was as follows:

I attended the Biography Workshop as a delegate. During the course I experienced an enormous depth and quality in the process, but the examples were all male examples and the only other woman in my group was overshadowed by her husband who was also attending the workshop. I gained great benefit from the workshop but felt it wasn't really aimed at me as a woman. So I talked with the male trainer and he was keen to develop the work to make it more appropriate for women as were two other women trainers that I knew. So we formed a study group. We met for a full day every six weeks over a period of a year, firstly sharing our biographies and secondly developing the Biography work in such a way that it would be as beneficial to women as to men. We decided to run a women-only course.

A tough decision followed. After years of development by the man and our year of preparation there was no way that we could leave him out. In any event, none of the rest of us felt competent or confident to run a programme on our own. The course went well, we learned a lot and we were also able to gauge the reactions of the women to having a man as part of the team. The result was sheer speculation: what would it have been like without him? Without him there would have been no course! He was very open-minded all through the development of the course and in the actual running of it to learning about working in depth with groups of women. So on this occasion it worked, but some women said that, despite liking and respecting our male colleague, they still felt inhibited by having a man present.

This anecdote demonstrates the exception that proves the rule. Usually, when we hear of men as trainers on women's development programmes they are men who have no unique contribution to make; one male trainer believed he could 'help women to catch up' and others are simply curious to see what happens on the programmes. So our preference at the moment is to say 'No' to men as trainers.

So, here is a summary of who you are, and who you aren't as a trainer:

Who you are	*Who you aren't*
a woman	a man
guide	'mother'
role model	career adviser
enabler	counsellor
catalyst	expert
energizer	problem solver
listener	lecturer
leader	guru
facilitator	dictator
source of encouragement	judge
supporter	agony aunt
challenger	magician

Co-training or not?

There are three occasions where it is helpful to have two or more trainers running the course together:

1 When the numbers are too big for one person.
2 If you want an internal trainer to work alongside an external trainer to provide a balance of internal/external views and background.
3 To give a less experienced or trainee trainer experience with a more experienced woman there to support and give feedback.

Co-training requires great trust and respect between trainers. We suggest that you draw up some form of 'contract', *before* you start working together, which clarifies some of the assumptions and values that you both have. It is a sensitive relationship, and one that needs a lot of commitment and work. It should not be entered into lightly—you don't want to discover that you don't get on together in front of a group of course participants! Here are some general do's and don'ts. These apply to any training, but belittle women's development training in particular if the relationship doesn't go well.

Do
- Clarify roles beforehand.
- Clear handovers to each other.
- Agree what the links are back/forward.
- Prepare material jointly.
- Both arrive early.
- Have each other's home telephone number.
- Be alert during your co-trainer's session.
- Be assertive with each other.
- Encourage each other.
- Control your body language so as not to distract the group.
- Look interested during your co-trainer's session.
- *Be* interested too.
- Look at the group when your co-trainer is working (you can judge their responses).

Don't
- Fidget during sessions.
- Go out of the room.
- Undermine your co-trainer or take the focus away from her.
- Contradict in public.
- Interrupt.
- Stand in front of co-trainer.
- Look bored.
- Do other work or the crossword while your colleague is on the platform.

This is the ideal; it's something to aim for, and to work towards. The final criterion when exploring the possibilities of a co-training relationship is to remember the role model element of your role, and to create duos and trios of trainers which offer a variety of examples. So, ideally, if you have children, work with someone who doesn't, if you're a graduate, work with someone who isn't, etc. When you get it right, co-training can be a most rewarding experience which works to everyone's mutual benefit. You'll learn from your co-trainer and contribute to her development too.

Developing trainers

The extent, nature and depth of any training will obviously depend on the experience and existing skills of the potential trainer.

Developing experienced trainers

If you are already an experienced trainer, but with no experience of running women's development programmes, here are some suggestions to develop yourself in the new role:

- Experience a women's development programme as a participant.
- Talk to your mentor, if you have one, about what particular attributes and skills you will need to develop.
- Co-train with an experienced women's development trainer and seek feedback.
- Attend a special women's development course for trainers for the programmes you intend to run.
- Have a go—preferably with a co-trainer—and learn as you go.

Developing new trainers

The extent of the training will depend upon the numbers involved so examine the key factors and decide what is practical for the numbers you have to train. There are three elements:

- experiencing the programme as a participant
- shadowing
- formal training programme

Experiencing the programme as participants

This is the ideal. It means that trainers will know what it is like to experience working on their own development. Ex-participants as trainers make good role models because current participants may see becoming a trainer as a major development step. They respect the achievement of someone who was where they are now. Also, if the trainer is an ex-participant, she will be able to contribute her own anecdotes and examples which will bring the programme alive and there is a rapport that develops when women have had similar experiences.

The only disadvantage for an ex-participant as trainer is when she is still a member of the target group, particularly in a small organization or unit. Participants may be so used to experiencing her in her job role that they have difficulty in accepting her 'expertise' as a trainer. This can be overcome by good development training.

For a pilot course, where there aren't any ex-participants, women who have attended other women's development training will also make good trainers.

Shadowing

This means experiencing the programme, not as a participant, but as a trainee. Most people listen in a different way when they step out of the participant role. Shadowing is helpful before any formal training of trainers, because it gives everyone a reference point and an experience to draw on for the training trainers sessions. Trainee trainers will also get a sense of how the group responds to particular exercises and activities. Shadowing helps them to soak up the atmosphere, and make notes on content, delivery and handling of situations, as well as building up familiarity and confidence with the material. Aim to give 'shadows' something specific to do on the course, as having an observer can inhibit the participants. Don't forget to explain to the participants why your shadow is there.

After a training trainers course, the shadowing exercise should include many small activities on the course, so that she can get her feet wet. It may be introducing and summing up a speaker, briefing an exercise, giving a short piece of input or coaching in role plays. Start where the trainee trainer feels confident and build from there. After working on a four-day training trainers programme, the trainees usually understand where they are competent and where they need to work more.

Asking questions is crucial in shadowing, both by the shadower and the shadowed.

- What does she see?
- What does she hear?
- What does it mean?
- What questions does it give rise to in her?
- What does she still need to find out as a result?
- Do her questions demonstrate her commitment?
- What does she still need to do to equip herself, e.g. collect her own examples.

Formal training programme

This is not about training women to be fully fledged all-round trainers, but training women to run a specific programme, e.g. an assertiveness course for women, women in management or a personal effectiveness course. This shouldn't be compared in any way with a full professional qualification as a trainer. These programmes are best run residentially over four or five days. This gives time for practice and supports net-working among the participants. A formal training programme needs to include:

- the philosophy/history of the course to be run
- the ground rules of the programme
- the course programme and what it means
- key content for each subject
- how to brief an exercise, run it and take feedback
- introducing and summing up profile speakers
- giving an input
- managing the logistics
- managing energy levels
  —yours
  —theirs

- practice in doing all the above
- coaching and feedback on the above
- many of the hints and tips from this book

A positive action programme

Here is an example of one organization's programme to develop more women as trainers.

In the 1980s when a large metropolitan council began providing positive action courses to enable women to move into management, their equal opportunities policy was clear:

- All courses should aim to have at least half the participants from ethnic minorities.
- Each programme should be run by one black and one white trainer working equally together.

In order to fulfil these objectives, more women (and especially women from ethnic minorities) had to be trained as trainers very quickly.

The course was called First Steps to Management and two external trainers developed the material on three pilot courses, with twelve delegates on each course. This gave a pool of ex-participants who were potential trainers and a plan was devised to enable some of these and more women to be trained as trainers to run the programme. The process was as follows:

Step 1 Advertise internally for potential trainers
Step 2 Potential trainers to experience the course as participants if they hadn't already
Step 3 Initial selection of trainee trainers
Step 4 Trainees to shadow courses run by existing trainers with participants' permission
- observe from trainer point of view
- build up own sets of notes
- collect own examples
- be part of trainers' progress discussions
- share insights about the process
Step 5 Trainee to work as co-trainer with experienced trainer. Here it was recognized that initially the relationship would be unequal and in some cases there was also a third trainee as trainer.
Step 6 Trainee trainers' workshop
- review experiences
- relationship of training to equal opportunities policy
- giving inputs
- briefing exercises
- coaching in exercises
- taking feedback
- building a course manual
Step 7 Trainees run course as equal trainer with experienced trainer
Step 8 Trainees run course as equal trainer with experienced trainer in supporting role

Step 9 Two trainee trainers run course equally together
Step 10 Review all trainees and trainers

It was hard work for all concerned. The trainees put tremendous efforts into becoming confident and competent. They knew they had arrived when they got good feedback from trainers and groups, developed their own materials and were able to coach each other. It was a slow process but established the following precedents:

- It is possible to develop more women in the organization as trainers (they welcomed the opportunity; some went on to do more training and others remained in their existing department).
- Development training can be designed to be effective *and* be delivered by non-specialists.
- The 'new' trainers often made better role models than the two original external consultants (both had left non-management jobs some time before and both were childless).
- It set a precedent for others to follow.
- It freed up budgets because internal resources were used and at that time not costed to the central training budget.
- It gave women an opportunity to become trainers where no opportunity existed before.
- It gave several black women a track record of success in training that enabled them to apply for and get training jobs.

For the mid-1980s it was an ambitious, radical forerunner to many women's development programmes today.

What if . . . ?   Whenever you're developing new trainers, keep a 'What if' chart going for all the questions that arise about the specific programme. It's a good measure of success of the trainers' programme if by the end of the week they can answer their own 'What ifs . . . '. Some of the 'what ifs' rarely happen, and some crop up regularly. Knowing what to do saves worry. Here are some examples of 'what if' questions from a Springboard trainers' programme:

What if . . .
A participant wants to drop out of the course?
Someone says she hasn't come to participate, she's just an observer?
A profile speaker directly contradicts something you've already said?
Someone has 'serious' problems?
Two women in the same group don't get on?
Someone is really cheeky and you're tempted to use a witty put-down?
Someone won't go along with the confidentiality ground rule?
You don't get any response when you ask about confidentiality?
One person 'hijacks' a group?
Someone dominates in a jolly and enthusiastic way?
You don't know the answer to a question?
A participant consistently refuses to join in the group work?
Someone makes a racist remark?

Your co-trainer doesn't turn up?
The profile speaker doesn't turn up?
Someone is talking about rushing back to work to resign?
Someone becomes angry and abusive in a plenary?
The group doesn't gel?
Someone bursts into tears in the group work?
A man who's had a sex change is in the group?
Halfway through briefing an exercise or an input, you realize you're doing it wrong?
Someone tells you at the end of a course that something you said previously has totally changed her life?

In case you're pondering over these, the answers are in Appendix 7.

Common pitfalls for the trainer

Women's development training has its own dangers for a trainer, just as any form of training has. However, because of the emphasis, flavour and form of women's development training, the common pitfalls are:

- The trainer overdoes being a role model and takes up too much time and space going on about herself.
- She plays down being a role model and hardly reveals anything about herself, while expecting everyone else to make themselves vulnerable.
- The trainer falls into counsellor mode.
- She becomes patronizing.
- She tries to relate personally to everything that crops up, thereby appearing to be auditioning for 'superwoman' and alienating the group.
- She doesn't listen enough.
- She gets too involved and doesn't give the group enough space.
- She underestimates the amount of personal energy needed to get a group moving.
- She doesn't recognize her own limitations.

After the course—your role

Thinking about your role after the course is particularly pertinent to internal trainers who are still available, visible and contactable afterwards. This can be an asset, as long as you're happy with ex-participants contacting you. Alternatively, you may need to develop a strategy for reducing any dependency.

- Be clear in your own mind where the limit of your responsibility lies.
- Be assertive—you have a right to your feelings, thoughts and privacy too.
- Encourage networking within the group itself.
- If you decide to continue contact, be clear about the boundaries of your responsibility, e.g. 'I'll come and talk to you about the problem that you're having with your Boss, but I'm coming as a friend and not as a trainer.'
- If you're comfortable with the relationship maturing into a mentoring role—fine. Otherwise explain assertively that that is not your role.

Summary

In this chapter we've looked at the issues around the trainer—her role and task, means of developing new trainers and the added dimension of co-training. We've also looked at some common pitfalls. The main points to remember from this chapter are:

- Only women can be trainers on women's development programmes.
- The trainer's role is crucial to the success of any programme and can make or break even the best-designed courses.
- New trainers can be successfully trained to run one specific programme.
- You are there as a role model as well as a trainer. This means you are being assessed as a person much more than when running conventional training. It also means you have to practise what you're preaching.
- Co-training relationships need managing.

Thames Television plc

Thames Television is a particularly intriguing example as it is one of the very rare organizations where success in women's development training has led directly to the implementation of a similar men-only course and mixed courses. This case study also shows how important the initial research and audit is, and how it provides a valuable foundation for training to take place.

Research findings

Thames Television has been involved in women's training and development since 1983, stemming from research undertaken in the Company in 1981/82. The research suggested that, contrary to popular assumptions, women were interested in career progression and development but often felt they lacked the confidence to apply for promotion or try new things, and lacked the appropriate skills and qualifications to move into non-traditional areas of work such as the technical roles.

The research led to the creation of a Women's Committee and the post of women's employment officer (subsequently redesignated equal opportunities adviser) who devoted their energies to coming up with practical ideas in which women's training played a major part.

In the light of this research, it was of course important for Thames to be seen to respond to the clearly identified needs. More importantly, however, there was a recognition of the value of women as an important resource within the Company and an acknowledgement of the shortcomings of the education system which had traditionally channelled girls' aspirations towards certain areas of work. It was recognized that the change process would be painfully slow if we waited for society to catch up with the wishes of our female staff. The need for an interventionist approach was clear.

Three particular training needs were identified:

- the need for a basic understanding of the programme-making process, important as so many female staff worked in administrative areas

- the need for an access course in basic science and television technology for those who might want to break with tradition and move into a technical job
- the need for confidence building/assertiveness training and career planning

Training was set up in response to all three of these needs, although it was only the Personal Effectiveness training which was exclusive to women. Courses addressing the other two needs were open to all staff. In practice, however, a very high percentage of participants were female.

Personal effectiveness training

The idea of Personal Effectiveness training was a completely new concept for Thames (and many other organizations!) in 1983 and was addressed initially by residential courses organized by the Independent Television Association (the industry's employers' federation). In 1986— 17 courses and 65 delegates later—the time had come to evaluate our position on this training for the following reasons:

- demand for places on courses far exceeded supply
- individuals had to be selected for the places available
- residential training could be prohibitive for certain groups of women
- rising costs

This resulted in the launch in 1987 of the Thames personal development workshops which are five-day courses (four days plus one follow-up day) run in-house in conjunction with an external consultant.

By this time we had had very positive feedback from delegates to the ITVA courses and men were beginning to ask whether we 'could do anything for them'. In response to this we offered the same course in a choice of single-sex or mixed workshops. The demand for these courses has resulted in seven mixed workshops, eight women-only workshops and one men-only workshop.

The workshop aims to enable participants to feel more confident in themselves and their abilities; to gain a better understanding of their behaviour; to communicate more clearly and effectively; to identify and build on their strengths; and to identify changes they would like to make in their lives. This is achieved through discussion, individual and group exercises, role play, tutor input and questionnaires. Our approach to the programme is holistic, based on the belief that an individual's life at work is influenced by her/his personal life and vice versa, hence the course title: 'Personal Effectiveness.'

What have been the results of this training, the benefits for Thames Television? This is always a difficult question because it is hard to make a direct link between the course and, say, promotion. We do know that when people come back for the follow-up day and talk about their achievements and how their lives are different three to four months on, participants themselves see very positive results from the course. Over the years some participants have left the Company, some have moved on within the Company, many are still in the same job. In any event if individuals, through the personal development workshops, are able to be more at ease with themselves with a greater confidence in their abilities and understanding of their behaviour, Thames Television is bound to be the beneficiary.

Christine Kerr, Personnel Manager,
Thames Television plc

9 Running the course

In this chapter we will take each element of a women's development course and look at exactly what to do and how to do it. We deal with the down-to-earth practical detail of the material, opening the course, giving inputs, running exercises, profile speakers, keeping the ground rules going, deviating from the programme, recaps/reviews, action sessions and closing the course.

The material

The material is the visible tip of the iceberg. It's the tangible part of the course—the course programme, the speakers' notes, the course handouts, the OHP slides. Anyone walking in on your course would see and hear the material being delivered, practised and discussed. The material has been dealt with in detail in Chapter 4.

However, underneath the material will be another level of objectives and subject matter. The difference between these various layers of impact will be determined and decided by your audit or analysis of needs, your own experience and the culture of the organization.

For example you may have diagnosed that building self-confidence is a need for the target group of women. How you choose to address this need is up to you. You can run a session on 'developing self-confidence' or you can run a session on something else that you know will develop self-confidence—public speaking skills, for instance. We often include presentation skills in women's development courses, as we find it is one of the most frightening things for people to tackle, and so has the greatest boost of self-confidence attached to it when it's achieved. It's almost irrelevant whether a participant needs to be able to give formal presentations or not; the boost in self-confidence transfers itself to whatever the most immediate hurdle is. So remember, as you run the course, why the material is there and the part it plays, but know that it is playing only one part. How you deliver it and work with it is crucial.

Opening the course

Each trainer has her own favourite way of opening a course, and we would not want to specify exactly what you do and say. However, the opening moments of any course set the tone and expectations for the whole course, so there are aspects of opening a women's development course that need to be emphasized and approached with greater sensitivity than may be needed generally.

The objectives of your opening remarks, opening exercises and opening session are:

- to generate a sense of occasion
- to reassure and support
- to whet appetites for what is to come
- to encourage and enthuse
- to clarify the objective of the course and remind participants what the course is all about
- to establish your own role
- to establish the ground rules
- to model and establish the style of behaviour that you're expecting from them
- to facilitate their getting to know each other
- to demonstrate your commitment

As the cliché says: 'You don't get a second chance to make a first impression'. Time spent preparing and polishing your opening is time well spent. The opening and closing encapsulate the whole spirit of a course, and are the moments most likely to be remembered and make an impact. Your style in the opening needs to be:

- energetic
- enthusiastic
- informal

The content of your opening will cover:

- welcome
- the objectives of the course
- how the objectives will be achieved
- a bit of background to the course
- introductions—them
- introductions—you and your style
- fire drill

Welcome Start promptly to set a professional tone and inject a sense of urgency. Give a warm friendly welcome to the workshop/course, a reminder of the course title and very brief explanation of who you are. Don't forget to smile!

Objectives Remind the participants about the formal stated course objectives, plus your own interpretation of what they mean in practice. By establishing these very clearly right at the beginning, it gives you something to refer to during the course.

If you have already produced a course programme or joining instructions, you are simply reminding them of the objectives and giving your interpretation. On courses which do not produce formal objectives beforehand, you need to expand a little more, to enable people to take them in.

Achieving the objectives
Set the ground rules for the course, to give an idea of the flavour of the course, and also let the group know what your expectations are, of them and of yourself. You can talk about some of the ground rules outlined in Chapter 2 and add any of your own that are specific to your course. It's also useful to explain and demystify the course programme at this point, as many people may feel threatened by a course programme or need reassurance on what some of it actually means.

This is the time to gain agreement for a contract of confidentiality. It's one of the ground rules, explain it and check that everyone agrees to honour it. Although confidentiality is a serious business, we find that broaching the contract is best done lightly and with an example such as: 'You may wish to discuss a problem that you have with your boss, but you wouldn't want your boss to hear about it from someone else—if we keep these things just between ourselves, you can feel more free to talk about them and get specific practical suggestions of how to deal with them'.

Asking for everyone's agreement is not a cosmetic exercise—you really need to check that everyone agrees because if just one person disagrees or abstains, it won't work. Our experience is that most women readily agree, indeed welcome the confidentiality, and the occasional dissenter only needs further explanation or reassurance to change her mind. So if someone isn't sure, take the time to discuss it and clarify her doubts—she may just be worried that she can't talk about any of the course back home.

This is a key moment in the course because, at this point, the individuals are accepting responsibility for each other and a bond can be formed. Make it clear that the contract of confidentiality also includes you, i.e. if anyone asks you how a participant got on or behaved on the course, you will not give any feedback, but ask the enquirer to ask the women herself. A women's development course is not an assessment centre.

Background
Give a very brief explanation of how the course came about and why the course is important. If it's the first course, say so and make an occasion of it. If it has a long track record, let them know how it's been well supported for years. If it is an in-house course, a few statistics about the position of women can focus on the reasons why it's a women-only course. If it is a public course, a few general statistics for the whole UK/industry/profession can have the same effect.

Introductions—them
The ground rule that says the course belongs to the participants provides a useful link into introductions. Every trainer has her own favourite ice-breaker. The important factor is that the ice-breaker should demonstrate the course principles and start the process of networking and hearing about real experiences; so ice-breakers which involve people's favourite food/colour, or their 'star sign' do not really go far enough.

For example   Check that everyone is sitting next to someone they don't know, and give them five minutes each to 'interview' their neighbour so that they can introduce her. Ask them to discover:

- what work she does, and how she feels about it, e.g. stuck? at a cross-roads? daunted? just promoted?
- as the course is holistic, what her personal circumstances are, e.g. does she have children? a partner? eldercare? lives with parents?
- what *her* objectives are for coming on the course. This is a key question for you, as you will then discover the range of issues that the group expects to tackle and the range and level of their expectations.

If they already know each other, you can add a fourth question—find out something you didn't know about her—it's amazing what people discover! After giving them five minutes each to talk to each other, take a report-back on everyone, going round the pairs at random. You may need to question a little if the objectives given are very vague, but keep questioning to a minimum and encourage crisp introductions.

At the end, you need to comment on their objectives for attending the course; make it absolutely clear which are realistic expectations and which are inappropriate. If anyone has objectives that will not be met by your course, say so.

Introductions—you and your style

By this time, the participants will have divulged quite a lot of personal information about themselves, while they know nothing about you and (if you've got one) your co-trainer. So it's only appropriate that you describe your background, both professional and personal, and explain why you're running the course, e.g. why you have a particular interest in/commitment to women's development training.

This is more than just a courtesy; the ground rules of women's development training include providing role models and working on real situations, and whether you like it or not, *you're* a role model! You will also be practising what you preach; by revealing personal information about yourself and your own issues and dilemmas, you are making it clear that you are serious in your request for them to do so; *you* provide a precedent.

This is not to say that you bare your soul or recite a detailed life history—five minutes will be plenty. Choose the content with care, and with thought for the participants. Do your introduction after everyone else because you may need to say slightly different things about yourself depending on what the participants say. Also, if you go first, there is a danger of them copying you and not answering the questions you've set.

Examples   If you're running a course for women in management, stress your own management experience. If it's a course for women at the most junior levels, then reinforce the fact that you've worked your way up from the bottom, if you have. If you know you have a room full of graduates and you're one too, mention it.

At the end of this introduction, explain *a little* of what your role is and what they can reasonably expect and not expect from you.

Fire drill After the introductions, brief them on the fire drill and any other points in the interest of health and safety.

You'll notice that, apart from pointing out the fire drill, there are *no administrative points* in your opening. The most important part of your opening is the course objectives. The trainer who starts a course by saying 'Now before we get started, I want to tell you about checking out on Friday' is a trainer who is demonstrating that her priorities are very different from those of the course. Keep other administrative points until just before your first break.

Giving input

Formal input is needed from time to time, usually to set up a session or introduce a new subject. There are many helpful books on preparing and delivering formal input so we won't replicate them here. The two aspects which are special to women's development training are:

- Use material and research developed by women if at all possible. If you are constantly quoting from male references, it simply reinforces the belief that men have all the ideas!
- Use lots of real examples from real women (including yourself) to illustrate the theory. Examples from other courses, anonymously, have especial credence, e.g. 'A woman on a course the other day said . . . '

Very few written examples of women at work exist, although it's getting better, so you'll have to collect and use your own, and be sure to use examples from your own experience—remember, you're a role model!

Briefing an exercise

The importance of a clear brief is multiplied by the size of the group. In other words, you can afford to get it wrong if there are only five of them; it wouldn't take too long to go round and brief them again. If you're talking to 100 and you get it wrong or they move before you've finished—you've had it!

When briefing an exercise, cover:

- why you're doing this exercise—the objective
- what you're going to do and what is expected
- the logistics
  —how much time you've got
  —how you're going to do it
  —where

As a generalization, women are more amenable than men, so it's even more important for your brief to be clear, particularly the objectives. While a group of men may challenge your brief, it's more likely that a group of women will do what you ask, but without being clear what the point is.

Staged briefings It is often helpful to give the briefing in stages, particularly where the final parts of the exercise are quite demanding and will stretch participants. Remember, many women come on women's development training to boost their confidence, so announcing that in half an hour some or all of them are going to come and stand at the front to give a short talk may give rise to attacks of nerves. It's easier on them to go through the preparation bit by bit, and then ask the group to decide who will report back, or to say 'You've done all the preparation for a two-minute talk about yourself—now let's do it'. Our experience shows that staging the briefing in this kind of exercise gets better results, as time isn't spent in the exercise worrying about the presentation.

During the exercise

If you're used to working with all-male or mixed groups, you'll find the group dynamics of an all-women group different. We often feel that during an exercise is when we do our hardest work. We sometimes use similar exercises when working with men, and we find that men and women tackle the exercises differently. Here are some of the key factors of working with women-only groups in group discussions/brainstorming sessions, role plays and individual exercises.

Group discussion/ brainstorming sessions

The hallmarks of an all-women group working on exercises are those of any underconfident group of people who have had their ideas and aspirations belittled and ignored for years. Not surprisingly, they tend to start off rather slowly, cautiously and negatively. The first few minutes can be quite difficult and you'll need to do a lot of pushing. Then, once they realize that what they're doing is OK, there can be an avalanche of ideas and positive thinking and you may have trouble stopping them!

This is particularly marked in a group of returners who may need special encouragement initially and will reward your perseverance with a rush of self-confidence. Watch out for:

- a reluctance to claim credit for achievements—they put them down to 'luck' or 'chance' or somebody else's efforts
- a tendency to use unexciting vocabulary to describe themselves, e.g. 'reliable', 'hardworking', 'punctual'
- feelings of powerlessness, and difficulty in thinking of anything positive about themselves and their circumstances, e.g. 'It's all hopeless', 'You don't know my boss', 'They won't take any notice of me'
- turning the discussion into an 'ain't-it-awful session' and spending time talking about why things are difficult rather than what can be done

To counteract this, during the group discussion/brainstorming session you will have to:

- Be especially positive and enthusiastic.
- Set them mini targets, e.g. 'Fill up the flip-chart', 'How about another piece of paper?'

- Prompt, e.g. 'That's fine on the work aspects—don't forget hobbies and your life outside work'.
- Make it clear what you expect, e.g. 'I want at least three OHP slides, *covered*'. If you do this as part of your briefing, it can be counter-productive, and become overwhelming. Doing it *during* the discussion makes it challenging and even fun!
- Be prepared to spend a bit of time with a group to get it going, but also know when to get out and leave them to it.
- Visit each group several times—little and often.
- Use their own words. Often the person with the felt pen will censor what is being said and not note it down, as being too obvious or not sounding important enough. As you approach a group, listen to what is being said and make sure it gets noted—nothing is too small or seemingly silly.
- Be prepared to do some friendly bullying!

Other things to do during this session are:

- Let the group settle and get going before you interrupt.
- Confer with your co-trainer to check that all the groups have been visited. If you haven't had much success with a group, ask her to try them—maybe they've had enough of you!
- As time begins to run out, ask them to decide on someone to report back on behalf of the whole group: *not* the person who's done the writing, and *not* someone who's done it before on this course. The aim is to give as many individuals as possible opportunities to speak in public. Doing a report-back is often seen as a nerve-wracking experience and it is a tremendous confidence boost to have done it and survived.
- Get an idea of which points you're going to focus on in the report-back, and where they will be giving you 'pegs' to hang your points on.
- Get an idea of a running order for feedback—not crucial, but you want to end on a positive note.

Role plays

The importance of role plays has been mentioned in Chapter 4. We regard them as absolutely essential for teaching assertiveness and some managerial situations. Playing with the concepts is great fun and intellectually satisfying, but no real changes in behaviour will take place unless the individual woman *feels* what it's like to put the ideas into practice. You could also use role plays in simulation interviews or as part of a problem-solving exercise.

Not everyone enjoys role plays; some feel threatened or embarrassed by them. Some women tell us stories of attending courses where role plays were used to expose a woman's behaviour in front of the whole group, with the negative aspects of her behaviour brought to everyone's attention. We've also heard of trainers role playing with course participants, where the object of the exercise seems to have been for the trainer to show off her superior skill. It's hardly surprising, therefore, that people are wary of role plays.

For all these reasons, role plays are best kept until well into the course, and used unannounced in small groups of three or four. On a returners programme of ten sessions (see Appendix 1), delay role playing for the first four weeks and then use it with care. Most people find it much less terrifying than they had anticipated and feel a great sense of achievement once they've tried.

Of course, role plays are not exclusive to women's development training, but the aspects that are particular to an all-women group are:

- a determined resistance to role playing; while men don't welcome role playing, they seem to accept that it's part of the course, and get on with it more readily
- a paralysing self-consciousness and lack of self-confidence
- once they steel themselves to start, they work in greater depth than a comparable group of men
- an astonishing openness with each other about their feelings and about the situation they're tackling
- difficulties in giving each other specific feedback—their concern for each other can become a hurdle, and it's often left to you to give the constructive criticism and the specific praise

Our guidelines for role plays for women are:

- Role plays are always of the real situations that they raise.
- Role plays are done in groups of three (the person whose situation it is, the other person, and an observer). If your group doesn't divide neatly into threes, you can always have an overflow group of four with two observers.
- Role plays are done with an element of privacy—ideally in a separate syndicate room, or in a corner of the main course room well away from other groups.
- The trainer only participates in the role play if the group is totally stuck and feeling negative about the outcome. If you do decide to join in the role play, be prepared to get feedback yourself (you are not superwoman!) and encourage the group to have another go after you.
- No one is forced to do it. They are, however, strongly encouraged!

While the role plays are taking place:

- Leave them to settle for a while and get into it.
- Confer with your co-trainer and decide the logistics of who's working with which groups, to ensure that they all get help at some stage.

To intervene in a group:

- 'Hover' outside the group to discover what they're doing and what is being said.
- At an appropriate pause, pull up a chair and join them. Do not stand over them.

- Ask them what's happening, use the observer if you can see who she is—you may have mis-read the roles.
- Check how many situations they've tried and move them on if they're discussing rather than doing.
- Listen on several levels—to the words and to the feelings.
- Give your observations of what you saw and heard and refer them back to the theories which were outlined in your input session.
- Suggest a positive course of action for them to try.
- Stay to coach in the role play, or withdraw if you feel your presence is making them self-conscious.
- Demonstrate, or join in briefly, if they need it or are stuck.
- Move on! Don't get stuck in one group. You have a responsibility to the others too.

Individual exercises There are four types of exercises which are inappropriate for groups and are done by people individually:

- those of a very personal nature
- where a woman needs individual feedback on, say, how she comes across to others
- where a woman needs time for individual thinking and preparation before being influenced by others
- where the exercise examines a woman's individual situation at work

Here are some examples of exercises that we ask women to do individually as part of women's development training:

- Values exercise: what really matters to you for your work/your relationships/yourself/the rest of the world?
- Success exercise: what is your personal definition of success for you?
- What would you regret not having achieved if you were to die today?
- What does it mean to you to be the sex/race/age that you are?
- Which five adjectives best describe you?
- What does it mean to you to be a woman with/without a disability?
- Prepare and deliver a two-minute talk about an achievement of yours that you're proud of.
- Prepare and deliver a two-minute talk on all the positive aspects of yourself.
- What are the most significant events in your life so far?
- What power/influences do you have in relation to the people closest to you at work—formal authority, expertise, resource control, interpersonal skills?

To get the best out of these exercises the trainer has to:

- be especially positive and encouraging
- give lots of examples, to stretch them and help them think bigger/ more positively
- be non-judgemental and build on what they first come up with
- stamp hard on negativity
- challenge

- be very sensitive and encourage people to take small steps
- reinforce all the positive aspects of their responses
- keep pushing for more quality and quantity

Taking a report-back

Report-backs are important in women's development training because:

- They reinforce the discovery that 'I'm not the only one who feels like this'.
- They provide ideas and inspiration.
- They validate ideas and experiences which an individual will see as being worthwhile when she finds they have also been discussed by another group.
- They give you pegs on which to hang points that haven't been made formally.
- The ideas are in the women's own words.
- They build confidence.
- They provide support.

Whether you're taking a report-back from flip-charts, on OHP slides or from notes, the sequence is always the same:

Report-backs from group discussions/brainstorming sessions

1 Call on someone to report back from the group. Ask her to stand and, if it is a big group, to come to the front or to where her flip-charts are. This provides a mini public speaking opportunity which, while possibly terrifying at the time, gives a confidence boost on achieving it.
2 Listen carefully to what she says and try to catch some of the words she uses which are not written down.
3 Thank and congratulate her.
4 Ask other groups for any questions for clarification.
5 Take the report-backs from all the groups before starting discussions.
6 Pull out any points you want to challenge or reinforce. For example, we will always challenge the word 'luck' in response to the question 'How did you get to where you are today?' and use it as an introduction to discuss to what extent we can make our own luck. You may also use the opportunity to introduce a new topic, or provide a link to the next session.
7 If you have a co-trainer, agree between you, before the report-back, which points each of you is going to major on, so that you have a smooth changeover.

Some do's and don'ts for report-backs

Do
- Go through everything.
- Move them on by reading the next one.
- Turn OHP off when summing up.
- Get them to face group.
- Enthuse.

- Pick out good points.
- Use positive language.
- Keep the momentum going.
- Encourage them if they dry up.

Don't
- Patronize.
- Stand in front of the speaker.
- Wave hands across slides.
- Look bored.
- Comment in the middle.
- Touch the person speaking.
- Assume that you understand the point.

Report-backs from role plays and/or individual exercises
This is much more informal, so you simply ask the whole group 'What came out of that?' or 'What were the main points from that?', 'What did you learn?', 'What surprises were there?'

Be prepared with some points of your own, based on your own observations, in case you meet with silence. Listen carefully to what is said, and build on it and/or introduce other ideas. At the end of any report-back, remind them of the objective of the exercise and summarize the main learning points before moving on.

Profile speakers

Of course, you can have speakers on your course to talk about anything, e.g. the new career-break scheme, further training opportunities, why this organization is keen to promote women. The area where women's development training needs specific action is in having profile speakers. The introducing and summing up of profile speakers who have come to speak about themselves is probably the aspect of a women's development course which is most taken for granted and therefore neglected, both by participants and by trainers.

In the middle or, worse, at the end of a hard day, the idea of an anecdotal speaking slot can all too easily become a bit of light relief—an hour off—an entertainment. This is not so. Profile speakers are asked along to talk about themselves as an important and integral part of the course material. It's important that you remember this and convey it to your participants.

These sessions are important: vital ingredients in any women's development course which we always include, whether it's a short session on a one-day workshop, or more than one speaker on a three-day course, or as after-dinner speakers on a residential course (the exceptions to this would be a one-day assertiveness course, as this is so tightly focused on one specific skill, or a biography workshop where participants hear the life stories of the other women in their small group in great detail). Unless you've heard the speaker before, these are also the sessions where you are mostly in the land of the unknown. And even if you have heard the speaker before, you cannot guarantee that she will stick to the same material, so in these sessions you really need to have your wits about you.

The huge advantage of these sessions, from your point of view, is that a profile speaker can reinforce ideas that you feel you haven't communicated well enough yourself, or can say things that you've forgotten, or that haven't emerged in the discussions so far. The speaker has novelty value and greater credibility than you have, for all your expertise.

The reason for these profiles is clear: to provide deliberate role models of women doing extraordinary and ordinary things. Role models don't need to be consciously provided for men. Men at work have lots of examples every day of men doing differnt types of work: men at the top of the organization; men as bosses; men taking on unusual responsibilities. Women have extremely few role models in their place of work of women in authority, of women as bosses, of women in positions of power, and of women doing unusual jobs. This is particularly so for returners, where it is especially important to choose profile speakers who understand their fears and doubts.

This is one of the reasons why women set their sights so low—they simply do not imagine themselves doing a more senior job, because no woman ever has—and the higher up the organization, the fewer the role models.

As part of your course organization and design you will have chosen your profile speaker with care and briefed her. You hope that she's prepared her notes and you make ready to introduce her. Here is a routine for dealing with profile speakers:

1 On her arrival, check that she understands the point of the session, and ask her how she'd like to be introduced. Some speakers have specific ideas; others will leave it to you. If she leaves it to you, ask her what her very first job was, and what her job is now; this usually provides sufficiently intriguing material for your introduction. Agree the length of her talk with her and the time left to take questions. Agree how you will signal if she overruns. Explain that you will chair any question and answer session.

2 Start your formal introduction of the session—it's your job in your introduction to set the tone:

   • Explain that this session is special.
   • Explain why you include profile speakers in the course.
   • Emphasize that it is an important and serious part of the course.
   • Explain the logistics and whether there will be an opportunity to ask questions.

3 Brief the group that you expect them to:

   • listen carefully
   • take notes
   • be considering 'How can I apply what she is saying to my own situation?'

 • be ready to ask questions at the end

4 Introduce the speaker in the way that you've agreed with her.

5 While she is speaking, you will also be very busy. You need to be:

 • keeping an eye on the time
 • taking copious notes yourself
 • noting what she says that reinforces the messages of the course
 • listening out for points that she makes in passing which you want to 'flesh out'

The speaker will not know in detail what has been going on during the course and may not know the course participants. This means that she may be delivering her material blind and won't know whether she is reinforcing or contradicting something that the group raised that morning.

Your job, following her talk, will be to dovetail her contribution into the rest of the course, and only you will know which of her points need to be reinforced and which quietly forgotten. You can also use this session to introduce a new subject or to make a point that you wanted to make yourself, but it sounds so much better if she has already mentioned it.

6 When she's finished, you need to take centre stage and chair the question session. Here are some tips:

 • Draw your chair into the middle or, if it's a big group, stand. You need to be clearly in control.
 • When you've asked for questions, be prepared for silence. You have to allow time for people's brains to go into reverse.
 • Have a question of your own up your sleeve, just in case the silence goes on too long.
 • Stay in control and keep a sharp eye on the time for questions.
 • Ensure that everyone hears the question—repeat it if necessary.
 • Beware of the speaker redelivering her speech; many speakers feel more relaxed during question sessions and start all over again. Be ready to interrupt.
 • Make it clear when you're taking the last question.

7 Sum up the session:

 • Draw out 3–4 points that you consider needed emphasizing or were particularly relevant for the group.
 • Thank the speaker for her contribution.
 • Start the applause.

Keeping the ground rules going

It's your job as trainer to keep all the ground rules (see Chapter 2) going during the course. This means making sure everyone gets a chance to bring in their personal or work examples, reminding the group of the confidentiality contract before they start role plays, and encouraging them to be assertive when faced with any prejudice, discrimination or assumptions. It means remembering to congratulate them on their successes and encouraging them to see how they are progressing. In short, it means being very familiar with all the ground rules so that you are able to keep them operating throughout the course.

Deviating from the programme

Having spent time and trouble designing your course programme, it may seem crazy to consider deviating from it. However, we believe there are times when it is important to do so. We don't mean wandering off your course programme or just being flexible with the timetable. By deviating, we mean introducing a session or a subject that you hadn't planned to include, which inevitably will be at the expense of something else.

If an issue crops up strongly and urgently in the early morning review, you can decide to put your programme for the day back and deal with it there and then. The other, potentially more difficult, occasion is when an issue won't go away, and it begins to feel as though the whole course is becoming obsessed with it. In this case, make it clear that you hadn't planned to cover this issue in any depth, and instigate a group brainstorming session to resolve it. You may also want to add any input that you feel comfortable doing without preparation.

Dealing with the issue reassures participants that they can raise *real* issues with you and reinforces the message that it's their course. It also clears the air and 'unsticks' the group, enabling them to move on.

For example On a three-day residential course for women managers, every problem seemed to have the one root: sexism inside the organization. Every new subject that the trainer introduced foundered with the response: 'That wouldn't work because of the sexism'. Almost overwhelmed with the negativity, and fast running out of ideas, the trainer in desperation decided to tackle the problem of sexism head-on and insisted that the group devise a checklist of action to deal with it. Much to her amazement and relief, within 10 minutes they drew up the following list, and the subject wasn't raised again; it had had its space, been digested and produced valuable action points.

Ways of dealing with sexism

- Tackle it one to one when it happens—take the person on one side.
- Assert ourselves one to one.
- Defuse it with humour one to one.
- Formally grieve to boss's boss.
- Don't reinforce it—no fluttering eyelids.
- Adopt a strategy.
- Lobby opinion-formers—informally, formally.
- Raise the issue.
- Discuss at equal opportunities meetings.
- Discuss with the union.
- Discuss at department meetings.

- Discuss with head of department.
- Promote more women.
- Build sexism awareness into mainstream courses.
- Wider recruitment.
- Reorganize the whole organization.
- Don't give up.
- Be patient.
- Start doing something!
- Remain optimistic.

Recaps and reviews

Progress checks, in the form of recaps and reviews, are important in women's development training to reassure, build confidence and give feedback. It's good training practice, anyway, to recap a session before moving on to a new subject. On a course of more than one day, start the day with a recap of what they've already done, and where you've got to in the programme, and follow this with a review:

- Impose a 'two-minute think', i.e. two minutes of silence in which to jot down the main points they've learnt, the main points still outstanding, and what they intend to apply after the course.
- Ask for some points to be shared in the whole group.
- Keep an eye on the time—10 minutes is about right.

Reviews are also helpful:

- after an activity or exercise
- at the end of a session
- at the end of a day

These reviews are valuable because they:

- provide reassurance and the relief of discovery that 'I'm not the only one who feels like that'
- provide you with an opportunity to correct misunderstandings
- give you feedback on your effectiveness
- build the confidence of the group and individuals
- give encouragement: 'We're getting there'
- enable participants to put issues on the agenda, although it's up to you to be clear about whether you plan to address them or not
- give you an opportunity to reinforce points that you feel may have got lost

Action session

As has already been said in Chapter 4, an action session is good training practice, but it is particularly important on a women's development course. However, don't leave it to the action session to talk about action! To ensure that your course is really effective, you need to encourage action right from the beginning—indeed you could mention the need for action points in your introduction to the course.

Action points are:

- small
- practical
- specific
- realistic
- with a real deadline (not wishful thinking)

You can suggest possible action points throughout the course:

- in recapping sessions
- in summing up speakers
- in summarizing report-backs
- in the early morning course reviews
- at any time one occurs to you!

To run an action session:

- Summarize the course.
- Remind participants what action points are.
- Give examples of action points and clarify the difference between good intentions and action points (see Figure 9.1).

Good intention	Action point
I am going to be more visible.	I am going to speak at the departmental meeting on Thursday.
I am going to be more assertive.	I am going to speak to Joan about her lateness, by Friday week.
I'm going to build up my network of contacts.	I will phone Asha in marketing and fix a date to have lunch with her, by the end of the week.

Figure 9.1 *Good intentions translated into action points*

- Give out 'action points' sheets. This is basically a blank sheet of paper. The action points could just as easily be written on ordinary notepaper, but special sheets confer more importance and a greater sense of commitment. In the example in Figure 9.2 the left-hand column is for the action point and the smaller right-hand column for the deadline the participant has set herself.
- Allow a few minutes for people to think and write—remind them about the 'by when' column.
- Stress that action points are their own responsibility and remain private.
- Ask everyone to choose just *one* action point to share with the whole group. If it's a workshop of more than 20 women, break them into groups to discuss their action points and ask for one point from each group.
- As individuals read out an action point each, ensure that they *are*

Action points

By when?

1		
2		
3		
4		
5		
6		
7		
8		
9		
10		

Figure 9.2 *An example of an action points sheet*

action points and not good intentions. Give ideas and information to help, and lots of encouragement.

Action points are the trainer's practical interpretation of the Chinese proverb: 'A journey of a thousand miles begins with a single step'. At this point you're looking for single steps, not whole journeys!

Closing the course

As with the opening, closing a course is very personal and everyone has their own favourite ways of closing. It is very much your session and whatever you say needs to come from the heart. Any administrative details should have been dealt with before you close the course. Information about claiming expenses, for example, can kill the end of the course. It's very challenging for a trainer to close each course afresh, rather than as a matter of routine, and to make sure the course ends on a high note.

The content of your closing remarks includes:

- a summary of what participants have done
- praise for what they've done
- putting the course into context and building links with the future
- reminding them
  —it's up to them
  —they're not alone
- your final remarks/special message

This is the obvious, visible part of *what* you say. Remembering the objectives of women's development training, *how* you say it is just as important. In preparing your notes, refer back to the objectives of the course and remember that, as well as the specific course objectives, the overall objectives of women's development training are to:

- provide support and encouragement
- build skills
- build confidence
- inspire
- give examples
- provoke networking
- raise awareness
- result in action

Your objectives in your closing remarks or special message are as they've been throughout the course, to:

- **energize**
- **encourage**
- **empower**
- **enthuse**

and to this list, we'd add one more for the closing:

- **inspire**

This is a tall order at the end of a heavy and demanding day, so you may want to prepare it well in advance. It's handy to have a selection of stories/anecdotes/quotes ready so that you can select the one you feel is appropriate for this particular group. Alternatively, you may want to wait and see what comes to you out of the course; you may conclude with something that one of the speakers or one of the participants said during the course, or with an image that comes to you on the spur of the moment.

Whatever you choose, you've got to mean it, and it's got to send them away knowing that you believe in them.

Summary

In this chapter, we've looked at all the particular aspects of running a women's development course which make a women-only course different from a men-only or mixed course.

The main messages from this chapter are:

- The actual material in women's development training is simply the visible tip of the iceberg. The vast bulk of the work is in how you deliver the material and facilitate the group.
- Women's development training needs you personally to put in a lot of effort and energy.
- Attention to detail and sensitivity to the group will pay off.
- If you're doing it well, it will look easy! Running women's development training is rather like looking at a swan floating across a lake—on the surface all is cool and effortless but underneath she's paddling like mad!

National Westminster Bank plc

This is a good example of an in-depth programme which includes project work and tutorial guidance as well as two separate weeks of courses. It is a well established programme, and it is interesting that National Westminster Bank offers places to other organizations, giving an added dimension to the networking aspect.

Background in banking

The first women came into the Bank at the turn of the century and, by 1907, 4 out of 3000 employees of the London and Westminster Bank were women. With the outbreak of the First World War, numbers increased dramatically and by 1919 women formed about 30 per cent of the workforce. During the following years, there was a gradual decline to under 20 per cent by 1939 but, once more, with the outbreak of the Second World War, there was a rapid increase. The proportion of women increased steadily after that to:

1960 – 40 per cent
1970 – 50 per cent
1980 – 55 per cent
1990 – 56 per cent

Until the mid-1960s, little encouragement was given and the majority of women showed no inclination to make a career of banking. Most women had resigned by age 21. Pre-war they were required to resign on marriage and from 1945–1960 married women were only on the 'temporary staff'.

Background within NatWest

Despite the barriers to advancement, from 1950 onwards women started to make inroads into the career stream, the main opportunities initially falling within the personnel function, then seen as a nursing/welfare function.

Mechanization and automation changed the face of banking and with it the tasks to be performed. Despite social pressure for change, progress for women was slow, although the introduction of legislation, particularly the Equal Pay Act 1970 and Sex Discrimination Act 1975, had some impact. Nevertheless, inherited attitudes and conscious/unconscious prejudices remained and unfortunately even in the 1980s some persisted.

Why start a programme?

Early in 1977 the Bank decided to make a full review of the situation of women in the organization. The general conclusions were:

- Progress was very slow. Even legislation was having little practical effect.
- In some areas opportunities were actually declining. Between 1973 and 1977 the percentage of junior supervisory posts held by women fell from 10.5 per cent to 8.5 per cent—in absolute terms, a decline of 100 women.

If it was to make the most of its human resources, the Bank could not ignore:

- statutory requirements and social trends
- the failure of existing policy to develop all existing talent
- the fact that the traditional source of future talent, male school leavers, was about to decline. Forecasts showed that the number of school leavers available for employment (male and female) would decline from 640 000 in 1981 to 480 000 in 1991, i.e. a drop of 25 per cent.
- the belief that managerial talent is not a male prerogative
- the recognition that a management team comprising both men and women is likely to be stronger than one comprising only the members of one sex

As a result of this review, research was conducted between 1978 and 1980 encompassing all areas of equal opportunity affecting women.

Action

A women's workshop was arranged at Heythrop Park where 15 women employees with identified potential were invited to a three-day think tank to consider the position of female staff and provide a comprehensive report on the way ahead. Their findings have been used to develop the equal opportunities policies subsequently implemented. For example:

1 As one of the initiatives taken forward, a special training course for women was introduced, Management Development for Women. This includes two separate weeks of full-time study at Heythrop Park, an intervening company-based project under tutorial guidance and a one-day follow-up workshop. It is aimed at women with potential and the accent is on personal development and on the integration of participants' training into the requirements of the organization. Examples

of bodies taking part are the Bank of England, British Airways, Marks and Spencer, and the Civil Service. A typical timetable would include:

- career and life planning
- goal setting
- assertiveness through communication
- financial policy on running a business
- a business game
- effective oral communication
- organizational power and culture

and, in addition, a work-related project which is reported on during the second week of the course, which normally takes place after a four-week gap.

2 The introduction of the Management Development Programme has ensured more objective selection of staff for development and more rapid advancement for the more able, ensuring equal opportunities to progress for women. Currently, those on the programme are split 50/ 50 men and women.

3 The introduction of a computer-based training programme, Equal Opportunities at Work, covering the legal and practical aspects of equal opportunities. This is available on a nationwide basis and all staff should be within 30 minutes travelling time of a distance learning station.

Outcome

Entering a new decade, we are seeing many more women in management positions, with a rise from 4 per cent in 1979 to 15.2 per cent in 1990.

Diana Balsdon, Equal Opportunities Unit
National Westminster Bank plc

10 Evaluation

Evaluation is an important part of your women's development training strategy. This chapter explains its relevance to women's development training, describes what can be done before, during and after the training, and gives examples of evaluation material. Common sense tells us that evaluation is particularly important to measure the success of pilot programmes and programmes that are in their infancy. It's equally important for programmes that have been running for several years and which may need reviewing, revitalizing or discontinuing.

For example   Evaluating a Career Development for Women course, which had been designed for women in management, the organization discovered that over a period of five years most of the women in the target group had attended. Women currently attending were in different roles and grades in the organization. As their needs were different, action was taken to redesign and relaunch the programme for this new target group.

Why evaluate women's development training?

As we've mentioned earlier, women's development training is always seen as controversial, so evaluation has a valuable part to play in:

- reassuring the organization
- silencing the cynics
- proving its cost effectiveness
- proving that it works
- providing you with examples of success
- encouraging its supporters
- providing examples to encourage potential participants
- convincing senior management that is it worthwhile
- demonstrating that it is addressing the business needs
- ensuring it continues to be supported
- giving you a sense of achievement
- supporting your overall strategy

The cost of evaluation needs to be set aside as part of your original budget, especially if you've been spending a lot of money. The interest in evaluation is usually in direct proportion to the amount of money you're spending on the training!

For example   Organization A invested £30 000 of direct budget and a further £20 000 of staff time in launching a substantial women's development training course. They aimed to write off all their development costs in the first three years. Investing at this level made them enter seriously into evaluation in the short term and, in the long term, to check the results against their corporate objectives of retention and promotion of women in the target group.

Organization B ran three pilot assertiveness courses at a budget cost of around £4000 and staff time of £1000. It was satisfied with information consisting of course evaluation sheets and informal feedback interviews held by the company training officer.

What are you looking for in evaluation?

Evaluation measures the effectiveness of your training against the specific objectives that you set in Chapter 3.

Peter Bramley, in his book *Evaluating the Effectiveness of Training*,[1] looks in detail at four main areas of change to be measured:

- changes in knowledge
- changes in skills
- changes in attitude and behaviour
- changes in levels of effectiveness

Bramley backs this up with detailed examples of processes for evaluating each area. He also includes a useful chapter on costing changes and a short and simple questionnaire to help you decide whether you really want to evaluate your training.

Within Bramley's four categories, the type of changes that you might expect to find in women's development training are:

Changes in knowledge—increased knowledge of the organization, policies and practices; increased knowledge of the position of women in the organization/business sector; increased knowledge of what other women have done/are doing; sources of further information and support.

Changes in skills—more effective professional skills, such as presentation skills.

Changes in attitude and behaviour—a great deal of women's development training is concerned almost exclusively with this category. Evidence of such changes would include: effective use of assertiveness; evidence of greater self-confidence; clearer goals, greater motivation and determination; dealing with people differently; evidence of an increased accepting of responsibility for herself. Evidence of a change in attitude is extremely difficult to measure—be open to changes which don't fit your course objectives or your evaluation criteria.

For example In a programme designed to develop personal effectiveness skills, aimed mainly at promotion and advancement, the outcome for one woman was the desired promotion, while another decided that she was perfectly happy in her present post and threw herself into her work with renewed vigour. Although she hadn't been promoted, she had become more effective in her post because she had 'realized how effective I am' and had made an attitude change 'to stop moaning'. A perfectly valid result, but one not initially set as an objective by the trainer in the pilot programme.

Changes in levels of effectiveness—achievement of goals; feedback from colleagues, managers and subordinates on changes; evidence of greater effectiveness in teams, departments and in the organization as a whole; completion of action points; networking activity.

The evaluation process itself consists of four phases:

- before the training
- during the training
- at the end of the training
- some time after the training

Before the training

Check that you are clear about the objectives, the desired results for the women, and the benefits to the organization. As women's development training deals with personal as well as work development, it may be difficult to set crystal-clear, detailed behavioural objectives. Be clear that achievements of personal goals are just as valid as work goals.

Meetings between trainer and potential participants rarely happen, but can be helpful, especially for returners who particularly need reassurance. Potential participants can be briefed on what to expect from a development course and may sharpen up their own objectives while the trainers can gauge their expectations.

In addition, a pre-training discussion between the participant and her boss can help to refine her objectives and enhance her learning.

During the training

Ongoing evaluation during the training is particularly useful for women, as they tend to:

- be over-modest about their achievements
- often overlook or even forget achievements
- regard small achievements as not worth mentioning (but later discover that an accumulation of small steps has resulted in a great leap forward)
- wait for someone else to recognize their achievements
- play down achievements for fear of embarrassment or looking bigheaded
- not mention small achievements made at the beginning of the training, as they feel they have been superseded by more impressive achievements later on

A formal evaluation process can take place part way through a training programme taking weeks or months, e.g. on an open learning or modular programme. On a shorter course of 1–5 days, informal evaluation processes can be built into the course and contribute greatly to learning.

Research by Peter Critten[2] in the hotel and catering industry showed conclusively that making evaluation part of the learning had the following benefits:

- The participants had their learning enhanced by being more aware of their progress.
- Participants who might have thought they were making slow progress were able to realize that their progress was OK and in some cases surpassing that of others.
- Participants were able to remember what they were learning, by being asked to recall and discuss learning points as they went through the training.
- It gave the trainers feedback so that they were able to adapt the design and content during the course.

As a result of these ideas, here are three simple ways of making evaluations during the training:

1 *The two-minute think*—two minutes of silence when participants are asked to think about what they have learned and what they are going to apply after the course (described further in Chapter 9).
2 *Learning diaries*—blank sheets of paper with prompt questions which encourage participants to note down what they've learned and ideas for transferring the learning to real situations (see Figure 10.1). Allow time on the course for this and then ask to hear a few learning points from the group at the beginning or end of a day. The learning diary and 'two-minute thinks' enable you to gauge the group's progress.
3 *Regular feedback*—having to give each other feedback on their performance means that participants have to evaluate each other. It also gives them a good opportunity to practise their assertiveness in giving and receiving the feedback. Use verbal feedback after an event or exercise. For example, when individuals are encouraged to make a positive presentation about themselves, ask the group to note and feed back on:

- What did she do well?
- Where did you feel she let herself down?

Use written feedback when more detailed or complicated feedback is needed. Having to stop to fill in a feedback form after an exercise enables participants to really take in, and learn from, what has just happened. It is particularly helpful for the reflectors and restrains the activists[3] from rushing headlong into the next activity.

Figure 10.2 shows a feedback form from a Women and Leadership course. It involves each woman assessing herself as the leader or as a team member, and team members in assessing the leader.

ITVA Learning Diary — Day 2

Leadership — Motivation — Decision making

1 *What are the key learning points for you from today?*

The need to stand back and monitor what the team is doing

Clear brief for the task

Everyone is motivated by opportunities for self-fulfilment

Better to make a decision than no decision

2 *What do you want to follow up and/or apply back at work?*

Have regular team meetings to talk about what we're doing

Stop and think more — not rush in and get my hands dirty without knowing what is going on

Talk to Peter about ways of developing his job

Listen to what Teresa has to say more

Figure 10.1   *A learning diary page from the Management Skills for Women course at the Independent Television Association*

Mid-programme evaluation

On longer programmes, mid-programme evaluation keeps you on track.

For example   On the pilot of a huge women's development programme, involving open learning, mid-programme evaluation was undertaken to assess:

- the effectiveness of the workbook and the time taken to work on it
- the effectiveness of the workshops
- the effectiveness of the networking and mentoring support systems
- the effectiveness of the programme's PR

The detailed questionnaire that was used is shown in Figure 10.3 (a) and (b). It was issued at the beginning of the programme to enable each woman to log her reactions as she went through and was collected in at the mid-point of the training.

Women and Leadership

Exercise Feedback Questionnaire

1 Did you achieve the task that was set?

- not at all
- partially
- completely

2 How did you feel about the result?

3 What percentage of your creative energies were being used?

4 How clear were you about what you were doing?

5 How involved were you in the task?

6 What did the leader do well?

7 What would you have liked her to do differently?

8 What will you do differently next time?

- as a team member?
- as team leader?

Thank you for completing this form.

Figure 10.2 *Feedback questionnaire*

The results revealed:

- some of the internal PR was not reaching the target group
- the programme was taking on average three hours a week to complete
- participants were contacting and helping each other
- they weren't using the mentoring network very much
- the least popular section
- the most beneficial section
- the range of actions which had already been taken
- the material was holding their interest
- the briefing of exercises on the workshops needed to be clearer
- participants were recommending the programme to others

These results enabled adjustments to be made to all aspects of the programme to ensure its success.

At the end of the training

Action points The final step of all women's development training is an action session which involves each participant deciding on the detail of proposed

Women's Development Programme: Evaluation Workshop Two

Name .... *Job title* ....

Can you help? We need to evaluate the programme to find out if it does what it is designed to do and if that has been worthwhile for you. Please complete this form, about the course and workbook to date, before the end of today and leave it with us before you go.

1   How did you hear about the course?

2   How much time per week have you spent on the workbook?

3   Were the four weeks between workshops 1 & 2
        Please tick   about right   ☐
                                                                  *too little time   ☐
                                                                  *too much time   ☐
*If too little or too much time, please say how many weeks you would prefer.

4   How many other women on the course have you contacted?
        _____ women   How often?   Reason for contact

5   Have you contacted any helpers?
        How many?   How often?   Reason for contact

6   How have you felt about contact with the helpers?
        Please tick   able to contact them all the way through   ☐
                                   able to contact them most of the time   ☐
                                   able to contact them some of the time   ☐
                                   not really able to contact them at all   ☐
                                   didn't feel the need to contact one   ☐

7   What have you found most helpful so far?
        e.g. particular section or part of section of the journal, helper,
        contact with other women, workshop etc.

8   What have you found least helpful so far?
        e.g. particular section or part of section of the workbook, helper,
        contact with other women, workshop, etc.

9   How has the workbook, up to section eight, held your interest?
        Please tick   all of the time   ☐
                                                  nearly all of the time   ☐
                                                  most of the time   ☐
                                                  some of the time   ☐
                                                  only very occasionally   ☐

10   In what constructive ways do you think the workbook could be
        improved?

11   What do you think of the course so far? *Please tick*
        I consider it is of: great use   ☐
                                                  considerable use   ☐
                                                  some use   ☐
                                                  not much use   ☐

12   What action have you taken so far as a result of the course?

13   Have you recommended this course to other women? If so, how many?

14   The next section of the questionnaire asks for comments on each section.
        Thank you for completing the questionnaire. Please use this space for any
        additional comments not covered by the questions.

Figure 10.3(a)   *Women's development programme evaluation form*

Section	Time taken	What helped you most?	What was most difficult?	What was the value to you? Not important Very important Circle your position on the scale
1				1 2 3 4 5 6 7 8 9 10
2				1 2 3 4 5 6 7 8 9 10
3				1 2 3 4 5 6 7 8 9 10
4				1 2 3 4 5 6 7 8 9 10
5				1 2 3 4 5 6 7 8 9 10
6				1 2 3 4 5 6 7 8 9 10
7				1 2 3 4 5 6 7 8 9 10
8				1 2 3 4 5 6 7 8 9 10

Figure 10.3 (b) Women's development programme evaluation form

actions. Details of an action session are given in Chapter 9. Action notes are evaluative evidence, as they give you an opportunity to assess the extent to which the trainer has achieved the objectives. For example, if assertiveness is included in the objectives and the action points consistently exclude assertiveness, then question why it is included in the programme and/or the trainer's effectiveness in delivering it.

Reaction charts
These are usually designed to log the participant's reactions at the end of the training and often include a curious mixture of questions about the programme itself, the logistics, course venue and end-of-course morale. They have dubious value because:

- They are usually completed when people are not concentrating and are distracted by wanting to get home.
- They can be too concerned with how people feel at that specific moment, hence the nickname of 'happy sheets'.
- The real effectiveness of the training will only be discovered when it is transferred back to the rest of the woman's life.

Reaction charts are only useful when:

- They collect any information that you need instantly.
- You have no way of being in touch with the participants later.

End-of-programme achievements
On longer programmes, participants will have achieved things within the life of the training. Recording these achievements gives you ongoing evaluation of the programme. Here are some examples of work and personal achievements from women at the end of a three-month programme:

Work achievements
- promotions and acting promotions
- gained an interview for promotion
- was assertive (and it worked)
- going on a technical course
- got job regraded
- wrote my own annual report
- followed up a career idea
- wrote CV
- formulated a business plan
- sorted out major computer headache
- arranged two days informal training
- broadened job content
- offered promotion
- headhunted into senior job
- learned from interview failure
- making more of an effort to get on with boss
- successfully proposed alternative system for paperwork
- negotiated contract with freelancers
- arranged to visit another department
- met up with people from another office

- taken on more responsibility
- offered a permanent job
- helped someone else get their qualifications evaluated
- negotiated leave within a busy schedule
- got an attachment to another department
- supervising a trainee
- work situation improved

Personal achievements
- starting degree course
- started driving again after six years
- decided to move flat
- organized a holiday
- encouraged others to do 'Springboard'
- passed exams including degree
- made positive decision to end unproductive relationship
- took up golf
- joined clubs
- lost weight
- go jogging regularly
- taking steps to be more independent
- feeling totally in control
- looking into Open University courses
- met other women on the programme for lunch
- gave up smoking
- applied to be a volunteer telephone counsellor
- concreted a wall
- learnt to dive
- feeling positive
- won a victory at the ante-natal clinic!
- more time for myself
- joined a gym—work out three times a week
- read book on assertiveness
- started working with mentally distressed people
- learnt that I'm satisfied with my life.

After the training

Post-course questionnaires These will form a substantial part of the evaluation of any training. They:

- consolidate learning
- give feedback about achievement of objectives
- measure the worth of women's development training to the organization
- influence the design of that specific programme and subsequent programmes
- encourage conversation with line managers, staff or other delegates

Figure 10.4 shows an example of a post-course questionnaire for a five-day Women and Leadership course. It is designed to be completed 3–6 weeks after the course.

Women and Leadership Course

Post-course Questionnaire

1 What was your overall impression of the course?

2 What did you specifically relate to your day-to-day work?

3 What did you think of the presentation style of the trainers? What was good? What could be improved?

4 Which sessions, if any, would you want to expand, and how?

5 Which sessions, if any, would you leave out? Why?

6 What, if anything, would you like to see introduced to the course?

7 How could the course be improved for other delegates? Please suggest ideas.

8 Was the course at the right level or did you find aspects of it either difficult to understand or too simple?

9 What were the main benefits of the course for you and your development as a leader?

10 What actions have you taken as a result of the course?

11 What other actions are you still planning to take?

12 What post-course discussions have you had with:

- your boss
- your staff
- other course delegates

13 Use this space to convey anything else not contained in the questions:

Figure 10.4 *Post-course questionnaire*

The results from this questionnaire showed that the participants had found the course challenging and very relevant to their day-to-day work (apart from two women who had temporarily found themselves without teams to lead). They wanted more time spent on team roles, and individual coaching/counselling from the tutors; as the course was already action-packed, they felt that there was no time for additional subjects. They appreciated the balance in intensity with some stress management activities. Several delegates were keen that the range of participants should be widened to include women from more than one region of the organization. Action was taken to accommodate all these suggestions.

Results in the weeks following the training had included:

- reallocating work to staff
- better briefings of staff
- improved contributions as team members
- resolution of one longstanding difficult relationship between two of the participants who could now see and respect each other's leadership styles
- more 'up front' leadership—speaking out more
- more effective motivation of staff

Figure 10.5 shows an evaluation form for a three-day career development course. It emphasizes the participant's responsibility for her own learning, and restricts the evaluation to the course activities.

Post-course discussions

An evaluation discussion has the advantage that it enables the interviewer to probe and obtain specific information. A disadvantage (particularly when the training covered personal issues) is that the interviewer needs to gain the confidence of the interviewee.

Post-course discussions can be held between participants and:

The trainer   This has the advantage that the trainer is included in the contract of confidentiality and can also pursue the points raised on the course. The disadvantage is that some participants may find it difficult to give negative feedback face to face with the trainer.

Immediate bosses   This can be very helpful if they are 'gardener bosses', i.e. they will help the woman to grow and apply the course learning to her whole life, but can be discouraging if the boss is negative or cynical.

Mentors   Individual mentors will usually know the woman's environment better than she does, believe in her more than she believes in herself, and will be able to give ideas, support and kicks to ensure that action points are carried out. Mentors can help participants to evaluate their attendance on a course.

Course mentors   Some organizations allocate more senior line managers to mentor a whole course. The idea is that there is someone who cares about what happens and is a source of support and ideas afterwards. The success of this will depend on the rapport between the mentor and the participant.

A training/personnel specialist   Discussions with a training/personnel special-

---

Career Development Programme

Evaluating the course

Which sessions did you find most useful?

Which session did you find least useful?

How would you improve the course?
(Consider content, speakers, written material, venue, administration, etc.)

Evaluating yourself

What were your objectives for coming on this course?

Were these objectives met?

What will you do differently as a result of this course?

What did you get out of the course?

Figure 10.5   *Course evaluation form*

ist other than the trainer can be helpful in evaluation if they are aware of the professional reasons and objectives of the training, but were not personally involved.

Other women from the course   This will probably provide the best source of support and encouragement—maybe just one meeting or through informal or formal networking. The fact that meetings take place evaluates any networking objectives. Also discussions with other women help participants to be aware of their own learning.

Follow-ups   The general value of follow-ups and their place in your design have been described in Chapter 4. They also contribute to the evaluation process because they enable you to gather evidence of the changes that have taken place and give you a measure of how effective the training has been. Lists of achievements and changes in attitudes can be used in evaluation reports, as long as the participants give you permission to use them in an anonymous form, thus preserving the contract of confidentiality.

Summary

In this chapter we've looked at why evaluation is so important for women's development training, what to look for when evaluating, and evaluation practices to use before, during, at the end of, and after the training.

The key messages from this chapter are:

- Women's development training is a vulnerable form of training. It is often questioned in a way that doesn't occur with other forms of development and training. So, as well as being good practice, evaluation is important to provide the organization with evidence of its effectiveness.
- Your evaluation results can contribute to your PR strategy and give other women the confidence to attend.
- There are lots of different ways of building evaluation into your training process.
- Evaluation processes can actively contribute to the learning.

References

1. Peter Bramley, *Evaluating the Effectiveness of Training* (McGraw-Hill, 1990).
2. Quoted in Len Holmes, *Design of Learning* (Hotel and Catering Industry Training Board, 1979).
3. Peter Honey and Alan Mumford, *The Manual of Learning Styles* (Peter Honey, 1986).

Bull HN Information Systems

The following case study is a good example of how women's development training can function within a very male-dominated, highly technological environment, with very few women at senior levels. It demonstrates how useful the evaluation process is and how women's development training can dovetail in with other developmental activities.

Introduction

Bull is a multinational organization which designs, manufactures, markets and sells computer solutions and services. The UK head office is in Brentford, Middlesex, and we have major centres and offices throughout the country. We employ approximately 2100 people, about a quarter of whom are women.

We have been running with an extensive portfolio of training courses over many years now. We obviously hold many technical, sales and marketing programmes. We also have a wide range of management and personal skills development offerings, ranging from presentation and interviewing skills to strategic management programmes at prestigious business schools in the UK, Europe and the USA. About three years ago we decided to strengthen these programmes by introducing one specifically for our female staff. The reason for this, as for all our training and development initiatives, was that we believed we could make better use of the abilities of our available workforce. We saw that women made up 20–25 per cent of our UK workforce, but recognized that they were concentrated in administrative roles or junior professional (through our 'A' level and graduate entry schemes), with very few progressing through to senior technical, consultant or management positions.

Women-only courses—why?

One of the problems in our industry is that career advancement goes to those people who push themselves forward, letting it be known that they want, and are willing to work for, senior positions. On the whole, women believe that, by keeping their heads down and doing a good job, recognition in the form of salary advancement and promotion will naturally follow. They do not project themselves as being self-confident and able to handle anything that is thrown their way, but tend to keep a low profile.

It becomes a vicious circle. Because there are so few women holding significant posts of responsibility there are a limited number of role models for younger women coming through and also, of course, few women who can act as mentor, coach or sponsor for experiential development. Also, the very few women who were in senior posts reported feelings of loneliness and isolation from being one of a few in a male-dominated environment.

We decided, therefore, that we should start to address these issues by running a women-only training course. This would provide a forum where matters of interest and concern to our female workforce could be aired, debated and worked upon in a non-threatening environment, where attitudes and values could be looked at and modes of behaviour and others' perceptions (male colleagues) examined.

The Self-Development in Careers for Women course

We selected Liz Willis to run a programme for us as our human resources director had previous knowledge and experience of her work. The aims and objectives, performance outcomes, content, and mode of delivery were fully discussed with Liz and a workshop tailored to Bull's requirements and needs designed. It is titled 'Self-Development in Careers for Women', and is a three-day residential programme with a one-day follow-up approximately three months later.

The first course was run in late 1987 with 15 participants. Since that time a further four programmes have been held which have been attended by a further 45 participants. Our HR director has taken a great interest in this activity and has come to each programme to discuss with course members issues of interest and concern to them. It is very important for any initiative like this to be given (and to be seen to be given) full and active support from top management.

The following are representative of comments taken from evaluation forms completed at the end of each workshop.

What were your objectives for attending this course?

To decide if I had a future with Bull. If so, how could I get promoted to a senior position? (There is a lack of women in senior positions in Bull.)

How would you evaluate your own performance during this course?

I contributed more on this course than other programmes that I have attended, as it was far more informal and completely non-technical.

What did you get out of the course?

I learnt that my opinions on subjects are varied and that I should work on putting them across effectively. I gained a more positive attitude to myself and how to evaluate myself fairly and realistically.

I have now developed a five-year career plan and know exactly what direction I am heading towards. Previously I didn't have a clue.

I have gained clarity of objectives and more direction for the future. It has renewed my enthusiasm for work in general.

I gained increased self-confidence. Also network links inside and outside the company.

What will you do differently as a result of the course?

I will work to improve my image and exposure at work.

I will tell people how good I am; make the effort to talk to senior management more and increase my visibility. Try to be less self-deprecating.

In addition to written feedback from the participants on immediate completion of the workshop, we have received further comments unsolicited from the attendees and from their managers who have reported significant differences in attitude and behaviour.

The training manager for the Systems Group reports:

In the past women have not had a very high profile within the Group as far as senior positions are concerned. Many progress to team leader level (first line management) but few have progressed beyond this stage.

By concentrating on raising the importance of women in business and focusing on increasing personal effectiveness the course has helped to encourage women's awareness of their potential. It has also helped to teach women how to cope with the prejudice and stereotyping which are a feature of business life.

Without exception all participants from this group have found the course to be of immense benefit.

Flexible work patterns

At the same time as we were promoting this development programme for our female employees we took a serious look at our work practices.

In one of our groups we introduced pilot schemes for more flexible working. These included homeworking (telecommuting), job sharing and part-time employment. The homeworking programme proved particularly successful and has since been extended to other parts of the company.

We also looked at our provisions for maternity leave and, a couple of years ago, introduced the Maternity Career Continuation Programme. This allows women to work on a part-time basis while their children are young for a period of up to five years, from the end of their maternity leave, with the assurance of a full-time post at completion.

Other development activities

Other activities and initiatives which we have actively encouraged women to participate in, and contribute to, in order to develop their interpersonal skills, have included:

- returning to their school, college, polytechnic or university to give

presentations on their own careers, opportunities within the computer industry, etc.
- participating as young managers in 'Insight to Industry' and 'Insight into Management', as run by CRAC and EITB
- attending, as representatives of Bull, careers conventions, exhibitions and conferences
- hosting visits from schools/colleges
- participating in the Prince's Trust Scheme
- acting as supervisors and mentors to junior staff

Results

The benefits of all these activities are manifold and include not only experience and development for our female employees, but the provision of information and role models for younger girls who may not currently see our industry as a particularly appropriate career outlet.

Looking at a few statistics on our workforce we find that, in the UK, 9 per cent of our middle managers and 4 per cent of our senior managers are women. Unfortunately, we still have no woman at management committee level.

We are beginning to see women moving into areas which were previously very much male preserves. For example, we have a woman account manager and sales manager in our Sales Group; we have a woman manager for our response centre in Customer Services and we see several women holding senior posts in our Systems Group.

It would be all too easy, but misleading, to attribute these moves solely to the development initiatives that we have put into place over the past few years. However, we do believe that these activities are making a significant contribution to the profile of our workforce.

People work for a variety of reasons. For many, the financial one comes at the top of the list, but work also conveys status and a place in society. Women have these needs as much as men, but often have to work twice as hard to achieve them. We in Bull believe that it is socially and commercially wrong not to capitalize on this untapped potential.

Anne Munroe, formerly Career Development Manager
Bull HN Information Systems Ltd
—now freelance consultant

11 Setting up networks

Networking is a key ingredient in any women's development training. It is a ground rule which will influence the strategy, the design, the way the training is run and what happens after the training. It can also be a formal subject on the course and provide material for discussion groups and other exercises.

Most of these aspects of networking have already been covered in earlier chapters. This chapter looks at the close link between women's development training and networks, and the different ways of networking after the training, and gives examples of networks which have grown out of women's development training.

The link between women's development training and networks

One of the hurdles to women's progression inside and outside work is their lack of contacts and their reluctance to use the contacts that they do have. In organizations, women often have an overdeveloped sense of loyalty to the department that they're in, and don't look outside for opportunities, such as sideways moves into other departments. When challenged about this, their reply is often that they don't know what is going on in other departments and have never had any contact with anyone in another department. (For 'department' you can also read organization, site, geographical area, industry, business sector.)

Women's family commitments also conspire against their ability to network and build contacts outside their immediate area. While their male colleagues are able to chat to their counterparts at professional group meetings, in the evening, at the company sports club on a Saturday, or in the pub on the way home, the women often have to rush home to collect the children from school, shop, cook, clean, and generally cope with their second job of looking after the family/home.

Men don't need to be encouraged to network—they do it automatically, and it gives them a headstart in hearing of opportunities and gaining ideas and encouragement.

Networking and attending a women-only course is inextricably linked because:

- The course creates a bond of support and encouragement.
- The group has been through a shared experience.

- It may be the first time individuals have been able to talk about many of the issues raised.
- The women become friends.
- It may be the first time they have met women from other specific departments and with very different experiences of life.
- They value the experience of sharing and support so much that they want to continue it.
- They recognize the value of a wide range of contacts.

As a result, it is very common for participants to want to meet again. If a follow-up day is planned, this will provide a formal opportunity, otherwise you need to make it clear that the training will not provide them with other opportunities to network—it is up to them to organize themselves if they want to meet again. Your encouragement is then from the sidelines. This can result in informal and formal networking, and often a mixture of both.

Informal networking

Informal networking means anything from just two women meeting, through to regular get-togethers of the whole group. Informal networking is an organic process, so decisions about when and where the meetings take place, what for, and whether other women are included are not usually consciously made. There is often a high social element in informal networking. Where the women networking are returners, it is helpful if the trainer can attend the first meeting to encourage and motivate.

For example After a personal effectiveness course, one woman undertook to organize one meeting for the group. Two years later the group is still active, has welcomed women from subsequent courses, and organized events to which women from other parts of the organization were invited. It needed only one woman to organize one meeting to get started. This way informal networks begin, tackle issues, grow or dwindle as the need arises.

For example A very successful network arose out of a series of six-day women's biography courses where 15 women with 3 tutors had worked in depth on their lives and their future, in the light of the fact that their organization was closing and they were facing redundancy. The women, of all ages and from a wide range of ethnic minorities, worked well together. The women from the first course decided to go on meeting and one woman undertook to organize it. While the second course was running, some women from the first course joined them over lunch one day and made contact. The original group of women were wary of the second group joining their network because they felt they might not be able to be so open with people with whom they hadn't shared a common experience. They took the risk and asked one of the trainers to visit and help facilitate the meeting of the two groups. The trainer paired each one up with someone unknown to share where they were in their lives and what the current questions were for their future. It worked!

The women were surprised to find how quickly they related to each other and found new views and experiences. In the year prior to the closure of the organization, five courses were run, and the network met regularly at the same time and in the same place, once a month. In addition, it issued newsletters to help and encourage each other, with news of job searches and of each other. Two years after the closure they decided that the network had done its work and would stop—members were now widely dispersed and found it difficult to get to meetings, and the network had lost its purpose. However, three women from the network who lived in the same area decided that they wanted to go on meeting together to look at new issues.

Formal networks

In addition, you can encourage the women who attend your women's development training to tap into the many existing women's networks. A complete list of women's organizations is available from the Women's National Commission.[1] There are so many excellent women's networks already functioning, crossing so many boundaries, that it is virtually impossible not to meet new people. The networks fall roughly into five categories:

- special interest groups
- professional sectors, e.g. Women in Banking, the Women's Engineering Society, Women in Management
- geographical areas, e.g. Women in the North East
- hierarchical levels, e.g. Network (only for senior women)
- inside specific organizations, e.g. Women in BP, Women in Midland, trade union groups

There are also those which defy categorizing, such as the network 'Women Mean Business', formed after the television documentary series of the same name. Some exist for a brief period of time, in order to address a specific short-term need. Others are well established over years, such as the Women's Institute and the Fawcett Society.

At the very least, have a few useful addresses to give the women on your course or issue a handout with a wider choice. However, if the main interest in networking is for that specific group to meet again, and they choose to network formally, then your role is to encourage, advise and maybe even facilitate. In some cases, organizations support women's networks by providing money, a room, facilities or activities to get them started. Here is a checklist from the Springboard workbook[2] for women thinking of starting their own network:

1 *What is your objective?*
   To give support, lobby, offer training, be consultative, have fun, campaign, etc? Write it down and keep it clear and brief.
2 *Who will be eligible to belong?*
   This needs to tie in specifically to your objective. Don't be afraid to keep the eligibility very tightly defined. There is a temptation to try

to be all things to all women. Are you going to include men?

3 *When are you going to meet?*

Take it one step at a time and don't be afraid to change the frequency or time to fit in with the current needs.

4 *Talk to your organization*

At the very least, inform them what you're doing. At best, persuade them to support you, give you a room to meet in, etc. It is extremely important to have a good relationship and two-way communication with the organization—usually through someone in personnel.

5 *What is the role of men?*

As members, allies, speakers, etc? Refer back to your objectives.

6 *Where are you going to meet?*

A room at work, local wine bar, hired conference room, someone's sitting-room, etc? Refer back to your objectives.

7 *What publicity do you need?*

If it's an informal support network among a group of women who, say, met on a course, you won't need any publicity, but if your objective is to act as, say, a forum for training, you may need to think of posters, circulars, notices on computers, etc.

8 *What about the trade unions?*

Talk to the relevant trade unions in your workplace before you start. They may have a women's group already, and so you need to be clear about how your network differs. Alternatively, networks can be misunderstood and called 'women's unions', especially if you speak up about issues such as workplace nurseries or pension rights. Trade unions can see you as a threat, so build a good relationship.

9 *Name?*

Whatever reflects your objectives and members. Most groups are called simply 'Women in BP', 'Women in ICL', 'Women in British Rail', etc. However, one network was called 'The Monday Moot' because they specifically wanted to include men in their meetings, and they met on Mondays!

10 *Start small and let it grow*

If there are three of you, you've started a network!

11 *Who's going to organize it?*

Networks that rely on one person only last as long as that one person can stand it, which is usually not long! Make sure responsibility and work is spread, and consider rotating responsibilities; Rank Xerox's network has rotating roles of chair and secretary for each meeting, to give everyone practice in dealing with meetings.

12 *Respond to the needs of the group*

Be flexible and ingenious in your activities in responding to the needs of the group. There is no set way of running a network, so do whatever works for you.

13 *Network with other networks*

You can learn a lot from linking with other women's networks in your profession, area, industry, etc. Give each other ideas, training opportunities and most importantly—support. See Appendix 5 for names of some of the big national networks who may have branches local to you.

14 *Start now!*

What are you going to do to extend and maintain your networks?

Below are two examples of formal networks which are openly supported by the organization, and are high-profile. Both of them were started by small groups of women who had attended women's development training courses, continued to meet, and lobbied for further support for women in the organization. To set these examples in context, read the case studies on Kent County Council (p. 88) and BBC Scotland (p. 55).

Kent County Council's LINK network

LINK was organized to give the women who work for Kent County Council an opportunity to form their own local and special interest networks. This extract from the leaflet launching LINK explains:

Whether part-time or full-time, LINK is for you. It is for every woman who wants to get the most out of herself and her work. LINK is:

- an open communications network for women across departments, areas, professions and grades
- a focus for women's development within Kent County Council
- an opportunity to make social and professional contacts
- a forum for discussion of employment issues relating to women
- a starting point for the organization of training and social events

LINK is a serious venture. It has grown out of an awareness that some women in KCC may feel isolated and overlooked when training, development and promotion opportunities come along.

LINK will supplement existing initiatives and promises to be supportive, stimulating and a lot of fun. Join us for one of our two inaugural meetings—each will begin with refreshments, followed by a series of short presentations, including one from chief executive, Paul Sabin, who is giving his support to this new venture.

Hundreds of women turned out for the two inaugural meetings, which resulted in twenty local networks being formed, with a variety of objectives.

BBC Scotland's network

Following a training course, a group of women in BBC Scotland continued to meet informally to give each other support. Encouraged by their discussions, they have raised women's career development issues with the personnel department, resulting in further training initiatives. The original group has grown and also supports and links up with other groups in BBC Scotland who have formed spontaneously, following their lead (see Case Study Two).

Summary

In this chapter, we've shown the links between women's development training and networks, looked at the different ways of networking and provided examples from the variety of women's networks which abound. The main messages from this chapter are:

- Women's development training often provokes the formation of networks. This should be encouraged.
- The impulse for forming a network has to come from the women. It is not part of the course, so your role is to provide encouragement, ideas and support.
- Networking is easy. It can be as simple as two women meeting over a coffee.
- Networking is a valid objective of women's development training.

References

1. 'Women's Organisations in the United Kingdom', from Women's National Commission, The Cabinet Office, Great George Street, Whitehall, London.
2. *Springboard: Women's Development Workbook*, by Liz Willis and Jenny Daisley (Hawthorn Press, 1990).

Sun Alliance Insurance Group

Sun Alliance Insurance Group is an organization with a long tradition of women's development training. This study is an excellent example of a women's network growing out of women's development training. From small beginnings and with a low profile, a group of women met to continue their development activities and discuss specific issues. Within two years it has become a thriving, active network with an established company budget.

'Women in International'

By 1988 Sun Alliance Insurance Group had already successfully run courses specifically for women in, or contemplating, management roles within the Group. The 'Women in Management' courses, as they are known, not only look at technical training and individual development but provide an opportunity to share experiences, and provide and receive support.

The initiative was taken a stage further by a few women who set up a support network involving women mainly from the London offices. At that time the group which was still very low-key, was known as Network South East (no relation to BR!). Meetings were arranged informally during lunch times and more women, working across all disciplines within the south-east region, soon became interested.

With corporate changes within Sun Alliance Insurance Group and the advent of Sun Alliance International in 1989, it was decided to change the name of the network to Women in International (WII). This seemed a more appropriate name—it is a better description of the intention of the group to include individuals in all our regions as well.

The Sun Alliance Insurance Group employs more than 9000 staff, 52 per cent of which are women. However, there are still only a few women in managerial positions. Not only is it important to have more women coming up through the ranks in order to achieve a more balanced company, but with the dramatic demographic changes anticipated during the nineties it is essential that good staff are attracted and retained.

With such a large proportion of women already working for Sun Alliance Insurance Group it is important that women are:

- encouraged to achieve their full potential
- encouraged to reach key senior positions
- given support and guidance on self-development
- encouraged to return to work after career breaks for children

Women in International collectively feels a responsibility to help achieve these aims by:

- helping with training and development
- providing a forum for the exchange of ideas and information
- acting as a support group, for women returners, etc.
- offering a line of communication to management on ideas that can be used to aid recruitment and improve conditions of employment.

During 1989 WII began to formalize its activities and in the summer of that year official status was obtained and with it a budget of £1000. A core group of about seven women organize meetings and these now take two forms:

1 Informal forums every 4–6 weeks, Monday lunchtimes
2 Formal meetings, with speakers, about once every 3 months, held in the evening

It was decided at the outset that all members of staff, women and men, would be invited to our meetings if they were interested in the topic. While WII was established initially to look at women's issues, it soon became apparent that we could also provide input to other matters affecting all members of staff. The following provides a flavour of the types of topics we have supported with the help of internal and external speakers.

Lunch-time meetings
As a result of discussions on career breaks and childcare a letter was sent to our personnel services department with suggestions for improvements. Feedback on this was provided at another meeting by a personnel officer who explained the progress and issues being considered by Sun Alliance. Another speaker came and explained her involvement in the Sun Alliance Women Returners Project.

We have had talks and demonstrations of self-defence, and personnel services used the WII forum to show a video on self-defence to all female staff.

With the change in taxation rules from 1 April 1990 we arranged for a speaker on independent taxation; this gave those who attended an opportunity not only to discuss this particular topic, but to obtain advice on financial planning generally. Another meeting has been arranged on pensions.

We have made contact with other networks and a speaker from Women in BP, a network established in 1982, was able to provide us with many good ideas and encouragement.

We have had a speaker from the Equal Opportunities Committee and one from Well Woman to discuss health screening. As a result of this second meeting WII is looking into the Sun Alliance policy for health screening, to see if there is room for improvement.

A more recent initiative by WII has been to address the problem of waste paper. We invited a member of Greenpeace along to discuss the possibilities of having our paper recycled and, having obtained management approval, WII has arranged an audit of the Sun Alliance head office to establish the cost effectiveness of such a project.

Evening meetings
Our first two evening meetings were particularly well supported by all members of staff, being of wide general appeal. To our first meeting we invited a member of senior management who spoke about our company in a new decade. This promoted lots of questions and a very useful and interesting evening.

Our second meeting will be hard to follow, as Edwina Currie MP was the speaker. Mrs Currie delivered an informative and lively speech on employment and women in the 1990s, covering the issues of the demographic time bomb and the role of women in the future. The audience was mixed, including members of senior management. As well as being a very entertaining evening, this particular meeting was important in raising the profile of WII.

WII is still in its infancy; for the future we hope to be able to provide regular newsletters and to expand by setting up groups in other regional offices, as well as continue with our schedule of lunch-time and evening meetings.

We have been fortunate in that from the beginning we have had support from management, enabling us to be open and positive in our initiatives, and we have gone some way in achieving some of our aims. We look to the future when we can see a truly balanced company with men and women working together in all disciplines at all levels.

Shelley Simmons, Women in International
Sun Alliance International

12 The future

In this book we have looked at every aspect of women's development training based on our own and others' experience of the past and present. As we approach the end of the book—what of the future? What will happen to women's development training? Will there be any place for it in the world of new order, and enlightened managers and organizations? And if there is, what form will it take?

In this chapter we look at the life of women's development training and some of the prospects for the future. We also look at the results of women's development training, your role in all this and what you can do to help yourself and others now.

The life of women's development training

The concept and practice of women-only training is relatively new. It was evolved through the 1960s and 1970s and given authority by the sex discrimination legislation of 1975. The idea of providing training specific to the needs and circumstances of women has often been considered marginal, rather quaint or rather threatening, depending on your role and your opinion. For years, women's development training was developed and piloted by a relatively small band of committed consultants, personnel and training professionals, senior management in organizations, trade unions, and active women's groups. Just as it was quietly maturing and coming of age, the demographic profile and all its attendant implications have hit us. Women's development training is now in grave danger of swiftly becoming fashionable. How it and all of us involved in women's development training deal with this overwhelming burst of interest will determine its future. Becoming fashionable is dangerous for any form of human development process. It can mean that:

- Organizations decide that they must have some of whatever their competitors are offering, to compete in the recruitment and retention race.
- Personnel and training managers may initiate women's development training without any commitment to it, or thought of the longer-term implications.
- Great things are expected of it, and quickly, so initiatives are not given time to develop and become part of the fabric of the organization.

• Women's development training may be bolted on from the outside.

Some women's development training done in these conditions will work, take root and grow. But much will fall away, losing the support of impatient managers who are keen to be associated with the next trend. Already there are organizations who say to us: 'Surely you're not *still* doing women's development training? That was an issue for the 1980s. It's not an issue now. We're now all into total quality management/ racism awareness/Outward Bound training, etc., etc.' But the statistics about women's status in these organizations remain almost totally unchanged. It is the managers' boredom level which has been reached.

If in-depth, long-term strategies such as women's development training can become fashionable quickly, they can just as quickly become unfashionable, and that's dangerous. Dangerous for organizations, for women themselves and for society. While we welcome an upsurge of interest in women's development training, we also need to keep an eye on the longer-term future.

The prospects for women's development training

So what are the alternative scenarios for women's development training and how will it develop? Here are our attempts at crystal-ball gazing:

Stop/fizzle out

The current rush of enthusiasm could just as easily dissolve away, leaving women's development training programmes with no roots. Programmes will either be abruptly cancelled or, without support, attention or energy put into them, left to fizzle out.

Continue unchanged

Women's development training could stagnate. Organizations that are currently running programmes may continue to do so, but little new work will be developed, and few new organizations will initiate training. For individual women, the courses will continue to be useful, and for individual organizations women's development training will continue to contribute greatly to the effectiveness of the organization. However, this scenario implies no further development or growth. A more optimistic view is that women's development training will change and develop.

Change and develop

There are signs that this is already taking place. There are two specific symptoms which indicate a significant shift and development in women's development training:

• Some organizations no longer see women's development training as an issue only for management level women. Women themselves have always known that women's development training has wider implications, but until recently have had greater difficulties in gaining access to training. Some organizations have provided notable exceptions to this, e.g. local authorities, trade unions and women's groups,

which have consciously extended access to non-management women.
- There is a move away from techniques-based women's development training to a more holistic approach. A training manager recently observed, 'Ten years ago women wanted to understand the game that was being played so that they could join in and win it. Now they're more interested in changing the game.'

We've seen too many women distort themselves to fit organizations, management styles and working practices. Women are now demanding that these change to fit *them*.

There is evidence of a new confidence and determination among women, to achieve and still be themselves. As a result, subject matters such as assertiveness and career planning are being used in women's development training in a different way, developing women from the inside out, not just developing a set of techniques.

Women's development training seems to be constantly metamorphosing and its organic ability to change and respond is one of its strengths. How it will continue to develop is unknown. Will there always be women's development training? While imbalances and injustices continue to exist to women's disadvantage, the answer has to be 'yes'. If society ever reaches the point when women's development training is superfluous, we can all cheer and celebrate, delighted to have been worked out of a job!

If women's development training continues to grow and develop, there is alongside it another optimistic scenario: it could become integrated into mainstream training and exert its own influence in the field.

Integrate and influence
At the moment, women's development training is still seen as something odd, on trial, strange. It can be initiated by equal opportunities units, using budgets and criteria which can be different from mainstream courses run by training or personnel departments. Women's development courses are often not found in mainstream directories of courses (usually because these directories are planned many months in advance, or because the target group would not be reached through such directories).

These factors conspire to marginalize women's development training, to treat it with suspicion and to make it vulnerable to budget cutbacks and changes of personnel.

Integration of women's development training is a long way off, but the future could hold the prospect of women's development training becoming sufficiently respected and recognized for it to be regarded as mainstream and uncontroversial. We consider this possible but unlikely.

The dynamic and creative way forward for women's development training lies in posing a challenge to traditional processes and materials in training, thereby influencing existing training as well as pioneering new forms and approaches to training. There are encouraging signs, in isolated pockets, that this has the potential to happen. Women's development training has provoked men's development training, and 'men and women working together' training (currently in its infancy and still to prove itself), as well as influencing the content of mainstream career planning and skills courses.

The lessons that women's development training offers mainstream training are:

- the value of the holistic approach—accepting the whole person, not just the bits that come to work
- the effectiveness of development from the inside out
- ownership of development by the individual with the organization acting in a facilitative and supportive role.

Of course, women's development training cannot claim to have discovered these issues for people-development. These are issues being increasingly validated in most personnel and training departments today. However, women's development training has had more experience than other forms of training of putting these ideas into practice. As such, women's development training has provided the testing ground for other forms of development.

This is certainly the most constructive and exciting scenario as it acknowledges the pathfinding work of women's development training and enables other training and development to develop and transform.

Natasha Josefowitz, in her book *Paths to Power*,[1] identified some of the shifts in values that she observed taking place, which would support this influence and integration:

Values are slowly changing in the world of business, and these are shifting in the direction of women's basic orientation. So while our male colleagues need to make an effort to encompass these new values, we feel more and more at home.

What are some of these changing values?

- placing a greater emphasis on collaboration as opposed to competition
- paying attention to process and not just to task
- trusting people
- sharing power
- being authentic as opposed to playing games
- appropriately expressing feelings rather than shutting them off
- viewing people as whole persons and not just in terms of a job description
- accepting and utilizing individual differences instead of resisting or fearing them
- showing many personality facets rather than only those related to work.

The results

We have seen that women's development training supports individuals and groups of women in seizing greater control over their own lives. This means that it results in women who:

- have greater self-confidence
- have a clearer sense of direction
- accept responsibility for their own lives
- actively seek opportunities for their own growth and advancement
- do not rely on the approval of others for their self-esteem
- are able to make choices for themselves
- are able to stand up for themselves
- are better bosses and better subordinates
- have more positive relationships
- speak out
- challenge and confront
- enjoy life more
- have more fun
- are more productive employees, more active members of communities, more pro-active citizens of the world

Where now?

In this book, we have taken all the ingredients of the women's development training cocktail apart, and examined and identified each one in great detail. There is a danger in this. Just as the ingredients of the most sumptuous and delicious banquet appear obvious, ordinary and run-of-the-mill in their raw and isolated state, so may the ingredients of women's development training.

Of course it's about strategy, design, publicity and recruitment. Obviously you have to give thought to the trainer's role, how to run the course and setting up networks, and everyone knows that it is good practice to evaluate training. So what's so special?

We have aimed to avoid duplicating books on mainstream training, and have tried to concentrate on the aspects that need particular attention, or assume greater importance, in women's development training. We've separated out the raw ingredients. The challenge now is to put them all together in such a way that they fuse and take on a joint identity. Having put all the ingredients of women's development training together, shake well and accept that they are inseparable, all relying on one another to contribute their particular quality, which results in the special challenge and excitement of women's development training.

Laying out the process in this book may make women's development training look like a lot of hard work and involve a lot of intricate detail. But the first time you mix your women's development training cocktail, stick to the recipe and measure the ingredients accurately. Having tasted the end result, we'd then urge you to be creative, ingenious, imaginative and even outrageous in developing your own blend!

You may be surrounded with supportive colleagues in a large enlightened organization. You may be one woman campaigning hard to get some form of women's development training started in your local community. You may feel you are fighting a losing battle against inertia and indifference. Whatever your circumstances and involvement in women's development training, do network with other women's development training providers, swap experiences and gain ideas and inspiration. Below are four useful organizations to help you tap into the network. Their addresses appear in Appendix 5:

The Equality Exchange of The Equal Opportunities Commission
Training 2000—The Scottish Alliance for Women's Training
Catalyst Integrating Women in the Workforce
EWMD (European Women's Management Development Network)

All these organizations welcome men as well as women to their meetings, and as members.

Everything in this book is common sense, but it is common sense that has been tried and tested and experimented with over the last twenty years. Having laid out the process in a linear form, it may not be possible for you to implement it in this neat, logical form. In which case, don't let that stop you from initiating, redeveloping and relaunching women's development training in your community group, or organization, in whatever way is possible for you.

Women's development training is a wonderful adventure, an adventure that you share with the women on your course. You will learn a lot about women and men, about organizations and about society, and one thing we can guarantee: you will also learn a great deal about yourself.

Just as we say to women on courses, so we'd say to you—start wherever you are, and take small steps. By taking the first small step, you have moved women's development training on. This is a very exciting time to be involved in women's development training; it has served its apprenticeship and has the potential to stand tall in its own right.

Whatever happens over the next few years will be an adventure, so whatever your involvement in women's development training—enjoy it!

Reference

1. Natasha Josefowitz, *Paths to Power* (Columbus Books, 1980).

Appendix 1

Course programmes

The course programmes given in this appendix show the wide range of training that is run under the women's development training banner. There are examples of:

1 Personal effectiveness workshop: 1 day, on-site
2 Career planning: Saturday workshop for women's groups
3 Women returners programmes: 10 weeks of 1 short day per week
4 Personal effectiveness seminar: 2 days, non-residential, off-site
5 Self-development in careers for women: 3 days residential plus follow-up day
6 Assertiveness: 2 days on-site, non-residential
7 Women and leadership: 5 days, residential
8 Biography workshop for women: 5 days, residential

They are given purely as examples and should not be used as 'masters' or regarded as perfect. They were all developed to fit the needs and circumstances of specific organizations and specific groups of women. We've included them to give you practical examples of design, ideas and inspiration.

Example 1   Personal effectiveness workshop: one day, run on-site
To start with, here is an example of a short, one-day workshop which was pitched as an introduction to many development issues for women.

Aim   To provide an opportunity to review personal progress and skills at work

Objectives
• To identify and use your ability to deal with people
• To identify progress so far and difficulties at present
• To look at the way we come across to others and to develop a more effective approach
• To draw up a plan of action to ensure greater effectiveness at work

Programme   9.30   Welcome, introductions and workshop objectives
10.00   Syndicate discussions to assess:

- How did I get to where I am now?
- Who and what helped me?
- How did I help myself?
- What are the difficulties to progress now?

10.30   Report-back

11.00   Coffee

11.15   *So what am I doing right?*
Input on personal power and influence, looking particularly at how things happen in organizations

12.00   *Launching my own PR campaign*
Marketing the product, that is—me!
Group discussion to look at:

- product
- customer
- packaging
- image
- advertising
- relaunch!

1.00   Lunch

2.00   *Practical exercise*
Individuals practise putting themselves across positively and gain feedback

3.15   Tea

3.30   *Managing my manager*
Finding the people who will give support, and finding ways of managing my manager positively
Input and group discussion

4.00   *Making it all happen*
Input—ideas to make things happen, incorporating a summary of the day

4.30   *Action session*
Delegates commit themselves to the practical actions they will take to become more effective at work

5.00   Close

Example 2   Career planning: Saturday workshop for women's group
Here is another one-day workshop, this time run on a Saturday for a small women's group and focusing on career planning.

Objective   A very participative workshop to enable members to assess where they are in their lives/careers, consider where they want to be in the future, and draw up some action points to enable it all to happen in practice.

Workshop approach   There is a minimum of input from the workshop leader, and the maximum of participation from workshop members in small groups and individually. A high level of mutual support and confidentiality is required to enable members to gain the most from the day. There should be no fewer than 10 and no more than 18 participants.

Programme   9.30   Welcome and introduction
                     Workshop objectives—input
              10.15 Syndicates to assess progress so far and to identify hurdles to
                     future progress
              11.00 Report-back
              11.30 Coffee
              11.45 *Where do we go from here?*
                     Career/life planning
                     Exercise in main group
              12.00 Life interests versus life space
                     Discussions in small groups
              12.15 Lunch
               1.00 Life-line exercise—individual work on our lives to date, and
                     looking to the future
               1.20 Discussion in small groups; problem solving
               2.00 Identifying skills, contacts and experience which will help
                     Individual exercise
               2.15 Lifestyle exercise—to pin down precise targets
                     Individuals and sharing in groups
               3.00 Tea
               3.15 Goal setting—individuals work on their own goals and actions
                     needed to get them to their targets
               4.00 Making it happen—input
               4.20 Action plans
               4.30 Report-back
               4.45 Close

Example 3   Women returners programme: 10 weeks, one short day per week

This is a good example of a programme from Jean Buswell of the
Gloucestershire and West of England Training Initiative (GWETI) for
women wanting to return to work. There are three specific features of
the design to tailor the materials for returners:

1 The course is spread out over 10 weeks, with participants attending
  for one day a week. Longer than 10 weeks can become dragged out
  and boring. Shorter than 10 weeks doesn't give enough material and
  support.
2 The days are short: 9.15 a.m. to 3.30 p.m. This is because returners
  are unused to having to study for long periods of time, and also to fit
  in with childcare arrangements.
3 All participants attend the first four weeks. Prior to Week 5 the whole
  group discusses and decides on the options for the following six
  weeks. This enables participants to identify their own needs and preferences, at a place in the programme where they will have developed
  enough self-confidence to speak out.

Programme

Week 1

9.15–10.45	Arrive and welcome
11.00–12.30	Self-assessment—taking stock
1.00–3.30	Difference between people
	Who am I?
	Beginning to identify strengths and weaknesses

Week 2

9.15–10.45	Discussion and review
11.00–12.30	Forum of working women
1.00–3.30	Job-seeking skills

Week 3

9.15–9.45	Discussion and review
9.45–12.00	Career and life planning
12.00–12.30	Job training opportunities
1.00–3.30	Visit

Week 4

9.15–9.45	Discussion and review
9.45–11.00	Introduction to assertiveness
11.15–12.30	Assertiveness practice
1.00–3.30	Job-seeking skills

Week 5

9.15–10.45	Job seeking continued
11.00–12.30	Time management
1.00–3.30	Successful selling

Week 6

9.15–9.45	Discussion and review
9.45–11.00	Setting up a business
11.15–12.30	Business ideas workshop
1.00–3.30	Forum of business owners

Week 7

9.15–9.45	Discussion and review
9.45–11.00	Computer hardware and software
11.15–12.30	Word processing
1.00–3.30	Computer applications

Week 8

9.15–9.45	Discussion and review
9.45–10.45	Preparing for an interview
11.00–12.30	Developing interviewee skills
1.00–3.30	Developing interviewee skills

Week 9

9.15–9.45	Discussion and review
9.45–11.00	Interviews
11.15–12.30	Interviews
1.00–3.30	Interviews

Week 10
 9.15–11.00   Reviewing interviews
11.15–12.30   Action plans
 1.00–3.30   Course review and farewells

Used with permission from Jean Buswell

Example 4   Personal effectiveness seminar: 2 days, non-residential, off-site

Here is a similar breadth of material over two days, non-residentially and off-site. There is a short introductory session the evening before which can cause difficulties with women getting delayed at work, but speeds things up the following morning as introductions have already been covered.

Programme

Day one 6.00 p.m.–7.00 p.m.	
5.45 p.m.	Tea and coffee
Session 1	The course objectives Introductions • participants • tutors
Day two 9.30 a.m.–9.30 p.m.	
9.15 a.m.	Tea and coffee
Session 2	Syndicate discussion • influential career factors to date • hurdles to further progress • strengths, weaknesses and values
Session 3	Report back and plenary discussion
1 p.m.–2 p.m.	Lunch
Session 4	Where am I in my career and where am I going? Practical exercises and plenary discussion to identify priorities, goals and the actions needed to achieve them
Session 5	Assertiveness—what it isn't; what it is; why it's not easy; the five basic ingredients
7.00 p.m.	Dinner
Session 6	Guest speaker A middle management woman who has worked her way up through the secretarial layers of an organization talks about her life and career
9.30 p.m.	Conclude
Day 3 9.30 a.m.–5.30 p.m.	
9.15 a.m.	Tea and coffee
Session 7	Assertiveness—applying the five ingredients to real situations
11.15 a.m.	Tea and coffee
Session 8	How we come across to others

	Plenary session on the importance of our own PR and ideas on how to come across positively
	Exercise in small groups
1 p.m.–2 p.m.	Lunch
Session 9	Making it all happen
	Input, followed by an action session in which participants commit themselves to the actions they will take
3.30 p.m.	Tea and coffee
Session 10	Close

Example 5 Self-development in careers for women: 3 days, residential plus follow-up day
Here is a course which covers much the same material as the previous programme, but in much greater depth and pitched at management level. Run over three days, residentially, it includes working in the evenings, and a follow-up day three months on.

Programme

Day one

9.45	Coffee and registration
11.00	Welcome; course objectives; introductions
11.30	Coffee
11.45	The self-development challenge
	Syndicate discussion to assess the positive and negative influences on our careers so far, and identify the hurdles to further progress
1.00	Lunch
2.00	*Learning from experience*
	Identifying themes and trends in our lives which can help us become more effective in the future
3.30	Tea
3.45	*Values* and their influence on our decisions
4.30	*Evaluating strengths and weaknesses*
5.00	*How organizations work*
	Setting our career plan into context
	A look at our ability to influence events
7.00	Dinner
8.30	*Trends and changes* in organizations and how they influence our careers

Day two

09.00	*Guest speaker*
	The personnel director explains the organization's attitude to the course, and its value to the organization, and outlines other career development opportunities
9.45	*Assertiveness*
	What it is, and what it isn't
	Definitions
10.30	Coffee

10.45	*Assertiveness* (continued)
	The five basic ingredients in assertiveness
	Practise in small groups
1.00	Lunch
2.00	*Assertiveness* (continued)
	Assertiveness in real situations
3.30	Tea
3.45	*Assertiveness* (continued)
	Additional techniques and group exercises
7.00	Dinner
	Guest speaker—a 'profile' speaker

Day three

9.00	*Promoting ourselves positively*
	Creating the right impression to back up our values and aspirations
	Input and discussion
10.30	Coffee
10.45	*Promoting ourselves positively* (continued)
	Exercise and feedback on the way we come across to others
1.00	Lunch
2.00	*Into the future*
	Developing a personal plan of action and setting goals to enable greater effectiveness
3.30	Tea
3.45	Summary and action session
4.30	Close

Follow-up day

10.00	Welcome and objectives of the day
10.15	*Progress review*
	Syndicate discussion to review progress and identify the effective strategies
11.15	Report-back on progress and strategies
	Discussion
12.15	What next?
	Clarifying the real hurdles to further progress
12.45	Lunch
1.30	(The afternoon programme will be developed in response to the delegates' needs and objectives. However, this usually includes such topics as further assertiveness, timing, and learning to learn.)
5.00	Close

Example 6   Assertiveness skills: 2 days, on-site

As a contrast, here is a straightforward two-day assertiveness skills workshop run on-site and non-residentially. Exactly the same programme could be run as a mixed or men-only course, but the course process and issues raised would be different.

Objective   To give delegates enough knowledge, understanding and experience in assertiveness to be more effective in their communications both at work and at home.

Programme   *Day one*

Session 1	Welcome; objectives; introductions
Session 2	What is assertiveness?
	Definitions of aggressive, assertive and passive behaviour
	Syndicate discussion
Session 3	Assertiveness
	Why it's difficult
	Theories connected with it
	Why bother with it?
Lunch	
Session 4	How to do it:
	The five basic ingredients in assertiveness
	Work on scenarios in syndicates
Session 5	Work on real situations in small groups
Session 6	The role and importance of words, tone of voice and body language
	Group exercises
Session 7	Listening skills
	Group exercises

Day two

Session 8	Review and recap
Session 9	Additional techniques • saying no
	• broken record
Session 10	Work on real situations in small groups
Lunch	
Session 11	Additional techniques • giving criticism
	• giving and receiving compliments
	• giving and receiving feedback
Session 12	Work on real situations in small groups
Session 13	Summary and action session
Close	

Example 7   Women and leadership: 5 days, residential

There are still significantly few women at senior levels in most organizations and most existing styles of leadership were developed by, and for, men. This course helps women develop a leadership style that they feel comfortable with, and which is effective in a faster-changing world.

Objective   To enable senior women in the organization to develop a management style which increases their effectiveness and fits their own personalities and values.

Process   The course is very participative. Participants will be responsible for developing their own management styles and for establishing their own development plans throughout the five days. Some theory will be introduced, but the main process is experiential and involves the participants in being open to ideas and feedback.

Content
- Old order/new order in organizations
- The changes in organizations
- The role of values in organizations
- Moving from vision into taking action
- Valuing differences
- Models of management
- Balancing professional and personal life
- Your own development within your team
- Understanding pressure
- Channelling energy—in yourself and others
- Managing in isolation and building support

Programme

Day one   11.30 a.m.–9 p.m.

Session 1	Welcome, introductions and objectives of the course
Session 2	A definition of leadership
	Group discussion and report-back
Lunch	
Session 3	Personal and professional value systems in leadership
Session 4	Taking action—transferring ideas into practice
	Exercise and feedback
Session 5	Building leadership models that work
	Exercise and feedback
Tea	
Session 6	Managing ourselves for stress prevention
	Practical work and discussion
Session 7	The importance of time for ourselves and how to use it effectively
	Discussion
Dinner	

Day two   9 a.m.–9 p.m.

Session 8	Changes and trends inside organizations
	The emergence of 'new-order' managers
	The impact of organizational culture on leadership styles
	Input and discussion
Coffee	
Session 9	Exercise and feedback
Lunch	
Session 10	Planning and delivering the plan!
	Exercise and feedback
Tea	
Session 11	Managing the balancing act
	Enhancing the quality of personal time
	Practical exercises

Dinner

Session 12	Working in teams—team roles and valuing individual contributions and differences
	Discussion and exercise

Day three   9 a.m.–9 p.m.

Session 13	Motivation—theory and practice
	Input and discussion
Coffee	
Session 14	Leading teams and communicating effectively
	Exercise
Lunch	
Session 15	Feedback and discussion from exercise
	Developing an effective leadership style from experience
Tea	
Session 16	Identifying your own stress symptoms and developing remedies
	Practical work
Session 17	Influences on leadership styles
Dinner	

Day four   9 a.m.–6.30 p.m.

Session 18	Vision to action
	An outline of the vision-to-action model and the leadership process that this provides
	Input and discussion
Coffee	
Session 19	Leadership and teams in action
	Project work to practise and try out the processes developed
Lunch	
Session 19 (continued)	
Tea	
Session 20	Managing time to ourselves
	Input discussion and practical work
Dinner	

Day five   9 a.m.–2 p.m.

Session 21	Presentation of project work
Coffee	
Session 22	Exercise
Session 23	Course summary
	Action session and close
Lunch	

Liz Willis and Jenny Daisley

Example 8 Biography work for women: 5 days, residential
This is the deepest form of development work and is therefore the exception to our philosophy of being able to train trainers specifically for a course. Biography work is a dynamic way of working with a person's life—past, present and future. Course leaders need specific and quite lengthy training as well as being committed to working on their own biographies.

Programme

Day one

Session 1	Introductions to each other and the programme
	Objectives; expectations
	Diaries
Session 2	Working with your biography
	• work
	• self
	• relationships
Session 3	Events—individual work
Session 4	Creative work
Session 5	Events—group work
Session 6	Plenary

Day two

Session 7	What's on top? (working in pairs, women briefly sharing their thoughts with each other)
Session 8	Being a woman
	• at home
	• at work
	• by myself
Session 9	Periods
	• individual work
	• group work
Session 10	Creative work
Session 11	Themes
	• individual work
	• group work
Session 12	Plenary

Day three

Session 13	What's on top?
Session 14	Life phases
Session 15	Relationships and current questions—individual work
Session 16	Creative work
Session 17	Relationships and current questions—group work
Session 18	Plenary

Day four

Session 19	What's on top?
Session 20	Barriers to development and how to lift them
Session 21	Options, consequences and deeper intentions— individual work

Session 22	Creative work
Session 23	Options, consequences and deeper intentions—group work
Session 24	Plenary and overnight choices
Day five	
Session 25	What's on top?
Session 26	Being myself
Session 27	Choices and first steps—individual work
Session 28	Creative work
Session 29	Choices and first steps—group work
Session 30	Plenary summary and action

Appendix 2

The Springboard programme

The Springboard Women's Development Programme is a three-month programme specifically developed and written by Liz Willis and Jenny Daisley for women in non-management areas in organizations and for women outside paid employment.

It is a personal development programme which provides the individual with a process which she can use to address whatever issues are relevant to her. Each woman sets her own agenda, so the Springboard programme can be used by women who are approaching retirement, aiming for promotion, wanting to return to work after a career break, or setting up their own business, as well as personal agendas such as building self-confidence, sorting out difficult relationships and developing assertiveness both at home and at work.

The Springboard programme is supported by a network of accredited Springboard trainers throughout the UK and is used both inside and outside organizations. It consists of five ingredients:

- a 300-page workbook which an individual woman works through on her own
- workshops or tutorial groups which complement and develop the material in the workbook
- encouragement of networking
- provision of role models
- provision of support back-up of mentors or 'helpers'

It can be used with small groups or in large workshops of more than a hundred. The material covered in a Springboard programme includes:

- assertiveness
- what you've got going for you
- the world about you
- more energy, less anxiety
- your personal resource bank
- networking
- setting goals

- finding support
- blowing your own trumpet
- making things happen
- balancing home and work
- CVs and interviews

The BBC was awarded the Lady Platt Award by The Institute of Training and Development for their pilot Springboard programme (known internally as the Women's Development Programme) as being the most innovative piece of equal opportunities training in 1989.

The Springboard programme is unusual because:

- It is specifically designed for women in *non*-management areas.
- It works well with large numbers such as 100 at a time.
- It brings together a great wealth of material all in one place.
- The five main ingredients are infinitely flexible, depending on the circumstances of the women and the culture of the organizations involved.

For more information on the Springboard programme, refer to p. 236.

Appendix 3

The Lady Platt Award

Valerie Hammond, director of research, Ashridge Management College, and chair of the panel of judges for the Lady Platt Awards introduces the scheme.

It was introduced in 1987 to recognize good training practices with regard to the development of equal opportunities. Since then organizations receiving the award have included the British Broadcasting Corporation, the National Westminster Bank, Birmingham City Council, the Metropolitan Police and East Leeds Women's Workshops.

The awards recognize commitment to measurably improved equal opportunities through training. It is not, however, necessary to be a large company or a high spender to achieve the award. The judges look for appropriateness of method as well as innovative approaches in the light of the circumstances of the organization.

The Institute of Training and Development issues the following guidelines:

The award carries the name of Baroness Platt of Writtle in recognition of her contribution to ITD during her period as President 1985 to 1987 and has regard for her special interest in the creation of equal opportunities and the office she held as Chairman of the Equal Opportunities Commission.

Aim
The Institute of Training and Development has introduced this annual award with the support of the Equal Opportunities Commission to recognize the contribution made by organizations and individuals to equal opportunities through the design and application of good training processes.

Eligibility
Employers—The award scheme is open to all employers—large or small organizations—in industry, commerce, public and community services in Great Britain. The judges will take into account the relevant resource and environmental situation of applicants.

Training providers—Provider Bodies, e.g. colleges, consultants, group training schemes, etc. may submit applications in respect of schemes they have designed and operate. However, such applications must include an endorsement from the client organization or representatives of those that have received training.

Criteria

To be considered, schemes must:

- demonstrate enhanced equal opportunities
- be currently operative or have been completed not earlier than 1 January 1988
- comply with the requirements of the Sex Discrimination Acts, 1975 and 1986
- have the expressed commitment of senior management
- exhibit good training practice and include monitoring and validation processes
- be designed and have learning objectives which take account of the needs of individuals as well as organizations

For further information and entry forms, see address in Appendix 5.

Sources of material

The following sources all have a selection of publications, videos and training packages, some of which are specifically for women. As catalogues change so often, we recommend that you contact these providers to check their current range and availability.

BBC Enterprises Limited
Woodlands
80 Wood Lane
LONDON W12 0TT

CFL Vision
P O Box 35
WETHERBY
Yorks LS23 7EX

Context Training Ltd
The Old Post Office
Northend
HENLEY ON THAMES
Oxon RG9 6LF

The Domino Consultancy Ltd
56 Charnwood Road
SHEPSHED
Leics LE12 9NP

Gower Training
Gower House
Croft Road
ALDERSHOT
Hants GU11 3HR

National Extension College
18 Brooklands Avenue
CAMBRIDGE
Cambs CB2 2HN

The Open College
Suite 470
St James Buildings
Oxford Street
MANCHESTER
Lancs M1 6FQ

Opportunities for Women
Centre Two
Ossian Mews
LONDON N4 4DX

The Springboard Consultancy
P O Box 69
STROUD
Glos GL5 5EE

Publications Department
Trade Union Congress
Congress House
23–28 Great Russell Street
LONDON WC1B 3LS

Department of Continuing Education
University of Bristol
Wills Memorial Building
Queens Road
BRISTOL
Avon BS8 1HR

Video Arts Ltd
Dumbarton House
68 Oxford Street
LONDON W1N 9LA

Appendix 5

Useful addresses

AMED
Association of Management Education and Development
21 Catherine Street
LONDON WC2B 5JS

Tel: 071 497 3264

CRAC
Careers Research and Advisory Centre
Bateman Street
CAMBRIDGE
Cambs CB2 1LZ

Tel: 0223 354551

Daycare Trust
Wesley House
4 Wild Court
LONDON WC2B 5AU

Tel: 071 405 5617/8

Educational Trust for Working Women
c/o Baroness Lickwood
Thorne House
Ruxley Ridge
Claygate
ESHER
Surrey

Equal Opportunities Commission
Overseas House
Quay Street
MANCHESTER
Lancs M3 3HN

Tel: 061 833 9244

European Women's Management Development Network
UK Representative, Sue Mathews
April Cottage
The Cross
Stonesfield
Oxon OX7 2PT

Tel: 0993 891720
Fax: 0993 891589

Gloucestershire and West of England Training Initiative (GWETI)
Contact: Jean Buswell

Tel: 0453 882643

The Hansard Society for Parliamentary Government
16 Gower Street
LONDON WC1E 6DP

Lady Platt Award
The Institute of Training and Development
Marlow House
Institute Road
MARLOW
Bucks SL7 1BN

National Childcare Campaign Ltd
Wesley House
4 Wild Court
LONDON WC2B 5AU

Tel: 071 405 5617/8

National Joint Committee of Working Women's Organisations
150 Walworth Road
LONDON SE17 1JT

Tel: 071 730 0833

New Ways to Work
309 Upper Street
LONDON N1 2TY

Tel: 071 226 4026

The Open Business School
Walton Hall
Bletchley
MILTON KEYNES
Bucks MK7 6AA

Tel: 0908 274066

The Open College
101 Wigmore Street
LONDON W1H 9AA

Tel: 071 935 8088

The Open University—School of Management
1 Coffenridge Close
MILTON KEYNES
Bucks MK11 1BY

Tel: 0908 274066

Oxford Women in Publishing
Contact for publishing training courses:
Sue Bennett, Training Matters
15 Pitts Road
Headington Quarry
OXFORD
Oxon OX3 8BA

Tel: 0865 66964

Pre-school Playgroups Association
61–63 Kings Cross Road
LONDON WC1X 9LL

Tel: 071 833 0991

Royal National Institute for the Blind
224 Great Portland Street
LONDON W1N 6AA

Tel: 071 388 1266

Royal National Institute for the Deaf
105 Gower Street
LONDON WC1E 6AH

Tel: 071 387 8033

The 300 Group
36–37 Charterhouse Square
LONDON EC1M 6EA

Training 2000
The Scottish Alliance for Women's Training
30 Rutland Square
EDINBURGH
Lothian EH1 2BW

Tel: 031 229 6775

TUC Equal Rights Department
Congress House
Great Russell Street
LONDON WC1B 3LS

Tel: 071 636 4030

The Wainwright Trust
45 College Cross
LONDON N1 1PT

Catalyst Integrating Women in the Workforce
Hewmar House
120 London Road
GLOUCESTER
Glos GL1 3PL

Tel: 0452 309330

Women in Construction Advisory Group
Southbank House
Black Prince Road
LONDON SE1 7SJ

Tel: 071 587 1128

Women's National Commission
c/o The Cabinet Office
Great George Street
Whitehall
LONDON

Women's Working Party, Industry Matters
Royal Society of Arts
8 St John Adam Street
LONDON WC2N 6EZ

Tel: 071 930 5115

Workers Educational Association (WEA)
Temple House
9 Upper Berkeley Street
LONDON W1H 8BY

Tel: 071 402 5608

Workplace Nurseries and Working for Childcare
77 Holloway Road
LONDON N7 8JZ

Tel: 071 700 0281

Useful books

Strongly recommended

Anne Dickson, *A Woman in your own Right* (Quartet, 1982).
Natasha Josefowitz, *Paths to Power* (Columbus Books, 1980).
Janice La Rouche and Regina Ryan, *Strategies for Women at Work* (Counter-
point, 1984).
Robin Norwood, *Women who love too much* (Arrow, 1986).
Marjorie Shaevitz, *The Superwoman Syndrome* (Fontana, 1984).
Liz Willis and Jenny Daisley, *Springboard: Women's Development Workbook*
(Hawthorn Press, 1990).

For management level courses

Roger Evans and Peter Russell, *The Creative Manager* (Unwin Hyman,
1989).
Margaret Hennig and Anne Jardim, *The Managerial Women* (Pan, 1978).
Leah Hertz, *The Business Amazons* (André Deutsch, 1986).
Rosalind Miles, *Women and Power* (MacDonald, 1985).

Some more useful books

Anna Alston, *Equal Opportunities, A Career Guide* (Penguin, 1984).
Ken and Kate Back with Terry Bates, *Assertiveness at Work* (McGraw-Hill,
1990).
Jane Beck and Maggie Steel, *Beyond the Great Divide* (Pitman, 1989).
Carrie Birch and Nina Houghton, *The ABC of Crêche Training* (The
Daycare Trust, 1990).
Equal Opportunities Commission, *Women and Men in Britain 1990*
(HMSO, 1990).
Nathalie Hadjifotiou, *Women and Harassment at Work* (Pluto Press, 1983).
Charles Handy, *The Future of Work* (Blackwell, 1985).
Charles Handy, *The Age of Unreason* (Arrow, 1989).
The Hansard Society Commission, *Women at the Top* (1990).
Beverley Hare, *Be Assertive* (Optima, 1988).

Francis Kinsman, *Millenium, Towards Tomorrow's Society* (W.H. Allen, 1990).

Margaret Korving, *Making a Comeback—A Woman's Guide to Returning to Work after a Break* (Business Books Ltd, 1991).

Rosabeth Moss Kanter, *Men and Women of the Corporation* (Basic, 1977).

Joni Seager and Ann Olson, *Women in the World* (Pan, 1986).

Lisa Tuttle, *Heroines* (Harrap, 1988).

Women in Management, *The Female Resource—an overview* (WIM, 1989).

Appendix 7

The answers to 'What if . . . ?'

Here are the answers to the 'What if' questions from Chapter 8.

A participant wants to drop out of the course?
Discuss it with her. If for organizational problems, coach her in
assertiveness to deal with it. If the programme or the timing is not right
for her, let her go.

Someone says she hasn't come to participate, she's just an observer?
Definitely not.

A profile speaker directly contradicts something you've already said?
Let her—she's entitled to her opinion. It also reinforces the point that
there are no set answers.

Someone has 'serious' problems?
Discuss sources of further help.

Two women in the same group don't get on?
Help them be assertive with each other about their difficulty.

Someone is really cheeky and you're tempted to use a witty put-down?
Don't! It is important that you use model assertive behaviour.

Someone won't go along with the confidentiality ground rule?
Stop, explain it again and check what her difficulty is.

You don't get any response when you ask about confidentiality?
Ask again and explain that you need to have an answer.

One person 'hijacks' a group?
Be assertive and make it clear that space is needed for everyone.

Someone dominates in a jolly and enthusiastic way?
Appreciate her support but be assertive.

You don't know the answer to a question?
Admit it.

A participant consistently refuses to join in the group work?
Encourage her, explain the importance of group work and the responsibility that she has to help the others.

Someone makes a racist remark?
Express your feelings about it—be assertive.

Your co-trainer doesn't turn up?
Make sure your notes cover all the sessions, have home and work phone numbers of other trainers for emergencies.

The profile speaker doesn't turn up?
Have relief emergency numbers. Be prepared for yourself or co-trainer to step in either to do a profile spot yourself or to introduce another exercise.

Someone is talking about rushing back to work to resign?
Talk to her about it, make sure she's thought it through and suggest a delay while she gives it another chance.

Someone becomes angry and abusive in a plenary?
Be assertive.

The group doesn't gel?
Try some group-building activities, otherwise—don't worry—not all groups gel.

Someone bursts into tears in the group work?
Don't overreact. People are often moved or upset by some of the more personal aspects of women's development training. Accept the tears and only take action if they persist.

A man who's had a sex change is in the group?
Be aware that, having been brought up as a man, she will not have experienced the same conditioning as women in the group.

Halfway through briefing an exercise or an input, you realize you're doing it wrong?
Stop and begin again.

Someone tells you at the end of a course that something you said previously has totally changed her life?
Thank her!

The authors would be very interested in being in touch about any of the issues, policies and practices mentioned in this book.

Please send me further information on women's development training. I am particularly interested in:

☐   The Springboard Programme for non-management women

☐   Women in Management

☐   Women and Leadership

☐   Short specific courses, e.g. Personal Effectiveness, Assertiveness, etc.

Name   ....

Organization   ....

Address   ....

.... Daytime tel no   ....

Please send to:

Liz Willis and Jenny Daisley
The Springboard Consultancy
P O Box 69
STROUD
Glos GL5 5EE

Index